A Political Companion
to
Marilynne Robinson

A POLITICAL COMPANION TO

Marilynne Robinson

EDITED BY

Shannon L. Mariotti

AND

Joseph H. Lane Jr.

UNIVERSITY PRESS OF KENTUCKY

Scholarly publisher for the Commonwealth,
serving Bellarmine University, Berea College, Centre College of Kentucky, Eastern Kentucky University, The Filson Historical Society, Georgetown College, Kentucky Historical Society, Kentucky State University, Morehead State University, Murray State University, Northern Kentucky University, Transylvania University, University of Kentucky, University of Louisville, and Western Kentucky University.

Editorial and Sales Offices: The University Press of Kentucky
663 South Limestone Street, Lexington, Kentucky 40508-4008
www.kentuckypress.com

Cataloging-in-Publication data is available from the Library of Congress.

ISBN 978-0-8131-6776-3 (hardcover : alk. paper)
ISBN 978-0-8131-6778-7 (epub)
ISBN 978-0-8131-6777-0 (pdf)

This book is printed on acid-free paper meeting the requirements of the American National Standard for Permanence in Paper for Printed Library Materials.

Manufactured in the United States of America.

Member of the Association of
American University Presses

Contents

Series Foreword

Those who undertake a study of American political thought must attend to the great theorists, philosophers, and essayists. Such a study is incomplete, however, if it neglects American literature, one of the greatest repositories of the nation's political thought and teachings.

America's literature is distinctive because it is, above all, intended for a democratic citizenry. In contrast to eras when an author would aim to inform or influence a select aristocratic audience, in democratic times, public influence and education must resonate with a more expansive, less leisured, and diverse audience to be effective. The great works of America's literary tradition are the natural locus of democratic political teaching. Invoking the interest and attention of citizens through the pleasures afforded by the literary form, many of America's great thinkers sought to forge a democratic public philosophy with subtle and often challenging teachings that unfolded in narrative, plot, and character development. Perhaps more than any other nation's literary tradition, American literature is ineluctably political—shaped by democracy as much as it has in turn shaped democracy.

The Political Companions to Great American Authors series highlights the teachings of the great authors in America's literary and belletristic tradition. An astute political interpretation of America's literary tradition requires careful, patient, and attentive readers who approach the text with a view to understanding its underlying messages about citizenship and democracy. Essayists in this series approach the classic texts not with a "hermeneutics of suspicion" but with the curiosity of fellow citizens who believe that the great authors have something of value to teach their readers. The series brings together essays from varied approaches and viewpoints for the common purpose of elucidating the political teachings of the nation's greatest authors for those seeking a better understanding of American democracy.

Patrick J. Deneen
Series Editor

INTRODUCTION

The Mystery of Experience: Marilynne Robinson's Political Theory

Shannon L. Mariotti and Joseph H. Lane Jr.

Something about Marilynne Robinson's voice seems so authentic as to be alien. In her fiction, her characters, towns, homes, and their happenings are so real, so grounded, so true, and so slowly, quietly, and beautifully ordinary that they seem to come to us from a different time and place. And the thinkers, themes, and topics she writes about in her essays have an honestly unfashionable quality to them. Even when she is writing about contemporary problems, as she very often does, her voice seems to come from another century, perhaps the nineteenth century, a touchstone for her thought. But the valuable experience of estrangement and alienation that we have when reading her is only because our own time is so unreal, so rushed, so breathlessly exuberant, where everything is extraordinary and also plastic, inflated, and ultimately empty. It is only a sad commentary on the state of things today that Robinson's writings seem to come to us from another planet. Her voice is wholly her own and immediately identifiable. No one else writes as vividly and convincingly from a place we inhabited before we became whatever we are now. But that is still the place that Robinson's voice comes from.

In her fiction and nonfiction essays, Marilynne Robinson speaks in this unassumingly iconoclastic voice to subtly weave together a consistent set of principles and practices. When drawn out and drawn together, they offer us what is, in essence, a political philosophy or a political theory: a sustained meditation on the problem of how we should live our individual lives and how we should live together with others. When surfaces are excavated, when depths are plumbed, her fiction and her essays give evidence of a core that we can piece together to articulate an ethos, a sensibility, a way of being in the world, that contains lessons for how to experience the world around us and how to approach each other with due reverence.

It might seem somewhat vulgar, though, to call what Robinson offers a "political theory," because her writings only rarely advocate for any conventional politics in a direct fashion and her unique constellation of beliefs, values, and advocacies don't fit into our usual categories of Republican or Democratic, red or blue, conservative or liberal. Indeed, that is the nature and that is the value of the unconventional philosophy her works embody and encourage. Her political theory, because that is what it is even if the label jars a bit, is communicated not by preaching lessons or giving advice, but just by showing, again and again, through the experiences of her characters and through the themes of her essays, the value of a particular kind of courage that is so difficult to achieve: the courage it takes to make ourselves vulnerable by facing the challenges and uncertainties of our ordinary lives with a spirit of open-mindedness and attentive perception to what our own eyes see and what our own ears hear and to grant the same respect to the experience of other humans. Like Emmanuel Levinas, Robinson takes seriously the idea that every other human being makes a legitimate claim on us and demands our consideration and respect. The unlikely heroes of Robinson's writings—characters like Sylvie and John Ames—enact her understanding of this democratic ethos. Through them and in her essays, she traces the value of an attitude of receptivity, a capacity to experience the world around us directly without the filters of conventional categories and dualisms, and an ability to recognize the grandeur that everyday ordinary life offers and that everyday ordinary people represent.

Robinson's views on democracy closely intertwine with her views on religion and social justice. The political theory described above is, ultimately, a deeply democratic theory, and Robinson is a thinker with strong commitments to democracy. She defines it in a characteristically unusual fashion: "To identify sacred mystery with every individual experience, every life, giving the word its largest sense, is to arrive at democracy as an ideal, and to accept the difficult obligation to honor others and oneself with something wholly approaching due reverence."[1] She makes a connection between this democratic ideal and religion because for Robinson, religion—though she thinks it is futile and impossible to try to define it—is most essentially that attitude of openness toward the mystery of daily life, an experience of direct perception, of really seeing and really hearing the world that surrounds us and attending to the people who inhabit that world as infinitely surprising beings who possess capable minds and meaningful souls. As she notes, "mindfulness is an attribute of God, as well as man, a statement of the sense of deep meaning inhering in mindfulness."[2] Indeed, "the locus of human mystery is the perception of this world."[3]

Robinson asserts that American religious traditions should not be seen as intolerant, punishing fundamentalisms; rather, in her view, religion is about the sacred mystery of individual experience, a vision that is "wholly open in that it anticipates and welcomes the disruption of present values in the course of finding truer ones. And it is as fully attested as America's old-time religion as is any exclusivist or backward-looking tradition."[4] She explores the often-abused trope of America as a "Christian" country in ways that remind us how many humanistic and democratic concepts are grounded in Calvinist theological traditions, but she also draws out the radicalism of that religious tradition. Robinson's writings, both her fiction and nonfiction, put the protest back in Protestantism and, in her sharp critiques of the contemporary religious right, assert that religion calls us to fight for social justice and equality. Robinson's religion prioritizes generosity to the poor and is deeply in tension with the tendencies of contemporary neoliberalism. Indeed, since she published *Mother Country* as a protest against the marginalization of the people on the periphery of British society in the 1980s, Robinson's most overtly political writings have been polemics against what she has called "austerity as ideology" and the policies of neglect and dismissal that she sees as direct attacks on the preconditions for democratic community. For Robinson, religion should motivate us to fight for tolerance, recognition of difference, and justice in terms of gender, class, and race.

Her "Gilead" novels explore these connections between religion, democracy, and social justice as they play out in terms of racial equality. *Gilead* and *Home* trace the stories of two men named John Ames who are both committed to fighting racism but are very different men living in very different times. The first John Ames was a nineteenth-century abolitionist, moving from Maine to the West in the cause of Free Soil, a fierce radical who fought alongside John Brown. But he was also a minister who stirred his congregation to take up the war against slavery. Three generations down the line, we meet the namesake of this first John Ames, a troubled man with a drinking problem who is living in the 1950s, a time of segregation and antimiscegenation laws. *Gilead* and *Home* explore these two complicated figures whose work toward racial justice takes very different forms, but whose shared commitment to racial justice and racial equality is part of what makes them both outsiders in their own homes. Neither figure is able to live according to his ideals in the conventional space of his hometown.

Robinson's work also features characters who yearn for the freedom of the frontier, and in her essays, she invokes the 1864 Homestead Act as an American holy writ, reminding us that this country is a home that was emphatically carved out of a wilderness. The settings of her novels unmistakably invoke the image of America as a frontier society. In her essay "Wilderness," Robinson identifies herself powerfully with Frederick Jackson Turner's familiar thesis that "pioneer roots" shape the American identity: "I am an American of the kind whose family sought out wilderness generation after generation. My great-grandparents finally settled in Idaho, much of which is wilderness now, in terms of its legal status."[5] In the very first pages of *Housekeeping*, Ruth identifies her family in much the same terms, telling the story of how her grandfather continued fleeing west until he found his place in Fingerbone, establishing a thin grasp on civilization in a narrow pass of the mountains where the hold of habitation was always so fragile that the storms and avalanches of the surrounding wilderness threatened to blow it away. Similarly, the narrator Reverend John Ames of *Gilead* cannot escape the moral obligations of abolitionist fervor that brought his grandfather to the broad plains of western Iowa.

Thus, Robinson's stories invoke a restless democracy, defined by a wild landscape and the requirements of the frontier. Robinson understands America as a place of remarkable fluidity and possibility, but as we negotiate the terms of our democracy, wild nature plays a role in the negotiation—or should do so. Indeed, Robinson fears that we are losing the natural referent that has long served as a uniquely American "escape from civilization, and a judgment upon it."[6] She fears for the consequences that the unlimited power of our technological prowess offers us, an unlimited authority that she fears might poison the relationships on which our personal and collective happiness depends: "It stirs the sad suspicion in me that we are of the Devil's party without even knowing it."[7]

We are also unwittingly of the Devil's party for the role many of us play in upholding neoliberalism. As we have seen, Robinson tends to pull "democracy" as a concept into the language of faith. She both defines and defends democracy as a political regime in terms of its consonance with a vision of what makes human souls worthy of grace and recognition. Consequently, Robinson has a particularly critical view of those public policy practices that undermine the realization of our faith in democracy or our practice of humanity. Since the publication of *Mother Country* in 1989, and even more pointedly since the public policy backlashes against the Affordable Care Act led to budgetary retrenchment in the United States and the restrictive monetary policies imposed by the European Central Bank after the onset of the Greek debt crisis, Robinson has focused her disapprobation upon what she calls "austerity as ideology," the practice of moving budgets toward balance by a progressive withdrawal of public safety-net guarantees that has been in evidence on both sides of the Atlantic. Robinson's unflinching critique of austerity policies is grounded in her theory of democracy and her conviction that at its deepest theoretical level democracy is grounded in a confidence in the importance of allowing all human beings to achieve their potential. She sees this as the core public commitment of each and every democracy worthy of the name, and she casts a critical eye on policies that categorize some as deserving of little or no social consideration.

As we have noted, Robinson first explored these issues in *Mother Country*—a little-read and yet much-critiqued book that set the stage for much of what would follow. Although this thin volume focused on the dumping of plutonium into the Irish Sea and the consequent environmental and economic degradation of the areas around the Sellafield nuclear station, Robinson connected this outrage to the broader range of Margaret Thatcher's economic policies, the deindustrialization of northern England, and the fraying safety net of the British social services. Her critique was renewed, this time directed at American policies, in the essays "Austerity as Ideology," "Open Thy Hand Wide," and "The Human Spirit and the Good Society," all of which are found in the 2012 collection of essays *When I Was a Child I Read Books*. In these essays, Robinson articulates her understanding of the connection between democracy and the spirit of generosity that she associates with American policy in the nineteenth century. She sets "austerity" again and again as a (perhaps as *the*) spiritual ill affecting our society. "Austerity is blasphemy," she writes. "It has become a sort of succubus on our national life"[8]

Her focus on the human costs of austerity politics and economics found expression in her literary works only very recently in the 2014 novel *Lila*. Unfortunately, as you can read later in our interview with Robinson, our volume was being finished quite literally as *Lila* was published, so this volume does not take that most recent work into account. But a brief word about *Lila* and austerity is certainly in order here: In that work, Robinson's protagonist and her vagabond associates wander—unwanted and unwelcome—through the seemingly apocalyptic landscape of the Depression-era Midwest. The looming shadow of "the crash," a disembodied term that they can scarcely comprehend or appreciate, hangs above them as a specter of a national economic system that is both in disarray and yet all-powerful, exercising massive control over the lives of those people who seem most distant and detached from its mechanisms and its comforts. *Lila* serves as Robinson's reflection on how even the harshest of conditions never fully annihilates the spark of human distinction or the capacity for wondrous action.

Lila is realistic fiction operating on the allegorical plane, serving as a reminder of the terrible human costs of policies that today mar the lives of migrant children and rural minorities trapped far from the technological marvels and economic largesse of modern life. And yet in the midst of despair, we are given a new vantage point for seeing the third Reverend John Ames as an exemplar of democratic tolerance and commitment. Ames's democratic vision is revealed in his ability to see in Lila something that she long ago lost the ability to see in herself—her capacity for human understanding, creativity, and love.

Lila is only the most recent example of how Robinson's writing subtly but consistently revolves around democratic questions concerning our being in the natural world, our relationship to the ideological space of "home," the character of our relationship with religion and access to divine authority, the limits of our abilities to recognize, respect, and live in peace with the "other," and the challenges of living in an increasingly neoliberal world marked by austerity measures and ideological commitments to a radical vision of individualism that paradoxically destroys individuals to vindicate and preserve theories. Given how these themes dominate so many of our political debates and divisions, their presence in the very fabric of Robinson's fiction and nonfiction lends credence to the argument that her thought can productively contribute to and intervene in key debates in both our political culture and our political theory.

Politics and Fiction: Political Theorists Read Robinson

Our contributors all are political theorists whose essays illuminate the political significance of a wide variety of themes and topics in the fiction and nonfiction of this novelist-essayist-philosopher: from the various models of racial justice that her work explores, to the democratic value of an ethos of homelessness, to the place of old people and old things in a democratic community, to the limits of secularism in contemporary life, to her unique version of modern humanism, and to her thoughts on the loss of wilderness in modern America. In different ways, the essays that make up this volume analyze the relationship between the spaces of nature, home, and democratic community, as they play out in terms of deep American engagements with religion, race, age, and freedom—our longings for transcendence, the tensions between our rights and obligations, our freedoms and responsibilities, and our uniquely American mission of establishing democratic homes and communities in the heart of an ever-shrinking wilderness.

Though Robinson's novels and essays are deeply political in terms of the themes they treat and the dilemmas they explore, thus far scholarly discussion of Robinson's works has been dominated by literary criticism. Marilynne Robinson's novel *Housekeeping* was quickly recognized as a modern classic when it was published in 1981 and was a runner-up for the Pulitzer Prize in 1982. But then, silence: general readers and literary critics would have to wait more than twenty years for Robinson to publish another major work of fiction. Her next novel, *Gilead,* came out in 2005, followed quickly by *Home* in 2008. Then, just as our book was going to press, *Lila* was published, in 2014. Robinson's reputation as a writer was cemented from the beginning, and fortunately, given the long wait for Robinson's next novel, *Housekeeping* kept scholars busy for years: its breadth and depth belied its slim size, and scores of articles analyzing it were published in the twenty-five years between Robinson's first novel and her second.

Literary critics found rich material in analyzing how themes of transience, absence, presence, loneliness, convention, and resistance play out in the gendered spaces of home that *Housekeeping* explores. *Housekeeping* has been analyzed with an eye toward art and metaphysics, its Far West location, female subjectivity, domestic spaces, and the subversion of women's roles, and students of literature have placed Robinson into productive conversations with other thinkers and philosophers ranging from

Henry David Thoreau and Emily Dickinson to Simone Weil and Michel de Certeau.[9]

More recently, literary critics have also begun to analyze *Gilead* (2005) and *Home* (2008).[10] These two novels continue to explore the themes of home, place, and gender that would be familiar to readers of *Housekeeping*, while also introducing new lines of inquiry concerning religion, redemption, and race. *Gilead* and *Home* are both set in the same town during the 1960s and deal with the same cast of characters, as they struggle with aging, death, homecomings, relationships between parents and children, the loss of illusions, failure, and the force of the past on the present. This question of history plays out especially in terms of the failed dreams of nineteenth-century abolitionists in Kansas and Iowa, in light of the experiences of racial marginalization, segregation, and antimiscegenation laws that characterize the 1950s-era present of the two novels: John Brown confronts the horror of Emmett Till, so to speak.

Today, Robinson is an established novelist whose work is popular with both literary critics and general audiences. In 2005, *Gilead* was awarded the Pulitzer Prize that eluded *Housekeeping*, and both *Home* and *Lila* were widely anticipated and reviewed in the popular national press. But Robinson's work has also increasingly turned toward nonfiction, and she has taken on the role of a public intellectual, with essays appearing in *Harper's* and the *Paris Review* as well as more mainstream media outlets. She was even featured on *The Daily Show with Jon Stewart* and interviewed by President Obama for *The New York Review of Books*. In addition to her three volumes of fiction, she now has four books of essays that deal with key questions in modern political thought, ranging from environmental issues to alienation: *Mother Country: Britain, the Welfare State, and Nuclear Pollution* (1989), *The Death of Adam: Essays on Modern Thought* (1998), *Absence of Mind: The Dispelling of Inwardness from the Modern Myth of the Self* (2010), and *When I Was a Child I Read Books: Essays* (2012). A fifth book of essays—*The Givenness of Things: Essays* (2015)—was announced for release in October 2015 even as this volume was in its final edits.

However, we are poised at a moment where interest in Robinson's work is spreading beyond literary criticism, and this volume is positioned to both capture and cultivate the work that political theorists in particular are beginning to do on Robinson. The time is ripe for this volume on Robinson because, as the success of the Political Companions to Great American Authors series attests, there is currently a literary turn in the field of political theory. This is especially true among scholars of American political thought, who are increasingly attuned to the importance of studying both the fictions of politics and the politics of fiction.[11] On the one hand, the study of fiction and narrative helps us better analyze the fictions of politics and the stories we tell ourselves about our political worlds. Political science is reliant on certain fictions and stories—of human nature, of the social contract, for example—whether they are acknowledged or disavowed.

But fiction and literature can also become active participants in the realm of politics. In American political thought, scholars have found it especially rich to analyze the role that literature plays in founding and constituting the American self, in cultivating identity and reforming the self, and in helping us understand the romance of nature in this country.[12] Nature is more complex when viewed from the perspective of literature, a romance of fantasies of pastoral harmony as well as a howling wilderness. And the founding as it plays out in literature also looks different, emphasizing identity conflicts, border problems, interracial encounters, and westward expansion. Robinson's work amply illustrates the payoff of this literary turn, and her writing gives us new insights into all of these themes as they unfold in both the intellectual discussion of American political thought and the evolving and contested language of American political culture.

Robinson also extends and enlarges the strengths of this particular series by placing a strongly female voice into conversation with the classic authors of the nineteenth century. The Political Companions series has been built on volumes analyzing Thoreau, Emerson, Whitman, and Melville. And as Robinson herself has said, she sees herself in conversation with these authors: "If to admire and to be influenced are more or less the same thing, I must be influenced most deeply by the 19th-century Americans—Dickinson, Melville, Thoreau, Whitman, Emerson and Poe. Nothing in literature appeals to me more than the rigor with which they fasten on problems of language, of consciousness. . . . I happen to have read these old aunts and uncles at an impressionable age, and so I will always answer to them in my mind."[13]

But these conversations occur with a difference, and much of her writing explores particularly female spaces, places, and times. In writing *Housekeeping*, for example, she notes that her hero, Sylvie, represents a female twist on the classic American hero who lights out for the territory:

"In Whitman the outsider is a visionary. In Thoreau he is a critic. In the vernacular tradition of Western myth he is a rescuer and avenger. In every version he expresses discontent with society. . . . Obviously, I have an ax to grind here. My one great objection to the American hero was that he was inevitably male—in decayed forms egregiously male. So I created a female hero, of sorts, also an outsider and a stranger."[14] Robinson brings the themes of classic American literature into conversation with political thought while speaking with a specific kind of female voice.

Overview of the Volume

A Political Companion to Marilynne Robinson is comprised of two major thematic sections. The first is titled "The Struggle to Live in Democratic Community: Home, Wilderness, Age, and Race," and the second section is titled "Faith and Skepticism: Religion, Secularism, and Humanism."

In the lead essay to our first section, "The Housekeeper of Homelessness: The Democratic Ethos of Marilynne Robinson's Novels and Essays," Shannon L. Mariotti offers a sweeping and synoptic account of Robinson's work. She explores a number of distinct ways in which Robinson's fictional protagonists enact the work of developing a democratic approach to others and to their communities and also shows how this unique ethos characterizes Robinson's nonfiction essays. Mariotti reveals Robinson's work as an articulation of a novel definition of democracy based on revering the experience of self and other, through cultivating an attitude of attunement, listening to our senses, trying to see, hear, think, and feel for ourselves, and through recognizing that the everyday, familiar, and ordinary experiences of all humans are equally worthy of dignity and respect. This democratic ethos is captured, in her fiction and nonfiction, through the paradoxical position of what Mariotti calls the "housekeeper of homelessness." She reveals the many different ways in which Robinson's writings argue for the political value of taking on an air of homelessness while never fully leaving the familiar places and spaces of home.

In "Our Home in the Wilderness: The American Experience with Wilderness and Frontier Democracy in Marilynne Robinson's Fiction and Essays," Joseph H. Lane Jr. explores a series of key concepts that illuminate Robinson's understanding of American democracy. Lane discusses Robinson's tendency to select narrators who are grandchildren of the American frontier experience—a position that she herself occupies—and to cast her novels as "hauntings" of those grandchildren by their ancestors. Lane connects tales of the closing frontier, especially in *Housekeeping* and in *Gilead*, to Robinson's essays on the American West, on environmentalism and abolitionism, and on the cultural threats to American democracy in order to show how Robinson's democratic vision is rooted in a certain, and somewhat problematic, valorization of the great motions of the nineteenth century and the American character those motions purportedly created. He argues that, while we certainly might raise valid questions about Robinson's sense of what makes the United States what it is, we can learn a great deal from Robinson's sense of how democratic communities must be grounded in a place and open to the experience of nature as a constitutive element of what makes us who we are.

In "*Gilead*'s Two Models of Action against Racial Injustice," Alex Zamalin and Daniel Skinner use Robinson's second novel and what we might call the political philosophy of John Ames to theorize different responses to racial injustice. John Ames reflects at length on the "strenuous" commitment in ethical matters that is exemplified by his grandfather, and his own struggles reveal some of the possibilities and limitations of putting this approach into practice in a variety of settings. Zamalin and Skinner describe Grandfather Ames's actions against slavery and racial discrimination as illuminating a "romantic-heroic" model that channels intensity of passion and personal commitment as the energy of creating social change. But more importantly, they illustrate the less obvious power of the life of Jack Boughton—the prodigal son of the Boughton family and the godson of the narrator John Ames—whose "everyday/tragic" action in countering racism and racist presuppositions is both more personal and more immediate in its practice. Ultimately, they argue that Robinson's novels teach citizens about different ways of confronting racial realities while also illuminating the limitations of each approach.

In an essay titled "'In Those Old Days': The Old and the Aging in Marilynne Robinson's *Gilead* and *Home*," Emily C. Nacol also takes up important questions about the creation of truly democratic communities by exploring the importance of the concepts of aging and the old in Robinson's work. "Old houses" and "old men" figure prominently in the Gilead novels and serve as a referent for understanding how our lives work and how meaning is preserved through human connection with the "old." More importantly,

Nacol brings these novels about the insights and experience of the old and the aging into dialogue with political theorists who have often noted democracy's penchant for the young, the new, and the novel. She argues that Robinson praises a certain type of old age that is marked by generosity and democratic piety that is personified in the narrator Reverend John Ames rather than a more fixed and traditionalist vision that can stifle necessary social change and that is personified in Reverend Robert Boughton. Nacol argues that Robinson's novels help us appreciate how democracy needs the old and not just the new, highlighting how old things and old people can help preserve certain virtues that are cultivated with the passage of time, the hope, generosity, and piety that are vital for democratic community to truly promote human dignity and flourishing.

In the last essay of our first section, titled "'Disabled and Dangerous': The Individual and Society in Marilynne Robinson's *Housekeeping*," Lorraine Krall McCrary explores the concept of "disability" in Robinson's first novel. Like "wilderness," "aging," "family," and "home," disability is a concept with both obvious public policy dimensions and much deeper political salience and power. McCrary shows how the seemingly simple question at the heart of *Housekeeping*—"Is Sylvie crazy?"—reveals multiple frames of discussion that have important political power but that too often escape our attention and our understanding. She argues that Robinson is to be commended for articulating an understanding of Sylvie that reveals the possibility for alternative ways of life and a democratic toleration of difference without dismissing the community's legitimate claims to provide safety and security for its citizens. The "polyphonic" approach that McCrary identifies in Robinson's writing allows us to give due weight to the claims of individualism, nonconformity, and tolerance of difference that is necessary in a democracy without neglecting the value of conventions and demands of social organization.

The second part of the volume begins with an essay by Matthew Scherer. Scherer's essay, "The Ministerial Exception," explores the relationship between religion and secularism, asking, "What place is there for faith in American public life?," and offering a response through the meditations, structure of address, metaphors, and context of the character of Reverend John Ames of the Gilead books. Scherer valuably shows how Robinson's fiction helps us think through the unintended consequences of mainstream secularism that imagines freedom as autonomy and isolation from the social world and public life. To remain rich and vital, Robinson suggests, spiritual life must be continuously connected to our shared world and entrenched in everyday life. Robinson's idiosyncratic view of religion is deeply situated in everyday ordinary life, and Scherer argues that her writings make a place for faith within public life, richly related to the care and commitments of community.

In "The Death of Jeremiah? Marilynne Robinson and Covenant Theology," Christie L. Maloyed explores the place of Puritanism in Robinson's thought. Maloyed argues that Robinson's valuably progressive reading of the Puritans, and the updated version of the theology that she offers as a guide to the twenty-first century, is really a reworking of Puritanism along key lines, specifically the concepts of covenant and jeremiad. For Maloyed, Robinson diminishes the role of covenant theology and reworks the jeremiad in ways that conflict with her profession to offer a more authentic and accurate interpretation of Calvin and Puritanism generally. Through an analysis of *Gilead* in particular and Robinson's essays generally, Maloyed shows how this picture of a more liberal, socially just, tolerant, and egalitarian vision of Puritanism is too sanitized, obscures too many problems, and reworks too many teachings. Ultimately, Robinson's Calvinism is updated in ways that make it more compatible with twentieth-century mores, but too much of the original is lost in the process.

Ralph C. Hancock's essay, "Transcendence and Human Purpose: Marilynne Robinson and the Travails of Liberal Calvinism," takes up elements of both Scherer's and Maloyed's arguments. Hancock also explores Robinson's more progressive reading of Puritanism, but he critiques her progressivism as opposed to her Calvinism. If Maloyed values Robinson's progressivism but wonders whether it can really still be called Puritanism, Hancock's avowedly conservative argument values her return to thinkers such as Calvin but questions the value of her liberal commitments and consequent adjustments. Hancock explores the costs of Robinson's concept of a "horizontal" and more egalitarian form of transcendence that finds value in the everyday, the ordinary, the beautiful, to argue that *Gilead* reveals the best of a certain liberal and aesthetic Protestantism as well as its limitations. Hancock sees Robinson's horizontal form of transcendence as vulnerable to modern strains of the secularism as well as materialism that she critiques in other moments.

Moving to a different place along this spectrum of explorations of Robinson's views on religion and secularism, Anna Hadfield and Roger Berkowitz's essay describes her as a modern humanist. In "The Romance of the Self: Marilynne Robinson's Existential Humanism," Hadfield and Berkowitz make a case for Robinson as a modern humanist who puts forward an aesthetic and romantic version of humanism that valuably works against the predominant reductive parascientific strain of this philosophy. In contrast to scientific humanism, Hadfield and Berkowitz show how Robinson values art, religion, and ethics, as well as thinking, writing, and reading, as part of what it means to be human, part of the culture of humans. Her romantic humanism places value on the mind, self, and soul as opposed to privileging the scientific truths of the brain, body, and biology. She gives us, they argue, a humanism for our times that puts faith in the ultimately mysterious and transcendental nature of human capabilities and capacities.

The final chapter in our volume is a new interview with Marilynne Robinson that we conducted at her home in Iowa on September 19, 2014. "Merism and the Mermaid in a Ship's Cabin: A Conversation with Marilynne Robinson" focuses on different political dimensions of her work. We studied all previous interviews with Robinson prior to conducting our own and tried to ask her questions that she had not been asked before, with rich and novel results. In many instances, we also asked questions specifically related to the themes of our contributors' essays. The result is a fascinating conversation with this incredibly articulate novelist-philosopher on topics ranging from democratic ideals to democratic realities, from American failures in the past to possibilities in the future, from Marx to environmentalism, from the purpose of government to the importance of the abolitionists.

Along the way, it becomes clear that the concept of "merism" is an important orienting concept for Robinson personally and as a writer. Merism is a rhetorical term where two opposing terms are used to indicate that an entirety is encompassed. For example, if you search "high" and "low," that indicates you've searched everywhere. Merisms are especially used in biblical criticism to refer to concepts like heaven and earth or good and evil, opposites that should nevertheless defy dualistic thinking and instead imply a continuum, an entirety. This concept of merism affirms and enriches many of our authors' readings and gives us a new way to understand Robinson's own life and work. In a way that, as she notes, is sympathetic to the concept of a merism, Robinson cultivates a habit of mind that questions the typical oppositions we tend to set up between different and disparate things, to work against dualistic thinking and instead approach seemingly different things as points along a continuum. She finds value in troubling our usual assumptions about the estrangement of disparate things. In a similar way, this volume hopes to trouble some conventional assumptions about the place of this novelist-philosopher and the relationship between politics and literature, facts and fiction, past and future, and our current political realities as well as our ascendant democratic aspirations.

Notes

1. Marilynne Robinson, *When I Was a Child I Read Books* (New York: Farrar, Straus and Giroux, 2012), xiv.

2. Marilynne Robinson, *Absence of Mind: The Dispelling of Inwardness from the Modern Myth of the Self* (New Haven: Yale University Press, 2010), 127.

3. Robinson, *When I Was a Child,* 9.

4. Ibid., xiv.

5. Marilynne Robinson, *The Death of Adam: Essays on Modern Thought* (1998; New York: Picador, 2005), 246.

6. Ibid., 254.

7. Ibid., 253.

8. Robinson, *When I Was a Child,* 41.

9. Joan Kirkby, "Is There Life after Art? The Metaphysics of Marilynne Robinson's *Housekeeping,*" *Tulsa Studies in Women's Literature* 5, no. 1 (Spring 1986): 91–109; Martha Ravits, "Extending the American Range: Marilynne Robinson's *Housekeeping,*" *American Literature* 61, no. 4 (December 1989): 644–66; Sarah D. Hartshorne, "Lake Fingerbone and Walden Pond: A Commentary on Marilynne Robinson's *Housekeeping,*" *Modern Language Studies* 20, no. 3 (Summer 1990): 50–57; Maureen Ryan, "Marilynne Robinson's *Housekeeping:* The Subversive Narrative and the New American Eve," *South Atlantic Review* 56, no. 1 (January 1991): 79–86; William M. Burke, "Border Crossings in Marilynne Robinson's *Housekeeping,*" *Modern Fiction Studies* 37, no. 4 (Winter 1991): 716–24; Heather Bohannan, "Quest-tioning Tradition: Spiritual Transformation Images in Women's Narratives and *Housekeeping,*" in "The Personal Narrative in Literature," special issue of *Western Folklore* 51, no. 1 (January 1992): 65–79; Paula E. Geyh, "Burning down the House? Domestic Space and Feminine Subjectivity in Marilynne Robinson's *Housekeeping,*" *Contemporary Literature* 34, no. 1 (Spring 1993): 103–22; Karen Kaivola, "The Pleasures and Perils of Merging: Female Subjectivity in Marilynne Robinson's *Housekeeping,*" *Contemporary Literature* 34, no. 4 (Winter 1993): 670–90; Christine Caver's "Nothing Left to Lose: *House-*

keeping's Strange Freedoms," in "Write Now: American Literature in the 1980s and 1990s," special issue, *American Literature* 68, no. 1 (March 1996): 111–37; Maggie Galehouse's "Their Own Private Idaho: Transience in Marilynne Robinson's *Housekeeping*," *Contemporary Literature* 41, no. 1 (Spring 2000): 117–37; Thomas Gardner, "Enlarging Loneliness: Marilynne Robinson's *Housekeeping* as a Reading of Emily Dickinson," *Emily Dickinson Journal* 10, no. 1 (Spring 2001): 9–33; Katy Ryan, "Horizons of Grace: Marilynne Robinson and Simone Weil," *Philosophy and Literature* 29, no. 2 (October 2005): 349–64; Christine Wilson, "Delinquent Housekeeping: Transforming the Regulations of Keeping House," *Legacy* 25, no. 2 (2008): 299–310; George B. Handley, "The Metaphysics of Ecology in Marilynne Robinson's *Housekeeping*," *Modern Fiction Studies* 55, no. 3 (Fall 2009): 496–521.

10. Christopher Leise, "'That Little Incandescence': Reading the Fragmentary and John Calvin in Marilynne Robinson's *Gilead*," *Studies in the Novel*, 41, no. 3 (Fall 2009): 348–67; Laura E. Tanner, "'Looking Back from the Grave': Sensory Perception and the Anticipation of Absence in Marilynne Robinson's *Gilead*," *Contemporary Literature* 48, no. 2 (Summer 2007): 227–52.

11. This literary turn in the study of American politics, and particularly American political thought, might be ascribed to a number of developments and sources. Surely the increasingly "political" character of literary criticism in the 1960s and 1970s played a role in bringing the political dimensions of literature to light. However, we should also note that a number of scholars played a role in advancing the idea that we can better understand the development of American politics through the careful reading of American literature. Wilson Carey McWilliams drew heavily on Mark Twain, Sinclair Lewis, James Baldwin, and many others to provide a political understanding of *The Idea of Fraternity in America* (1973). Robert Penn Warren, himself the author of one of the most influential political novels in American letters, articulated a theory of the relationship of the poet to the prospects for democracy in his Jefferson Lectures, published as *Democracy and Poetry* (1976). Catherine Zuckert used a reading of novels to demonstrate the deeply modern character of American politics in *Natural Right and the American Imagination* (1990). See also the work of Patrick Deneen generally, and his coedited volume in particular, *Democracy's Literature: Politics and Fiction in America* (2005). In addition, the very existence of the series Political Companions to Great American Authors testifies to the growing importance of this line of political inquiry.

12. In a classic essay titled "Nature as Politics and Nature as Romance in America," Michael Rogin shows how a split in the American self-image has manifest itself as a split between politics and literature. On the one hand, the vocabulary of American political thought, since the Puritans, has been the language of the contract, the economic exchange, of the exterior, of the marketplace. But there has

always been another logic, another language, circulating at the same time, of the family, the interior, the religious, of fantasy, illusion, rebirth, and regeneration. As Rogin notes, the language of the contract came to be the language of politics while the other logic was relegated to literature (Rogin, "Nature as Politics and Nature as Romance in America," *Political Theory* 5, no. 1 [1977]: 5–30).

13. Marilynne Robinson, "The Hum inside the Skull—A Symposium," *New York Times Book Review,* May 13, 1984, 30.

14. Robinson, *When I Was a Child,* 92.

PART I

The Struggle to Live in Democratic Community

Home, Wilderness, Age, and Race

CHAPTER 1

The Housekeeper of Homelessness

The Democratic Ethos of Marilynne Robinson's Novels and Essays

Shannon L. Mariotti

Contemporary democratic theorists have tended to see the ideological space of "home" as something dangerous, while ascribing democratic value to states of psychic "homelessness." For example, Bonnie Honig characterizes "home" as a place removed from political involvement, as a space of "safety and withdrawal from the tumult of politics."[1] For Honig, democratic politics requires that we "give up on the dream of a place called home, a place free of power, conflict, and struggle, a place—an identity, a form of life, a group vision—unmarked or unriven by difference or untouched by the power brought to bear upon it by the identities that strive to ground themselves in its place."[2] She sees the "dream of home" as dangerous because it excuses our withdrawal from the agonistic world of democratic politics and exacerbates our tendency to ignore internal and external conflict, difference, and division. Thomas L. Dumm also depicts the dangers of home in a similar way and connects democracy with an ethos of homelessness.[3] For Dumm, "home" is figured today as an easy solution rather than a difficult challenge, a comfortable place where we might seek refuge from politics: it is a "place of withdrawal from the demands of common life, a place of fixed meaning, where one is protected from disorientation, but also from the possibility of democratic involvement" (155). Being at home relieves us of the hard work of having "to think for ourselves, think impertinently" (177). Accordingly, "fear of democracy is associated with a desire for home, which remains, as it has for the history of our experience of united states, the solution to all of our problems, the comfort we might find when the demands and challenges of political life become too great" (177).

Marilynne Robinson's book of essays *When I Was a Child I Read Books* (2012) gives us insights into how her writings as a whole productively intervene in these debates regarding the ideological space of home and the ethos of homelessness.[4] Both her fiction and nonfiction writings, as I will show, explore the cultivation of an unusual ethos that she sees as politically beneficial. Her writings consistently illuminate a democratic value in the paradoxical position of what I will call the housekeeper of homelessness.[5] The figures populating this position exhibit a capacity to recognize the illusory nature of the seemingly firm structures and foundations that surround them—whether those be social norms, conventions, doctrines, houses, or towns. They adopt an attitude of open perception and mindful awareness of the unfathomably mysterious and ultimately unknowable world around them, apart from the disciplining and comforting constraints of assumptions and categories. Her heroes work carefully to avoid being judgmental, and their own attitudes of acceptance, flexibility, and forgiveness powerfully highlight the repressive judgments and constraining conventions of others. In this way, Robinson shows how certain modes of perception and ways of experiencing the world further the goals of democracy.

If democracy means that the people (the *demos*) have power and authority (*kratos*), then Robinson says we need to truly respect individual experience: "To identify sacred mystery with every individual experience, every life, giving the word its largest sense, is to arrive at democracy as an ideal, and to accept the difficult obligation to honor others and oneself with something wholly approaching due reverence."[6] She makes a connection between this democratic ideal and religion because for Robinson, religion—though she thinks it is futile and impossible to try to define it—is most essentially that attitude of openness toward the mystery of daily life, an experience of direct perception, of really seeing and really hearing the world that surrounds us and attending to the people who inhabit that world as infinitely surprising and capable minds and souls. Indeed, "The locus of human mystery is the perception of this world" (*Child,* xiv). So her democratic ideal of recognizing the sacred mystery of individual experience "is a vision that is wholly religious though by no means sectarian, wholly realist in acknowledging the great truth of the centrality of human consciousness, wholly open in that it anticipates and welcomes the disruption of present values in the course of finding truer ones. And it is as fully attested as America's old-time religion as is any exclusivist or backward-looking tradition, though our ill-informed nostalgias elevate what is called fundamentalism to that place, with the result that those who cannot endorse fundamentalist religion scorn the past while those who embrace it despise the present" (*Child,* xiv). Robinson's understanding of the democratic ideal is similar to her understanding of religion in that both are highly idiosyncratic and concerned primarily with cultivating a form of perception and attunement that avoids fundamentalisms and foundations. We should remember that we are mysteries to each other and to ourselves, and "if it is agreed that we are in this respect mysterious, then we should certainly abandon easy formulas of judgment."[7] As she notes, "Those who would employ reductive definitions of utility or reality credit their own perceptions of truth with fundamentalist simple-heartedness, brooking no allusion to complexities and ambiguities and countervailing experience" (*Adam,* 3). Especially in the modern era, she thinks that we are plagued by a "tendency to fit a tight and awkward carapace of definition over humankind, and to try to trim the living creature to fit the dead shell. . . . [F]orget definition, forget assumption, watch. We inhabit, we are part of, a reality for which explanation is much too poor and small" (*Child,* 7). Our "attempt to impose definitions on indeterminacy and degree and exception," she writes, "is about the straightest road to mischief that I know of, very deeply worn, very well-traveled to this day" (*Adam,* 87).

She abides by the imperative that "Everything always bears looking into, astonishing as that fact is" (*Adam,* 12). And so we fulfill her democratic ideal by trying to see what is immediately around us in new ways: "So I have spent my life watching, not to see beyond the world, merely to see, great mystery, what is plainly before my eyes" (*Adam,* 243). But this democratic ethos of homelessness, for Robinson, uniquely takes place within the spaces and places of home. She values the attunement to wonder and mystery and openness to possibility that can come from the small, near, local, and mundane acts of housekeeping. And she means this quite literally. She values houses and homes. As she says: "It is the sad tendency of domesticity—as of piety—to contract and of grace to decay into rigor and peace into tedium. Still it should be clear why I find the Homestead Act all in all the most poetic piece of legislation since Deuteronomy, which it resembles" (*Child,*

93). But she has an unusual and unconventional prescription for *how* those houses and homes should be kept: with an air of homelessness.

Ultimately, for Robinson, homelessness and housekeeping can ideally be contained within the same space, as we see in different ways in *Housekeeping, Gilead,* and *Home.* The figure that exemplifies the democratic ideal in Robinson's work is an outsider, a homeless stranger, where "home" represents the ideological space of settled conventions, firm foundations, comfort, and certainty. But this figure never engages in any simplistic lighting out for the territory. The heroes of Robinson's writings, those who exemplify this democratic ethos, take on an air of homelessness all the while never fully leaving the more familiar places and spaces of home. Through their open perception, her heroes find the new, the strange, the unexpected, the disruptive, the unusual, in what lies close at hand. Her heroes exemplify this democratic ethos by reminding us that what is local and familiar is always also exotic and exciting, that what seems known and comfortable can always also be strange and mysterious, and by emphasizing how the new can spring up within the terrain of the old. This democratic ethos of acting as a housekeeper of homelessness performs a kind of immanent critique on the landscape of home, finding active, vital, and vibrant contradictory value in what might initially seem given, natural, and inert, or even pathological and problematic.

Robinson's work explores the realization that any true home—a space of complete comfort, stability, firm foundations—is an illusion. Realizing this is a process of maturation. But we don't need to abandon our homes to live in them with this realization. We can be homeless—recognize and appreciate our essential instability, foundationlessness—while still housekeeping, while still within the space of the home. As I will show, her three works of fiction lay out the value found in this paradoxical position of the housekeeper of homelessness in different ways, while her three volumes of essays illuminate the value of this position in an entirely different register from the novels.

Housekeeping

Of all of Robinson's fiction, *Housekeeping* is the novel where houses are kept the least and where transience figures most prominently. Here, there is a less complete overlap between housekeeping and homelessness than we see in the two later novels; rather, these two ways of life are starkly opposed to each other at many points in the novel. And whereas in *Gilead* and in *Home,* the same characters can act as housekeepers while maintaining an air of homelessness, in *Housekeeping* these two dispositions are predominantly represented within different characters. This seems due, in large part, to the nature of the town of Fingerbone itself and to the fact that the story deals with the care of children. As we will see, the conventional authorities of the town essentially made it impossible for Sylvie to occupy the dual position of acting as a housekeeper of homelessness and continue to live out her semi-transient lifestyle while caring for her two young charges, Ruth and Lucille. The town tries to force Sylvie—and Ruth—into conventional roles that felt highly restrictive to them, until they were left with no other options than to wholly adapt to the town's expectations or leave the town completely. Because the position of acting as housekeepers of homelessness is not available to Sylvie or to Ruth, they are forced into a more radically transient lifestyle. This will also happen to the character Jack, of *Gilead* and *Home.* The townspeople prevent him from occupying the desired position of housekeeper of homelessness, and he has to leave town. But this leaving, in both cases, is presented not as a heroic ideal but as a sad necessity. Home is not gleefully abandoned for a life on the railroads, and in *Housekeeping,* it remains powerfully present in its absence, and Sylvie and Ruth's thoughts continually turn toward this home that had to be lost because they were not allowed to keep it as they saw fit.

The town of Fingerbone itself is so hostile to transience because it is a town where things are easily lost. This is a town built on uncertain and insecure ground. The houses of Fingerbone are constantly threatened with floods and with snow and are always on the verge of falling down. It's easy to imagine the town emptied of all its houses. As Ruth says, "If every house in Fingerbone were to fall before our eyes, snuffing every light, the event would touch our sense as softly as a shifting among embers, and then the bitter darkness would step nearer."[8] The town is especially vigilant against transience because it is especially prone to it: "There was not a soul there but knew how shallow-rooted the whole town was. It flooded yearly, and had burned once. There were reports that things were otherwise elsewhere, and anyone, on a melancholy evening might feel that Fingerbone was a meager and difficult place. So a diaspora threatened always" (177). The emphasis on housekeeping is a mask to cover the illusion that home doesn't actually exist in reality in the same way it might in our imagination. Housekeeping is an injunction and an imperative in Fingerbone because home is being everywhere revealed as an illusion. Fingerbone attacks transience, then, and attacks Sylvie, in an effort to preserve itself against the pervasive uprootedness. As Ruth says, "Fingerbone lived always among the dispossessed" (179). Fingerbone marshals its forces to work against transience in an effort at self-preservation. The "transients" who "wandered through Fingerbone like ghosts" were "terrifying as ghosts are because they were not very different from us" (179). Because of this, "it was important to the town to believe that" the narrator of the novel, Ruth, "should be rescued, and that rescue was possible" (179).

So Fingerbone itself forces the choice between housekeeping and homelessness that closes off the ideal democratic space of a kind of transience-at-home that Robinson values and that we could imagine Sylvie occupying. On the one side, there are the housekeepers, like the two girls' maiden aunts, Lily and Nona, who initially come to take care of them after their grandmother dies. Lily and Nona hate the disruption of their routine that comes with caring for the two girls. They yearn for the ideological space of home: "Lily and Nona, I think, enjoyed nothing except habit and familiarity, the precise replication of one day in the next" (32). They leave as soon as they can get in touch with Sylvie to ask her to care for the girls instead. Ruth's sister, Lucille, also becomes strongly aligned with the forces of normalcy and the conventional ideology of home. Lucille was "of the common persuasion. . . . She wanted worsted mittens, brown oxfords, red rubber boots" (93). Lucille increasingly disciplines herself to fit into the world of conventional normality. By spring, Ruth says, "I had begun to sense that Lucille's loyalties were with the other world. With fall began her intense and passionate campaign to naturalize herself to it" (95). Lucille had a friend named Rosette Brown "whom she feared and admired, and through whose eyes she continually imagined she saw" (95). Rosette Brown and her mother become the measure of conventional normality through which Lucille comes to judge herself and the rest of the world, especially Sylvie. Lucille even starts a notebook where she writes field entries from the land of normality, about how grace is said or how plates are supposed to be passed at table.

Sylvie, the girls' aunt and new caretaker, on the other hand, is described by Lily and Nona in the following terms: "An itinerant"; "A migrant worker";

"A drifter" (31). Sylvie is a transient, a woman who rides the rails. She is the opposite of housekeepers like Lily and Nona in every way, yearning neither for the ideological space of home nor for the actual comforts of a house. As the girls notice, "she seldom removed her coat, and every story she told had to do with a train or a bus station" (68). Sylvie kept her things, not in the dresser, but "in a cardboard box under the bed." She slept in her clothes, on top of the covers, "at first with her shoes on, and then, after a month or two, with her shoes under her pillow" (103). Sylvie is eccentric, but she is never neglectful or abusive in any way. She is sweet and pleasant and truly enjoys the girls and doesn't seem to have hesitated at all when asked to come care for them. She's just very different, not quite housebroken.

When the girls are supposed to be at school but are playing truant to spy on Sylvie, they discover that she spends her days wandering around the rails and the lake. She doesn't always stay in the house during the night: "We thought we sometimes heard her leave the house, and once when we got out of bed, we found her sitting on the back porch steps, and once we found her standing in the orchard" (83). Sylvie will hold herself quietly, listening and looking. To give one example of the kind of thing that she does often, Sylvie goes out to get wood and is entranced by the darkness and just stands there outside listening: "I've never seen such a dark night. . . . It's like the end of the world!" The girls want her to come back inside, "but Sylvie had fallen silent again. Guessing that she must be listening to something, we were silent too. . . . We all stood there silently for a long moment" (70). Sylvie experiences, perceives, attends: "Sylvie always walked with her head down, to one side, with an abstracted and considered expression, as if someone were speaking to her in a soft voice" (48). She lived always in the now, not in the past or future, and "inhabited a millennial present" (94). Ruth feels an affinity with Sylvie and knows that they are similar to each other. Like Sylvie, Ruth is a watcher, a listener. In these ways, Sylvie models the qualities Robinson associates, in her essays, with a democratically valuable ethos: attentiveness to the mystery of the world, mindful openness to what is given. Sylvie is accepting, open, kind, generous, forgiving, and she avoids judging others even though they judge her so harshly.

Despite her persistent transience, Sylvie does make itinerant stabs at housekeeping, of a strange but delightful kind. If it is cold outside, she always has a fire going inside and warms up soup and sandwiches for the girls over the blaze. She plays Monopoly with them, and cards, and brushes their hair for them. She listens to them and tells them stories. She sings "Goodnight, Irene" for them. She brings the girls presents from the five-and-dime store, "treasures" that are wholly impractical such as atomizers, gilt dresser sets, angora-trimmed anklets, and scalloped nylon gloves (94). She feeds them crackers in cellophane, "watermelon pickles and canned meats, apples and jelly donuts and shoestring potatoes, a block of pre-sliced cheese, a bottle of milk, a bottle of catsup, a raisin bread in a stack. Sylvie liked cold food, sardines aswim in oil, little fruit pies in paper envelopes" (87). She also saves newspapers and stacks up cleaned, washed-out tin cans.

But her efforts at housekeeping seem aimed mainly toward minimizing the differences between indoors and outdoors, toward bringing the outdoors inside. As Ruth says:

> I remember Sylvie walking through the house with a scarf tied around her hair, carrying a broom. Yet this was the time that leaves began to gather in the corners. . . . Thus finely did our house become attuned to the orchard and to the particularities of weather, even in the first days of Sylvie's housekeeping. Thus did she begin by littles and perhaps unawares to ready it for the wasps and bats and barn swallows. Sylvie talked a great deal about housekeeping. She soaked all the tea towels for a number of weeks in a tub of water and bleach. She emptied several cupboards and left them open to air, and once she washed half the kitchen ceiling and a door. Sylvie believed in stern solvents, and most of all in air. It was for the sake of air that she opened doors and windows, though it was probably through forgetfulness that she left them open. (85)

So it's not that Sylvie rejects housekeeping. She simply has an unconventional view about what housekeeping means. For example, Sylvie liked to leave the lights off as long as possible as the evening rolled in, so they would eat their dinner looking outside, instead of having their sight closed off to the gloaming by the brightness of interior lights: "We looked at the window as we ate, and we listened to the crickets and the nighthawks, which were always unusually loud then" (86). Sylvie "seemed to dislike the disequilibrium of counterpoising a roomful of light against a worldful of darkness. Sylvie in a house was more or less like a mermaid in a ship's cabin. She preferred it sunk into the very element it was meant to exclude" (99).

For Ruth, if not for Lucille, living with Sylvie in this way fills a void inside her. Lucille is always trying to improve herself, hanging out at the drugstore, learning the habits of the conventional world, normalizing herself, "to slip across the wide frontiers into that other world, where it seemed to me that I could never wish to go" (124). But for Ruth, living like a mermaid in a ship's cabin with Sylvie is fulfilling, even (especially?) as the house becomes less and less aligned with the conventional space of home: "It seemed that something I had lost might be found in Sylvie's house . . . as I approached the house I was newly aware of the changes that had overtaken it. The lawn was knee high, an oily, dank green, and the wind sent ripples across it. It had swamped the smaller bushes and the walk and the first step and had risen to the height of the foundation. And it seems that if the house were not to founder, it must soon begin to float" (124). In Sylvie's house, or at least in the house Sylvie temporarily is able to make as a housekeeper of homelessness, Ruth finds something she thought she had lost: herself. But for Lucille, Sylvie's unusual house is no home at all.

The sharp contrast between the life Lucille chooses and the life Ruth and Sylvie strive toward is captured in the difference between huckleberries and home economics. At one point in the novel, Ruth and Lucille find Sylvie sleeping on a park bench with a newspaper over her face. Lucille is horrified, saying: "I don't know what keeps her here. I think she'd really rather jump on a train" (107). And soon after, Sylvie comes back with huckleberries, which she found growing over by the train station, and they make huckleberry pancakes (108). Here, the huckleberries seem an allusion to Sylvie's uncultivated and undomesticated state. As I have shown elsewhere, huckleberries are a classic symbol of a kind of wildness and resistance to civilization because they are very difficult to grow in artificial conditions and resist commodification as well. They wilt soon after being picked, can't be shipped or grown elsewhere, and are best eaten in their native wild habitat, right off the branch.[9] Thoreau writes extensively about huckleberries and huckleberrying throughout his corpus.[10] And lest we forget, Huckleberry is also the first name of Huck Finn, the boy who wouldn't be "*sivilized*." One night soon after Sylvie comes home bearing huckleberries, Lucille leaves the house forever and—in a true testament of her desire for conventional housekeeping—moves in with her home economics teacher. Lucille essentially talks her unmarried, spinsterly teacher into letting her move in: "Miss Royce gave her the spare room. In effect, she adopted her, and I had no sister after that night" (140). And the same night that Lucille leaves, Sylvie tells Ruth her plan to take her on an adventure to an abandoned house up in the north. Two very different kinds of homes are chosen at this point in the novel.

When Sylvie and Ruth go to this abandoned cabin in the woods, far north of the lake, it becomes clear that Sylvie has come here often and dreams of living in this strange place. Sylvie says there are families that live in the area, hunting and fishing: "Sometimes you'll see a little smoke in the woods. There might be a cabin with ten children in it" (148). But it seems like these cabins in the woods with ten children are fantasies or imaginings of Sylvie's, not real. She describes how she has tried to lure the children toward her with marshmallows, though she recognizes they might be kind of wild, living out there in the woods: "A child like that might claw or bite. But I did want to look at it" (148). Chasing this fantasy, Sylvie says: "If I think I see smoke I go walking toward it, and now and then I'm sure there are children around me. I can practically hear them. . . . That's one reason I keep crackers in my pockets" (148). Sylvie seems to be attracted to the idea of the cabin in the woods with ten children in it—though she laughs, "What would I do with another child?"—but this really seems a manifestation of her desire to create her own paradoxical home that society does not make available to her.

While Ruth is at the abandoned house, another extended meditation takes place on how housekeeping and homelessness might exist on a simultaneous plane. A new narrative voice in the novel, unnamed but not Ruth's, writes of how we can find surprising richness even in a homeless and seemingly desolate place like Carthage, where we thought there was nothing. If approached the right way, even homeless spaces can flower into a world made whole, giving us back what we thought we had lost: "Imagine a Carthage sown with salt, and all the sowers gone, and the seeds lain however long in the earth, till there rose finally in vegetable profusion leaves and trees of rime and brine. What flowering would there be in such a garden? Light would force each salt calyx to open into prisms, and to fruit heavily with bright globes of water—peaches and grapes are little more than that, and where the world was salt there would be greater need of slaking" (152). Emptiness blooms into fullness; homelessness and housekeeping intermingle, like Sylvie's home that is submerged in the element it was meant to exclude. Ruth and Sylvie both long for that middle place and wish they could have continued as they had once, mermaids in the ship's cabin, occupying the position as housekeepers of homelessness and making things bloom in a seemingly barren landscape. The abandoned house represents their last attempt to find a middle place outside of conventional society. This is a recurring theme in the works I explore in this essay. Each character who occupies the position of housekeeper of homelessness also has a home away from home, an imaginary home, a space of escape that is like a second home, or even just a tent in the barn, as we will see.

Soon after they return from this trip to the abandoned house, the sheriff comes to talk with them: "It was not the theft of the boat he came about, though that had been reported, not my truancy, since I was almost old enough to leave school if I chose to. It was not that Sylvie had kept me out on the lake all night, because no one knew just where we had been. It was that we returned to Fingerbone in a freight car. Sylvie was an unredeemed transient, and she was making a transient out of me" (177). There will be a hearing regarding Ruth's welfare, and Ruth and Sylvie know that the hearing will not turn out well. The sheriff asks her if she wants to come home with him, to his wife's apple pie, to be with "nice folks" (206). Here we have the last temptation of home, but Ruth rejects it. It is not her native land, and she cannot imagine inhabiting such a space. The sheriff issues a veiled threat, making it clear that Ruth will be taken away from Sylvie tomorrow: "All right, then. But I'm going to be keeping an eye on you. I want you in school tomorrow, you hear? . . . I want you to be here tomorrow, now. I want to talk to you tomorrow,' he called back to us" (206–7). So Sylvie and Ruth both go into the house and Sylvie immediately sets it on fire: "One moment I had no idea where Sylvie was, and the next moment the parlor curtains were sheet of flames." But Ruth joins in and they act as if they were "almost a single person" (208).

They burn the house down not because they detest it but because they cannot occupy it in the manner they desire. Nor can they leave it behind, filled with sentimental objects like Ruth's mother's gray purse, the grandmother's lock of girlhood hair: "In the equal light of disinterested scrutiny such things are not themselves. They are transformed into pure object, and are horrible, and must be burned" (209). They burn the house because they don't want these objects to become even more present in their absence, to haunt them because they have been lost. They leave because the sheriff is clearly going to take Ruth away in the morning: "For we had to leave. I could not stay, and Sylvie would not stay without me. Now truly we were cast out to wander, and there was an end to housekeeping" (209). They pull on their boots and dash out of the still-burning house. There is something so ephemeral about this book that we are apt to forget that Ruth and Sylvie are essentially being driven out of town because Ruth is about to be taken away from Sylvie by the sheriff, by the judge, for nothing more than not being conventional. We are apt to forget, amid the poetic descriptions of this final breaking up of housekeeping, that Sylvie has done nothing really wrong, that she is really being persecuted here for reminding Fingerbone of the illusory nature of home, for reminding them of their own transience, which they would rather deny and try to forget.

And they leave and run away as the house burns, and the townspeople think that they fell into the lake or committed suicide: "Lake Claims Two," the newspaper headline reads (213). Ruth and Sylvie never tell Lucille the truth, never tell her that they are alive, at first waiting for the seven-year statute of limitations to pass but then figuring it's better to just let it go. So they ride the rails, and they never return to Fingerbone, though they ride past it sometimes and indulge in fantasies that they know are untrue, imagining that Lucille is now living in their old house, pruning the trees and neatly taking care of it and making it look presentable. So this home is still present for them in its absence, just as an air of homelessness was present in their temporary housekeeping. Sylvie keeps the newspaper story about their apparent death pinned under her lapel, out of sight, but still there.

Ultimately, Sylvie only becomes a kind of democratic hero for the story because of how her own way of life contrasts with the townspeople's, as well as Lucille's and Lily's and Nona's. Sylvie exemplifies a kind of reverence for her own experience, over and against conventions and expectations. She seems to find mystery in the small pleasures of daily life and lives with curiosity and a sense of wonder. She simply wants to be left to live her own life according to her own sensibilities. But Sylvie's nonconformity brings out the worst in others, and their reactions to her—their desire to force her to fit into existing conventions, their judgment of her, and their ultimate refusal to let her live in her own way—highlight the violence that stems from *not* having the kinds of qualities that Sylvie exemplifies. The dangers and deficits of the townspeople's behavior serve to illuminate the value of Robinson's understanding of—and Sylvie's performance of—this democratic ideal.

Gilead and *Home*

Gilead and *Home* involve the same characters and take place in the same town, occur during the same time period, and even analyze the same events from the viewpoints of different characters. In both of these novels, there are figures who, like Sylvie from *Housekeeping,* are not allowed to keep house as they see fit because of the conventions of the town and so must abandon the paradoxical position that Robinson idealizes for a more radical form of homelessness. The elder Reverend Ames and Jack, in their resistance to the racist conventions of their days, take up this more extreme form of homelessness. But they leave home with lament, regrettably. For the elder Reverend Ames and Jack, as for Sylvie and Ruth ultimately, the conventional authorities of the town close off the possibility of acting as housekeepers of homelessness. But there are also figures, like Ames, the first-person narrator of *Gilead,* and like Glory, the third-person narrator of *Home,* who do manage to occupy this paradoxical middle place that Robinson values. Both model the modes of perception that Robinson sees as furthering the democratic ideal.

In *Gilead,* the narrator Ames embodies this desired position. Ames faces death in the near future. In his late seventies, he has recently learned he has a bad heart. He lives in a house that is literally insecure. He is a pastor who lives in church housing but knows that when he dies his home will revert back to the church and his young wife and son (he married very late in life) will be turned out. Ames is also an outsider, though he is an important figure in the town. He spent the vast majority of his life living alone, and because of his position with the church, he was never quite one of the townspeople and felt that difference strongly. In addition, quite unusually, he fell in love, married, and had a child, all in his late sixties, which contributes to his dual insider/outsider position, always a productive space of insights for Robinson.

Ames combines the occupations of housekeeping with the spirit of homelessness in an exemplary way. When asked what death is like, he says it is "like going home. We have no home in this world, I used to say, and then I'd walk back up the road to this old place and make myself a pot of coffee and a fried egg sandwich and listen to the radio, when I got one, in the dark."[11] Like Sylvie, Ames lets the darkness of the outside into the house at night, minimizing the border between inside and outside by eating dinner with the lights off as the night comes in. He never leaves Gilead, yet he also never fully feels *of* Gilead. He describes himself as "the good son, so to speak, the one who never left his father's house—even when his father did, a fact which surely puts my credentials beyond all challenge"—but who is also "homesick for a place I never left" (238, 235).

And like other characters in Robinson's novels, Ames has a home away from home: his church. When troubled by his conscience, worried, or unable to sleep, Ames will walk down to the church—often in the middle of the night—and sit quietly in the pews. This has been his habit for years. This space is like Sylvie's abandoned house in the woods. The church represents a place of solace for him, a home apart from his actual house. Ames speaks of "how pleasant it was to walk through the streets in the dark and let myself into the church and watch the dawn come in the sanctuary" (70). When he was troubled, after walking through the town, perceiving, wide awake, noting that "trees sound different at night, and they smell different too," Ames would "go into the church and pray some more and wait for daylight" (71).

Ames's most notable quality is his attempt to be continually open to the mystery of daily experience, to see, hear, and perceive in a concentrated way: "This is an interesting planet. It deserves all the attention you can give it" (28). As he says, "Wherever you turn your eyes the world can shine like transfiguration. You don't have to bring a thing except a little willingness to see. Only, who could have the courage to see it?" (245). He opens himself up to the groundless nature of experience: "My point here is that you never do know the actual nature even of your own experience. Or perhaps it has no fixed and certain nature" (95). He recognizes that the spirit of homelessness that we build homes to protect against may wall out the quality of uprootedness that sharpens our perception. As he says at one point, "when we think we are protecting ourselves, we are struggling against our rescuer" (154). So he tries to open himself up to experience, difficult though that is: "Well, see and see but do not perceive, hear and hear but do not understand, as the Lord says. I can't claim to understand that saying, as many times as I've heard it, and even preached on it. It simply states a deeply mysterious fact. You can know a thing to death and be for all purposes completely ignorant of it" (7). This openness to the mystery of experience is the kind of attunement that comes from occupying the paradoxically dual position of the housekeeper of homelessness:

> In every important way we are such secrets from each other, and I do believe that there is a separate language in each of us, also a separate aesthetics and a separate jurisprudence. Every single one of us is a little civilization built on the ruins of any number of preceding civilizations, but with our own variant notions of what is beautiful and what is acceptable—which, I hasten to add, we generally do not satisfy and by which we struggle to live. We take fortuitous resemblances among us to be actual likeness, because those around us have also fallen heir to the same customs, trade in the same coin, acknowledge, more or less, the same notions of decency and sanity. But all that really just allows us to coexist with the inviolable, untraversable, and utterly vast spaces between us. (197)

So Ames models a respect for other individuals, a respect for the differences that lie beneath a superficial appearance of similarity, a flexibility in his judgments, and a willingness to change his mind. But where Jack is concerned, the democratic value of Ames's way of being becomes all the more pronounced. Jack is someone who tests Ames's commitment to these principles. Jack brings out the worst in him, but Ames is wise enough to be deeply troubled over and worried about these failings in himself. And Ames ultimately masters his doubts about Jack and comes to accept him with open generosity, sees the good in him, forgives him, and is even thankful to Jack for giving him the opportunity to consistently live out his principles even when tested.

In *Home,* Glory comes to occupy a space that is similar to Ames's position. Unlike some of the characters, like Jack and like the elder Reverend Ames, who are forced into a position of homelessness, Glory is pushed against her will into a position of housekeeping, returning home to the house she grew up in because her own life has fallen apart and because her sick father needs nursing. But because Glory no longer has any illusions about "home," she performs these acts of housekeeping with a spirit of homelessness in a way that proves valuable as the story unfolds. Glory had been a schoolteacher, seemingly successful and engaged to be married, but she gives up her job and returns home after the relationship ends. She was engaged to a man who in fact was just sucking her finances dry for years. Finally he broke up with her—after the money was gone?—and she realizes she had been living with a complete illusion: they hardly spent any time together, and she didn't really even love him. But she loved the illusion of him and the future children they might have and the life they might make together: "What does it mean to come home? . . . She had dreamed of a real home for herself and the babies, and the fiancé, a home very different from this good and blessed and fustian and oppressive tabernacle of Boughton probity and kind intent. She knew, she had known for years, that she would never open a door in that home, never cross that threshold, never scoop up a child and set it on her hip and feel it lean into her breast and eye the world from her arms with the complacency of utter trust. Ah well."[12]

She realizes she was actually happiest when the fiancé was gone—he was a traveling salesman—because then she could have the ideal illusion of him rather than the harsher reality. Glory also, like Sylvie, imagines invisible children playing in an invisible house. She put up with the fiancé so she could continue this fantasy. Glory even recognizes at one point that she much prefers the illusion to the reality: "She gave him the money so he would stop talking, maybe even so he would go away. He might have known this. He would go away and leave her with her thoughts of him" (312). But ultimately, that illusion could not be sustained, and Glory had to face up to the fact that her supposed fiancé was not actually going to marry her or have children with her. And so Glory goes home to her father's house that is now no home at all. Her family, however, actually thinks she has gotten married, quickly, without fuss. Though her own father has hoped to officiate the ceremony, she sent a letter explaining that "on impulse, just to get things settled, they had gone to a justice of the peace" (25). That wasn't true, but she is too embarrassed to say they had never gotten married, and when she returns home, sensing her feelings, her father never actually asks her why she is home or what happened but simply welcomes her and lets things fall into their own pattern. Here, in the first line, is all the complexity of home: "'Home to stay, Glory! Yes!' her father said, and her heart sank. He attempted a twinkle of joy at this thought, but his eyes were damp with commiserations. 'To stay for a while this time!' he amended, and took her bag from her, first shifting his cane to his weaker hand. Dear God, she thought, dear God in heaven" (3).

In this novel, the ideological space of home is captured in the Boughton family home in Gilead, Iowa, where all eight children grew up. The Boughton family home represents the forces of convention and normality, and their father especially was deeply invested in maintaining the appearance of happiness, prosperity, and stability. As the father says, as he must tell himself, it seems, showing Glory to her room: "'Well, it's a good house.' The house embodied for him the general blessedness of his life, which was manifest, really indisputable" (3). Glory sees the house differently, as does Jack. Glory is the youngest of the children, and Jack was always the outcast, but the two of them share a position of alienation in this novel. Glory always felt apart from the rest of the family. Her experiences of alienation intensify as she grows older and give her insight into Jack's position and sympathy for him. As Glory says, "Why should this staunch and upright house seem to her so abandoned? So heartbroken? The eye of the beholder, she thought. Still, seven of her father's children came home as often as they could manage to, and telephoned, and sent notes and gifts and crates of grapefruit" (4–5). Glory increasingly realizes that she is not one of those seven, that her attitude toward home has changed. She realizes that home is just an illusion that must be kept up, sustained. But for her father's comfort, she tries to extend the lie and re-create the sense of home that her father remembers from when the children were young. Glory cooks, cleans, and bakes because that was what her mother always did and this comforts her father. But, as we will see, Glory does, by the end of *Home,* develop her own strategy for a more sincere kind of housekeeping that does not require her to give up the valuable spirit of homelessness that also came with the evaporation of her illusions.

Before we can understand how Glory will combine housekeeping with homelessness, though, we have to analyze the role Jack plays in both *Gilead* and *Home.* And before we can understand Jack, we need to explore the nineteenth-century abolitionist Reverend Ames. Throughout the book, parallels are drawn between this earlier Reverend Ames and Jack Boughton, named John Ames Boughton, after the narrator of *Gilead,* who was never expected to have any children of his own. The grandfather's radicalism and commitment to racial justice is not reflected in his son or his grandson so much as in his distant namesake who is not actually a blood relative at all.

Grandfather Ames is a radical figure, who seemed continually "stricken and afflicted, and indeed he was, like a man everlastingly struck by lightning, so that there was an ashiness about his clothes and his hair never settled and his eye had a look of tragic alarm when he wasn't actually sleeping. He was the most unreposeful human being I ever knew" (*Gilead,* 49). Ames says, "I believe he was a saint of some kind" (31). He had had a vision when he was young, in Maine, not yet sixteen: "Someone touched him on the shoulder, and when he looked up, there was the Lord, holding out His arms to him, which were bound in chains. . . . He said he knew then that he had to come to Kansas and make himself useful to the cause of abolition" (49). His grandfather joined the Union army and "preached his people into the war, saying while there was slavery there was no peace, but only a war of the armed and powerful against the captive and defenseless. He would say, Peace will come only when that war ends, so the God of peace calls upon us to end it. He said all this with that gun in his belt. And everyone there always shouted amen, even the littlest children" (101). He knew John Brown and Jim Lane, and "In course of time," Ames "learned that my grandfather was involved pretty deeply in the violence in Kansas before the war" (85). When he was in town and not off helping John Brown, engaging in other abolitionist activities, or aiding the war effort, he used to call his congregation in to hear him preach, sometimes in a bloodstained shirt, by firing his rifle into the air. At one point, the grandfather sheltered John Brown and his wounded men, along with their horses, in the church, dripping blood over the pews. There is deep suspicion that the grandfather also killed the Union soldier who was tracking down Brown, in part because they had to keep the authorities away from the town because of all the secret underground tunnels and hollow walls designed for helping escaped slaves—none of that could be discovered without endangering their abolitionist activities.

In his old age, the elder Reverend Ames was always taking money to give to the poor, anything he had, and anything he felt other people had but didn't need. He even stole from the Presbyterians' collection plate because he felt that they hoarded their money too much. Ultimately, the grandfather ran off to Kansas at the end of his life in part because he had nowhere to "spend his courage" and in part because someone set the Negro church on fire. Just before he takes off, the grandfather is asked, just as a formality, to give what everyone expects will be a banal address at a July Fourth event. Instead he preaches: "Children—When I was a young man the Lord came to me and put His hand on my right shoulder. I can feel it still. And he spoke to me, very clearly. The words went right through me. He said, Free the captive. Preach good news to the poor. Proclaim liberty throughout the land. . . . No one lives by them, unless the Lord takes him in hand. . . . The President, General Grant, once called Iowa the shining star of radicalism.

But what is left here in Iowa? What is left here in Gilead? Dust. Dust and ashes" (176).

Then he takes off for parts unknown, old and alone: "He was just afire with old certainties, and he couldn't bear all the patience that was required of him by the peace and by the aging of his body and by the forgetfulness that had settled over everything. He thought we should all be living at a dead run" (32). He leaves his family a note: "No good has come, no evil has ended. That is your peace. Without vision the people perish. The Lord bless and keep you" (85). He ultimately dies far from family and from Gilead and is laid to rest in a grave that is marked in the humblest of ways, that his son and Ames, while only a boy, go off to find in a pilgrimage or sorts. The grave is in a poor, drought-stricken part of the West, an entirely homeless and inhospitable place: "It was the most natural thing in the world that my grandfather's grave would look like a place where they tried to smother a fire" (50).

Jack Boughton, the unrelated namesake, embodies a similar kind of radicalism and an inability to abide by the hypocrisies of conventional society. In *Gilead,* we only really know Jack as a troubled child who has grown into a troubled man—he's been known to steal, he drinks, he's tried to kill himself, he's been in jail. But Jack had always been the outsider in the family—a strange child who was never at home in his own family. And he turns into a troubled teenager who, home for a visit from college, takes advantage of an extremely young girl. The girl becomes pregnant, but Jack never acknowledges the baby. Horrified by what has happened, his family does acknowledge the child and tries to care for her, but she dies very young from an infection. After this, Jack leaves home, and no one sees him for a very long time—twenty years—though they try to track him down, and they do send money. After Glory moves home, they get a letter from him, out of the blue one day, saying that he is coming home for a while. When he finally shows up, he is hungover but also embarrassed, like Glory was. Both homecomings feel like embarrassing failures.

Steadily throughout *Home,* Jack's status as an outsider is complicated and continually reframed. In the beginning of the book, Jack appears as the outcast of the family because he was a thief, a liar, a drunk. Jack was never at home in his house, never at home with his family. Even after he returns home, Glory describes his transient habits, his "boarding house" habits: "After a few days she might find him sitting in the porch, reading a magazine. And sometimes, if she was busy in the kitchen, he would bring his magazine to the kitchen table and read in there. A stray, she thought, learning the terms of domestication. Testing the comforts, weighing the costs" (52). Robinson also highlights the artificiality of the process of normalization, both through Jack's study of the ordinary world as though he was a foreigner to it and through Lucille's habit of taking notes on other people's habits and composing a field guide to that conventional world. A friend of the family invites Jack to dinner, and he isn't sure how to respond. Glory says, "'It's the most ordinary thing in the world.' He nodded. 'There it is. My lifelong exile from the ordinary world. I have to learn the customs. And somehow persuade myself that they pertain to me'" (210). Jack and Glory, in their illusory homecomings, both become homeless. But this is familiar terrain for Jack, indeed, the only one he has ever known. Jack is described as having had, from the beginning, an "inaccessible strangeness," and "estrangement" is described as "his oldest habit" (230). Upon returning home, Jack remarks: "I've thought about this place so many times. When I was a kid I used to wish I lived here. I used to wish I could walk in the door just like the rest of you did and, you know, sit down at the table and do my homework or something" (276).

Like Glory's dream home, Jack also builds an alternative to his father's house. Once he starts drinking again, he reconstructs a tent in the barn that he used to use as a home away from home when he was a kid, hanging clothesline from beam to beam and throwing a tarp over it: "The dark little room smelled strongly of whiskey and sweat. It seemed almost domestic, and yet there was a potency of loneliness about it like a dark spirit lurking in it, a soul that had improvised this crude tabernacle to stand in place of other shelter, flesh" (285). Jack's father's house is also described as a "tabernacle." Glory thinks that his tent is a way of making a statement, even immature. She wondered as a child what gave him the right to be so strange, and, as an adult, she still sees the estrangement he clings to as a sort of privilege that she can't afford. She is as alienated as Jack but doesn't enact it as spectacularly as Jack always has: "And then that hiding place he had made, comforting himself in concealment as he had always done. Or hiding his loneliness, or making his estrangement literal, visible" (300). Even at the end of the book, Jack leaves home for true homelessness—setting out with only a few dollars in his pocket, practically like a hobo with a bindle over his shoulder. His is a kind of extravagant performance of homelessness, while Glory's ultimate homelessness is experienced and performed in a less visible, more mundane, but no less real, way.

These two figures are inversely sympathetic to each other. If Jack yearns to, in some degree, escape homelessness for home, Glory wants to escape housekeeping for greater homelessness. She finds inheriting the Boughton house as oppressive as Jack finds his own homelessness at times:

> "Well, Jack, I've just found out that I will inherit this house. I never meant to stay in Gilead. I mean I positively intended to leave Gilead. I don't want to sound ungrateful, but I'm—'horrified' is too strong a word, but it's the one that comes to mind. . . . This is a nightmare I've had a hundred times. The one where all the rest of you go off and begin your lives and I am left in an empty house full of ridiculous furniture and unreadable books, waiting for someone to notice I'm missing and come back for me. And nobody does." He laughed. "Poor pigtails." Then he said, "When I have that dream, I'm hiding in the barn hoping someone will find me, and nobody does." (298)

Both Glory and Jack want to be found, but the circumstances of where they are lost and found are opposed given their different native lands, so to speak.

But as we learn more about Jack, especially in *Home,* we find out that he is troubled, in large part, by the racist and segregationist practices of the day. We learn that he's been married, at least in the eyes of God if not of the state, to an African American woman named Della. They haven't been actually able to live together as man and wife except for short spells because no rooming houses will have a mixed-race couple. They have a child together, named Robert Miles Boughton. Jack is also engaged in antisegregationist activities of the twentieth century in a way that recalls the grandfather's nineteenth-century abolitionism. And like the grandfather's commitment to fighting class inequality by liberally taking from the haves and giving to the have-nots, we learn that Jack has read W. E. B. Du Bois and is sympathetic to Marx and Engels.

The connections between the grandfather and Jack are further strengthened by a conversation that happens between Della's father and Jack. Della's family disapproves of Jack, but at one point, her father thinks he is actually a literal descendent of the grandfather, whose courageous abolitionist activities have been remembered in the African American community. As Jack later relates the story to Ames:

> "He said, 'I understand you are descended from John Ames, of Kansas.' Of course anyone else would have put that right, but I thought there might be some advantage in letting him believe it—he was referring to your grandfather, of course. It was the first slightly positive thing he had ever said to me. He said he knew people whose families came north from Missouri before the war, and apparently they told him some remarkable stories about him, about raids and ambushes. . . . I said my family had turned pacifist after the war. And didn't encourage discussion of it. That's correct, I believe?" (*Gilead*, 227)

But though he may not have been as active in the civil rights movement as Reverend Ames was in the abolitionist movement, Jack clearly supports the desegregation efforts of his own day, as we learn when Jack and his father are watching their new television. The news reports that "a colored woman wants to go to the University of Alabama" (*Home*, 155). A conversation ensues between Jack and his father, where Jack reveals himself to have a deep investment with the civil rights movements, whereas his father thinks that if African Americans want to be accepted, they just need to improve themselves. As his father says: "I have nothing against the colored people. I do think they're going to need to improve themselves, though, if they want to be accepted. I believe that is the only solution" (155). And Jack responds:

> "I'm a little unimproved myself. I've known a good many Negroes who are more respectable than I am."
>
> His father looked at him. "I don't know where you get such a terrible opinion of yourself, Jack. . . . There's a lot you could do if you put your mind to it."
>
> Jack laughed. "True enough. I could stay in a hotel. I could eat in a cafeteria. I could hail a cab. I could exercise my franchise. Unworthy as I am." (155)

The conversation continues, and Jack's father says that "the colored people" create a lot of trouble and commotion: "they bring it on themselves" (155). Jack just looks at his father.

> He drew a long breath, then another. He asked softly, "Have you heard of Emmett Till?"
>
> "Emmett Till. Wasn't he that negro fellow that—attacked the white woman?"
>
> Jack said, "He was a kid. He was fourteen. Somebody said he whistled at a white woman."
>
> His father said, "I think there must have been more to it, Jack. As I remember, he was executed. There was a trial."
>
> Jack said, "There was no trial. He was murdered. He was a child, and they murdered him." He cleared his throat to recover control of his voice.
>
> "Yes, that is upsetting. I had another memory of it."
>
> Jack said, "We read different newspapers." (155)

This exchange also seems to confirm that Gilead is not yet a place where Jack and his wife, Della, and their son, Robert, can live as a family, in peace. Gilead is not a place where this interracial family can create the home that Jack desires. It turns out that Jack has returned home to Gilead to investigate whether it would be possible, in this town that was founded on a commitment to racial justice, to bring back his wife and son to live. He wants to settle his family, to find a kind of home where they can live in the space between inside and outside. Jack asks: "What about this town? If we came here and got married, could we live here? Would people leave us alone?" (*Gilead*, 231). The answer seems to be "not yet," but Jack and Della never have a chance to test the strength of Gilead's supposed commitment to social justice.

At the end of *Home*, Della sends Jack a kind letter that also seems to indicate he shouldn't wait for her any longer, and he gives up hope and decides to leave. He will only take ten dollars from Glory, knowing that if he has more money on him, he will be too tempted to spend it all on drink. Jack leaves. Glory watches: "She went to the porch to watch him walk away down the road. He was too thin and his clothes were weary, weary. There was nothing of youth about him, only the transient vigor of a man acting on a decision he refused to reconsider or regret" (318). After Jack leaves, his father collapses fully into dementia and senility, a process that began slightly before he left. As soon as Jack leaves, Della shows up. Della and Glory can only talk briefly, but they are so happy to have met each other, immediately seem to recognize each other as friends, as two women who love, and to some extent understand, Jack. Glory promises to let Della know if she hears from Jack. They exchange phone numbers. Della and her son need to leave, but Glory wants to give them something from the house, something to take with them. She takes a framed picture of a river that has hung in Jack's room since he was a boy and gives it to Della and to Robert, his son: "Jack had a beautiful child, a beautiful son, who would some time turn Boughton, no doubt, and lose his prettiness to what they called distinction" (322).

The book also ends just as *Housekeeping* ends, with a vision, an imagining of the lost one returning home. Just as Ruth imagines Lucille returning to the house that was almost lost, almost burned, that Sylvie and Ruth left, Glory imagines Robert returning to his father's house:

> What of Jack will there be in him? And I will be almost old. I will see him standing in the road by the oak tree, and I will know him by his tall man's slouch, the hand on the hips. . . . And he will be very kind to me. He is Jack's son. . . . He will be curious about the old place, though his curiosity will not override his good manners. He will talk to me a little while, too shy to tell me why he has come, and he will thank me and leave, walking backwards a few steps, thinking, Yes, the barn is still there, yes, the lilacs, even the pot of petunias. This was my father's house. And I will think, He is young. He cannot know that my whole life had come down to this moment.
>
> That he has answered his father's prayers.
>
> The lord is wonderful. (325)

Glory realizes her lot in life is to keep the house ready for the return of Jack's son, Robert. But now she takes up a more sincere and less illusory form of housekeeping, now with a productive rather than destitute spirit of homelessness. Thus in this novel, Glory and Jack take on different positions with respect to housekeeping and homelessness. Whereas Jack has always had the ethos of homelessness, in *Home*, he is searching for home, seeking to ground himself and hopefully his family in a new home in Gilead. Jack comes from a landscape of homelessness and is looking to put down roots and set up some (minimal) degree of housekeeping. Jack hopes to find a way to live with his family, probably still in the margins of society in Gilead, positioning him as a kind of aspirant housekeeper of homelessness. Glory, on the other hand, moves in the opposite direction as Jack, to end up aspiring toward the same middle place. Glory goes through a process of maturation throughout the book that moves her from the landscape of home into the region of homelessness. She realizes that she has lived her life so far, as a child in the Boughton home and then as an adult with her supposed fiancé, with an image of the conventional home that was always an illusion, an appearance, a fiction, a lie. During the course of the story, she frees herself from this illusion and increasingly cultivates an ethos of homelessness where she simply confronts the present as it comes, open to her experiences, without the disciplining categories of convention. Glory has been trapped by "home" in various ways, not least because of her gender, her necessary role as caretaker for her ailing father, and the fact that she will inherit the family home. But she ultimately finds a way to escape home without leaving the house. She will keep the house, but now she undertakes this occupation without being deluded by the illusory conventions of home.

But for both, Robinson's democratic ideal is tied to this combining of housekeeping with homelessness. The values that Glory and Jack exemplify, despite their human flaws, humble them away from dangerous certainties and make them both open-minded, forgiving, accepting of other ways of life, and skeptical about conventional assumptions. In Glory's case, she becomes aware of her own conventional assumptions and is liberated from her own obedience to conventional authorities and desires. And the heroes of Robinson's fiction—figures like the elder Reverend Ames, the narrator John Ames, Glory, and Jack—are able to think and act against the racial prejudices of their day because of their mode of perception and their ways of being. Thus again, Robinson makes explicit connections between how we see, hear, sense, and experience and how we live in the social and political worlds. Her heroes are critical of conventions in a way that leads them to reject racial injustice. Robinson shows us, again in *Gilead* and in *Home*, how our ways of being in the world, our modes of experience, are deeply related to our ability to live out a democratic ideal where we embrace otherness, question conventional authorities, and do not judge other ways of life.

The Essays

Robinson herself takes on the role of the housekeeper of the democratic ethos of homelessness in her essays, and this paradoxical position is part of what makes them so difficult to categorize, and so rich. She can seem like a conservative writer given the topics she treats and the terrain her writing explores: John Calvin, the Bible, Moses, Puritanism, Family, Darwin, Science, to give a few examples. Furthermore, Robinson's essays can seem conservative because of the way they are recognizably rooted in a traditional and recognizably "American" terrain. Her writing is strongly marked by her own origins as a descendant of Protestants from the western states, and before that, from England. Indeed, her book about Britain is titled *Mother Country*. In these ways, Robinson's essays can seem to inhabit a settled, familiar, stable space that maps onto the ideological space of "home." But we are never allowed to get too comfortable within the themes, texts, and topics that Robinson treats in her essays because she courts an attitude of homelessness *within* these seemingly familiar landscapes of home. In these ways, Robinson complicates the ways we might usually think about conservatism and radicalism, traditional and progressive, old and new, home and a radical democratic ethos of homelessness. She works at defamiliarizing spaces that seem known, at denaturalizing that which we tend to take for granted, at cultivating a sense of homelessness in the terrain of one's own home, however defined. And as in her novels, the mode of perception that identifies "sacred mystery with every individual experience"—the way of being that she characterizes as a democratic ideal—shapes how the self interacts with others too (*Child,* xiv). As the essays also demonstrate, this democratic ideal requires that we "honor others and oneself with something wholly approaching due reverence" (*Child,* xiv).

To give one example of the way Robinson acts as a housekeeper of homelessness—with important outcomes for democracy—she is deeply religious but identifies religion with mystery, with an antifoundationalist uncertainty and openness. In fact, she thinks real science and religion have a lot more in common—in their devotion to a search for meaning but also an understanding of uncertainty and ambiguity—than contemporary "parascience," which makes strong assertions and grounds itself in certainty and a kind of fundamentalism. She will make a traditional statement and assert that there is value in the idea that human beings were created in God's image, but then twist that seemingly familiar idea. She sees the idea of "God," like religion, as difficult to define, because both strain against limits and containment. So Robinson uses this, at first glance, very conventional idea that humans are created in God's image to ultimately make a case for the limitlessness of human potential, to argue for human potentialities, to fight against the modern idea of a human being which she thinks "has grown oppressively small and dull":

> I would like to propose a solution of sorts. . . . What if we were to say that human beings are created in the image of God? It will certainly be objected that we have no secure definitions of major terms. How much do we know about God, after all? How are we to understand this word "created"? . . . But it is just on these grounds that this conception would rescue us from the problems that come from our tendency to create definitions of human nature that are small and closed. It would allow us to acknowledge the fact, manifest in culture and history, that we are both terrible and very wonderful. (159)

She acts as the housekeeper of homelessness by reading the Bible and writes about theology, but with wonder and openness to newness and the unexpected: "I do not understand the Bible. I study theology as one would watch a solar eclipse in a shadow. In church, the devout old custom persists of merely repeating verses, one or another luminous fragment, a hymn before and a hymn afterward. By grace of my abiding ignorance, it is always new to me. I am never not instructed" (*Adam,* 231). Regarding the Gospels, she thinks, "It is as true of these old texts as it is of anything that we do not really know what they are" (*Adam,* 241). For her, "the text itself always remains almost entirely elusive. So I must come back to hear it again; in the old phrase, to have it opened for me again" (*Adam,* 231).

She draws lessons from the Old Testament, but her reading of it, and the instruction she draws from Moses, is not about hellfire and damnation. Rather, she sees Moses as an exemplar of the spirit of generosity and liberality toward the poor that is, for her, certainly an essential part of Christianity and a major influence on Calvin, noting: "It is often said that Europeans learned religious intolerance from the Old Testament. Then how did we happen to skip over the parts where the laws protect and provide for the poor, and where the oppression of them is most fiercely forbidden?" (*Child,* 102). God's largesse toward the poor is unconditional: "They need not be pious, or Jewish, or worthy, or conspicuously in need, or intent on removing themselves from their condition of dependency" (*Child,* 107). She wants us to learn something, today, from the "absolute biblical imperative of respectful generosity toward the poor and the stranger" and reminds us that when "Jesus describes Judgment, the famous separation of the sheep from the goats, he does not mention religious affiliation, or sexual orientation or family values. He says 'I was hungry, and ye fed me not'" (*Child,* 124). In Robinson's Bible, "Jesus does *not* say, 'I was hungry and you fed me, though not in such a way as to interfere with free-market principles'" (*Child,* 139).

So Robinson wants to return to the past, not to preserve traditions but to correct misconceptions that have sedimented into truths. But she emphasizes: "I do not wish to suggest in these essays that the past was better than the present, simply that whatever in the past happens to have been of significance or value ought to be held in memory, insofar as that is possible, so that it can give us guidance" (*Adam,* 6). She returns to the past to set the record straight, on many different topics, and launches into "what looks in retrospect to have been a campaign of revisionism, because contemporary discourse feels to me empty and false" (*Adam,* 2). She thinks that we need to "look at the past again, because it matters, and because it has so often been dealt with badly" (*Adam,* 4). The "struggle to own the past so that it can be made to serve contemporary interests has led to gross distortions" (*Child,* 172). So despite the way this return to the past might seem aimed at conserving tradition, her treatment of the past aims at a radical unsettling of the stories we tell ourselves about how things used to be that is intended to shift contemporary practices in a progressive way. She retells the story of American political thought and culture, but outside of the narrow confines of selfish individualism, oppressive Puritanism, and liberal capitalism.

If Robinson writes primarily about the familiar figures of American culture, classic nineteenth-century American writers such as Emerson, Thoreau, Whitman, and Melville, she writes of these traditional heroes to remind us of the radicalism—especially a kind of religious radicalism—that is also part of the legacy of American culture. As she notes, religious revivals have not always been "hostile to reform and to the kind of education we call liberal, have not always been obscurantist, antifeminist, and presumptively racist," as they seem to be in the conservative Christian movements of the twentieth-century" (*Child,* 173). She calls our attention to the nineteenth-century radical figures of religion: "The Second Great Awakening has been remembered in history for its excesses and eccentricities. Associated with it were millennialism, spiritualism, and experiments with plural marriage. In many respects, notably the proliferation of communal societies, this period resembled the 1960s" (*Child,* 171). In short, she values nineteenth-century religious culture for its radicalism and progressivism, for its commitment to equality of classes, races, and genders, but especially for its commitment to abolitionism. She is deeply critical of those who treat the abolitionists as crazy and too extreme: "The inevitability of the association of abolitionism with sick and devious motives and with hypocrisy is very nearly absolute. What is the opposite of abolition? Tolerance for chattel slavery, for human bondage. Why should pathology be associated with the cause of human freedom rather than with slavery?" (*Child,* 178). The urgency that characterized these thinkers, "sometimes verging on desperation, is understandable in light of the overwhelming difficulty of the task they set themselves" (*Child,* 180).

She also, at first glance, might seem to praise American exceptionalism, but it becomes immediately apparent that she sees it as a double-edged sword and appreciates that many aspects of American culture are "exceptions" in negative ways as well. The best aspects of American culture have been "the serene sort of courage that allows us to grant one another real safety, real autonomy, the means to think and act as judgment and conscience dictate" and the assumption that "this great mutual courtesy will bear its best fruit if we respect, educate, inform, and trust one another" (*Child,* 45). But this country has also often fallen short of the goal, and an attitude of openness toward others has closed down into xenophobia: "This often manifests itself as a bold willingness to be rid of problem populations—intellectuals, for example. Or Gypsies or Cherokees or Albigensians or Carthaginians, or sturdy beggars, or degenerates and social parasites. Anyone could add clearances and pogroms and outright extirpations to this brief list" (*Child,* 37). Today, this attitude of openness toward others is threatened by the current economic climate and the ideology of Austerity: "After so much history, those very irritations at certain elements of society, certain problem populations, have never gone away and are now clearly resurgent, becoming normalized and respectable, as they have done so often in the past" (*Child,* 37). Today, in this climate of Austerity, there is "a dearth of humane imagination for the integrity and mystery of other lives" (*Child,* 45). "Everywhere the crisis of the private financial system has been transformed into a tale of slovenly and overweening government that perpetuates and is perpetuated by a dependent and demanding population. This is an amazing transformation of the terms in which our circumstance is to be understood. For about ten days the crisis was interpreted as a consequence of the ineptitude of the highly paid, and then it transmogrified into a grudge against the populace at large, whose lassitude was bearing the society down to ruin" (*Child*, 45). Market economics has come to function as truth, as nature, as an ideology, but "it does not represent or conform to or even address reality. It is a straight-edge ruler in a fractal universe" (*Child*, 49).

She is also, in a seemingly traditional way, critical of Darwin. But her critique is not based on the reasons we might expect, given how deeply religious she is. Robinson fully subscribes to the theory of evolution but doesn't think Darwin invented it—the theory predates his work. And she doesn't reject Darwin because she is a "creationist"—she doesn't see science or the theory of evolution as in conflict with her capacious experience of religion, at all. She rejects Darwin because of the impoverished and limiting view of humanity and nature that he puts forward, as only about survival and competition and for the way his theory has been used to underwrite the primitive economics of free market capitalism, social Darwinism, and modern eugenics programs. She thinks we have been distracted by a fairly ridiculous debate between creationism and Darwin, when the real problem is the way that Darwinism underwrites a doctrine of ruthless competition. For Robinson, "Creationism is the best thing that could have happened to Darwinism, the caricature of religion that has seemed to justify Darwinist contempt for the whole of religion" (*Adam*, 40). All this sound and fury serves to distract us from the fact that "Darwinism is, intrinsically, a chilling doctrine" (*Adam*, 36).

> We are to believe the world will be better if people are forced into severe and continuous competition. If they work themselves weary making a part for a gadget assembled on the other side of the earth, in fear of the loss of their livelihoods, the world will be better for it. If economic forces recombine and shed these workers for cheaper ones, the world will be better still. In what sense better? To ask is to refuse to accept the supposedly inevitable, to deny the all-overriding reality of self-interest and raw competition, which will certainly overwhelm us if we allow ourselves some sentimental dream of a humane collective life. This economics implies progress and has no progress to show. (*Adam*, 30)

If we would place "humane limits" on this "exploitation of people," this might solve the problem but would "interfere with competition, which is the great law of nature, supposedly, and which therefore functions as a value, because 'science' has supplanted religion" (*Adam,* 74). But we should ask ourselves, Robinson says, "How much misery and premature death (most of it out of sight, granted) do we agree to when we accept this new economic order? Is it in any way an advance on colonialism?" (*Adam,* 74).

To give one final example of how Robinson herself takes on this dual position as a housekeeper of homelessness, she places great value on family but doesn't define it in any kind of traditional way. She sees "family," like "religion" and like "America," as a word that "eludes definition, as do other important things, like nation, race, culture, gender, species; like art, science, virtue, vice, beauty, truth, justice, happiness, religion; like success; like intelligence" (*Adam,* 87). But "just for the purpose of this discussion," she goes ahead to offer a definition of family that eschews any limited notion of "traditional family values" and opens "family" up to an antifoundational capaciousness: "Let us say: one's family are those toward whom one feels loyalty and obligation, and/or from whom one derives identity, and/or to whom one gives identity, and/or with whom one shares habits, tastes, stories, customs, memories. This definition allows for families of circumstance and affinity as well as kinship, and it also allows for the existence of people who are incapable of family, though they may have parents and siblings and spouses and children" (*Adam,* 87). She defends unconventional definitions of the family, in part, to protect segments of the population, like single mothers, who are so often attacked in a perverse defense of the traditional family: "We are conditioned to think that the issue for single mothers, say, is work or welfare. In fact the issue is decent working hours and reasonable pay. These are important people, holding the world together for children who in many circumstances have been half abandoned. It is grotesque that their lives should be made impossible because of some unexamined fealty to economic principles that are, if we would pause to consider, impoverishing us all in so many ways, some of them extremely straightforward" (*Adam,* 97).

In contrast, Robinson counsels the greatest respect for other individuals. She rejects the idea that "sympathy and identification are allowable only within certain limits" (*Child,* 26). This is the real danger: "When definitions of 'us' and 'them' begin to contract, there seems to be no limit to how narrow these definitions can become. As they shrink and narrow, they become increasingly inflamed, more dangerous and inhumane. . . . I am convinced that the broadest possible exercise of imagination is the thing most conducive to human health, individual and global" (*Child,* 26).

On the one hand, Robinson participates in key conversations in contemporary political theory that explore how affect, disposition, comportment, and modes of being are part of the theory and practice of democracy. She defines democracy in terms of an attitude of openness to the mystery of individual experience and an appreciation of the strangeness of daily life, combining a posture of direct perception with an abiding attentiveness that eschews fundamentalisms and certainties. But beyond this dispositional definition of democracy as a kind of experience, she also productively intervenes in related discussion regarding democracy and the ethos of homelessness. With remarkable persistence and innovation, Robinson shows how democracy should be associated, not just with an ethos of homelessness, as some strains of contemporary political theory would have it, but with a way of being that unsettles itself even as it courts the spaces of home. Through her fiction and essays, Robinson advances a subtle critique of those who would associate democracy solely with an ethos of homelessness. She argues that we don't actually need to leave the spaces and places of home to experience them with an attitude of productive homelessness. She reminds us how much of what seems familiar, conventional, and traditional—much of what would seem to compose the ideological space of home—is far less certain, settled, and known that it appears at first glance. Many of those things that we take for granted can actually appear strange and new when experienced with an attitude of curiosity and a sense of mystery.

But beyond this, she shows how a kind of privilege can attach to these assertions about the value of an ethos of homelessness that is more wholly detached from the spaces and places of home. Robinson reminds us of the powerful pull of the familiar, the traditional, the known, in a way that makes arguments for a more radical ethos of homelessness seem cold, sterile, somehow unhuman, and even gendered as masculine. Robinson brings a specifically female voice to bear on these discussions of home and homelessness, not just because many of her characters have too many obligations to light out for the territories even if they wanted to, but because of the ways she reinvents the space of home itself as a kind of uncharted wilderness. Home and domesticity, as well as many other things that seem tedious in their familiarity or repressive in their traditions, are portrayed by Robinson as places of discovery and reinvention. Robinson's heroes find adventure and wilderness in unexpectedly familiar places, often at home.

In this way, she highlights how our own communities might be improved by an antifoundational openness to what direct experience teaches us, as opposed to what the conventional authorities say. Robinson's writings show us that how we live in the world affects how we live with others in the world: living with curiosity, with an eagerness to be surprised, with a sense of wonder at the mystery of daily life, can help make us accepting as opposed to judgmental, forgiving as opposed to rigid, and flexible as opposed to fundamental. Like mermaids in a ship's cabin, sunk down in the element they were meant to exclude, Robinson's heroes illuminate the democratic value in acting as housekeepers of homelessness.

Notes

1. Bonnie Honig, "Difference, Dilemmas, and the Politics of Home," in *Democracy and Difference: Contesting the Boundaries of the Political,* ed. Seyla Benhabib (Princeton: Princeton University Press, 1996), 260. See also Bonnie Honig, *Democracy and the Foreigner* (Princeton: Princeton University Press, 2001).

2. Honig, "Difference, Dilemmas, and the Politics of Home," 258.

3. Thomas L. Dumm, "Joyce Brown, or Democracy and Homelessness," in *United States* (Ithaca, NY: Cornell University Press, 1994), 155. Hereafter cited parenthetically.

4. Her works of fiction are: *Housekeeping* (New York: Farrar, Straus and Giroux, 1981); *Gilead* (New York: Farrar, Straus and Giroux, 2004); *Home* (New York: Farrar, Straus and Giroux, 2008); and *Lila* (New York: Farrar, Straus and Giroux, 2014). Her works of nonfiction are: *Mother Country: Britain, the Welfare State, and Nuclear Pollution* (New York: Farrar, Straus and Giroux, 1989); *The Death of Adam: Essays on Modern Thought* (1998; New York: Picador, 2005); *Absence of Mind: The Dispelling of Inwardness from the Modern Myth of the Self* (New Haven: Yale University Press, 2011); *When I Was a Child I Read Books: Essays* (New York: Farrar, Straus and Giroux, 2012); *The Givenness of Things: Essays* (New York: Farrar, Straus and Giroux, 2015).

5. Thus far, there has not been an exploration of these democratic themes in Robinson's work. The existing scholarly analysis of Marilynne Robinson's work has been confined to literary critics writing about her fiction, especially *Housekeeping.* Nearly all of the existing scholarship on Robinson is confined to *Housekeeping.* See Joan Kirkby, "Is There Life after Art? The Metaphysics of Marilynne Robinson's *Housekeeping,*" *Tulsa Studies in Women's Literature* 5, no. 1 (Spring 1986):

91–109; Martha Ravits, "Extending the American Range: Marilynne Robinson's *Housekeeping*," *American Literature* 61, no. 4 (December 1989): 644–66; Sarah D. Hartshorne, "Lake Fingerbone and Walden Pond: A Commentary on Marilynne Robinson's *Housekeeping*," *Modern Language Studies* 20, no. 3 (Summer 1990): 50–57; Maureen Ryan, "Marilynne Robinson's *Housekeeping:* The Subversive Narrative and the New American Eve," *South Atlantic Review* 56, no. 1 (January 1991): 79–86; William M. Burke, "Border Crossings in Marilynne Robinson's *Housekeeping*," *Modern Fiction Studies* 37, no. 4 (Winter 1991): 716–24; Heather Bohannan, "Quest-tioning Tradition: Spiritual Transformation Images in Women's Narratives and *Housekeeping*," in "The Personal Narrative in Literature," special issue, *Western Folklore,* 51, no. 1 (January 1992): 65–79; Paula E. Geyh, "Burning down the House? Domestic Space and Feminine Subjectivity in Marilynne Robinson's *Housekeeping*," *Contemporary Literature* 34, no. 1 (Spring 1993): 103–22; Karen Kaivola, "The Pleasures and Perils of Merging: Female Subjectivity in Marilynne Robinson's *Housekeeping*," *Contemporary Literature* 34, no. 4 (Winter 1993): 670–90; Christine Caver, "Nothing Left to Lose: *Housekeeping*'s Strange Freedoms," in "Write Now: American Literature in the 1980s and 1990s," special issue, *American Literature* 68, no. 1 (March 1996): 111–37; Maggie Galehouse, "Their Own Private Idaho: Transience in Marilynne Robinson's *Housekeeping*," *Contemporary Literature* 41, no. 1 (Spring 2000): 117–37; Thomas Gardner, "Enlarging Loneliness: Marilynne Robinson's *Housekeeping* as a Reading of Emily Dickinson," *Emily Dickinson Journal* 10, no. 1 (Spring 2001): 9–33; Katy Ryan, "Horizons of Grace: Marilynne Robinson and Simone Weil," *Philosophy and Literature* 29, no. 2 (October 2005): 349–64; Christine Wilson, "Delinquent Housekeeping: Transforming the Regulations of Keeping House," *Legacy* 25, no. 2 (2008): 299–310; George B. Handley, "The Metaphysics of Ecology in Marilynne Robinson's *Housekeeping*," *Modern Fiction Studies* 55, no. 3 (Fall 2009): 496–521; Christopher Leise, "'That Little Incandescence': Reading the Fragmentary and John Calvin in Marilynne Robinson's *Gilead*," *Studies in the Novel* 41, no. 3 (Fall 2009): 348–67; and Laura E. Tanner, "'Looking Back from the Grave': Sensory Perception and the Anticipation of Absence in Marilynne Robinson's *Gilead*," *Contemporary Literature* 48, no. 2 (Summer 2007): 227–52.

6. *When I Was a Child I Read Books: Essays* (New York: Farrar, Straus and Giroux, 2012), iv. Hereafter cited parenthetically.

7. Marilynne Robinson, *The Death of Adam: Essays on Modern Thought* (1998; New York: Picador, 2005), 171. Hereafter cited parenthetically.

8. Marilynne Robinson, *Housekeeping* (New York: Farrar, Straus and Giroux, 1981), 35. Hereafter cited parenthetically.

9. See Shannon Mariotti, *Thoreau's Democratic Withdrawal: Alienation, Participation, and Democracy* (Madison: University of Wisconsin Press, 2010),

especially the chapter titled "Huckleberrying toward Democracy: Thoreau's Practices of Withdrawal."

10. We know that Thoreau was an influence on Robinson. As she said in an interview, "If to admire and to be influenced are more or less the same thing, I must be influenced most deeply by the 19th-century Americans—Dickinson, Melville, Thoreau, Whitman, Emerson and Poe. Nothing in literature appeals to me more than the rigor with which they fasten on problems of language, of consciousness. . . . I happen to have read these old aunts and uncles at an impressionable age, and so I will always answer to them in my mind" (Marilynne Robinson, "The Hum inside the Skull—A Symposium." *New York Times Book Review,* May 13, 1984, 30).

11. Marilynne Robinson, *Gilead* (New York: Farrar, Straus and Giroux, 2004), 4. Hereafter cited parenthetically.

12. Marilynne Robinson, *Home* (New York: Farrar, Straus and Giroux, 2008), 102. Hereafter cited parenthetically.

CHAPTER 2

Our Home in the Wilderness

The American Experience with Wilderness and Frontier Democracy in Marilynne Robinson's Fiction and Essays

Joseph H. Lane Jr.

In this chapter, I explore "wilderness" as a concept in Marilynne Robinson's fiction and essays. I argue that Robinson situates her characters and her thought in the wilderness, or, perhaps more precisely, she reflects upon those who occupy the permeable frontier that divides American habitation from the wild. Robinson sees the human interaction with the American landscape, the American wilderness, as a uniquely revealing activity that defines our civilization and our democracy, a struggle that is constitutive of our American identity and that helps define our aspirations. The reciprocal self-definition of the American people with the lands that we have come to occupy is fraught with consequences—both good and ill—and Robinson is characteristically unflinching in her willingness to see both the best and the worst that our encounters with the wilderness and the West have brought us. In doing so, she urges us to reconsider the self-defining interrelationships of people to land and land to people that make it possible for us to understand who we are, where we have come from, and what might be required of us. Robinson encourages us to look around—to scan the horizons from the places where we are situated—in order to understand both ourselves and our nation.

Robinson explores the concept of "wilderness" directly in the essay of that name in the collection *The Death of Adam* as well as in several of the essays in *When I Was a Child I Read Books.* Electrifying descriptions of the landscape surrounding Fingerbone serve as the backbone of her celebrated first novel, *Housekeeping*, and even though it might be less pronounced or obvious, I will argue that understanding the settlement history, frontier commitments, physical landscape, and human relationship to the wilderness is equally vital for understanding *Gilead*. Drawing on each of these works, I argue that the concept of wilderness may serve as a critical referent for understanding how Robinson situates human communities in a landscape and how she understands the character of democracy and community as fundamental constituents of our existence.

Robinson's fiction and essays focus on how we live in the land, and the settings of her novels are replete with reflections of the landscapes that define people's lives. The mountains of Idaho and the plains of Iowa both shape and reflect the lives of the people who live there, and Robinson invites us to think deeply about how people and place become so intertwined that it proves difficult to say that we can ever leave a place without being forever changed by our having been there as well as by our having left.

We should not be surprised to discover that Robinson is fascinated with the relationship between landscape and the structures of human society. This assumption pervades her first major nonfiction work—*Mother Country*. That work, which Robinson herself has identified as her most important book, is a polemic against the pollution of northwest England and western Scotland by the British nuclear industry in the 1980s. In *Mother Country*, Robinson indirectly articulates a theory of the interrelationship of the people of that region and the land and sea that has defined them for generations, and she laments (even decries) the transformations that have been worked by an industry imposed by outsiders that has served the needs of distant urban areas at the expense of the health and livelihood of local communities. I argue that Robinson's suggestive title drives home the fundamental connection between the threats posed to people and landscapes in England and those she foresees in the United States. We can read *Mother Country* as a lesson that is aimed as squarely at us as her works about the United States. In fact, her most obvious treatment of "wilderness" as a concept—the essay that carries that single word as its name—is first and foremost an extension of the logic of *Mother Country* to reconceptualizing the potentially tragic consequences of using the American West as the final repository for the radioactive wastes generated elsewhere in the United States.

As many of the authors in this volume note, Marilynne Robinson situates herself very emphatically in the literary culture of the American nineteenth century, and her rapturous and evocative reflections on lakes and mountains; sunrises, sunsets, and nighttime walks; and the songs of wild birds and insects rival those of Thoreau and other early American nature writers whom she obviously admires. Her understanding of our imposition on the natural world simultaneously invokes and critiques classic theories about the meaning of the wilderness and the frontier for American life and self-identity.

Americans as a people have long drawn our understanding of ourselves from our struggle against the wilderness, and yet, Robinson suggests, as we have acquired, transformed, and subjugated our great western expanses, far more than landscape is lost or damaged. Robinson is clearly establishing herself as one voice in that chorus of American writers who view "the interaction between settlers and raw wilderness as the central reality of American life."[1] Characteristic of that line of thought, Robinson sees human society both as profiting immensely from the effort and innovation necessary to survive in this great vastness and as suffering from developmental distortions that harm our relationships with both our neighbors and the land. In Robinson's understanding, the great western wilderness into which we poured our ever-increasing population, our newly empowering technologies, and our proverbial ingenuity over the course of that great nineteenth century defined us as a people and incubated the democracy of which we are (in Robinson's view) quite justifiably proud.[2]

And yet, even as "we," the American people, forged a unique identity in our struggle with the wilderness, there are decisive ways in which we were diminished by our victories over it. Robinson presents the American landscape and wilderness as both a rebuke to society and an alternative source of value that we ignore or destroy at our peril.[3] Nor is she willing to domesticate the American wilderness into a series of literary national parks—mountains with handrails that are full of sublime visions but neutered of any threat.[4] She describes a vision of the American wilderness that is both beautiful and terrible—unbelievably scenic and tragically fragile, subject to our increasing technological power to destroy and yet wholly beyond our capacity to possess or tame. The wilderness that Robinson describes is a space in which we might form remarkably democratic associations and that simultaneously threatens to separate us from community, thus undermining our commitment to society and, ultimately, to our humanity. To live in the wilderness, or on the frontier, is to struggle, but it is a struggle that can benefit us and might teach us habits of responsibility, self-sufficiency, and citizenship that are necessary building blocks of the democracy that we might install there.

Thus, in contemporary political debates, Robinson proves to be an advocate for the wilderness and an environmentalist, but not of the most widely recognized variety. She is both seduced by the allure of wilderness but wary of the nature that lies beyond our social structures and connections. She does not practice a solicitude for nature that is born of some untenable ecocentric concern with the value of "nature" in and of itself, and she does not write about or seek to preserve some wilderness that is forever inviolate and distinct from any human influence. Quite the contrary, she recognizes that the American wilderness has always been and likely always will be a place of human engagement with landscape. In fact, she warns us about the terrible human and environmental tragedies that could follow from placing our western wilderness out of mind and out of reach as a convenient repository for the deadly wastes that our modern ways of life produce. She fears a walling off of the wilderness as a reservation beyond human settlement will only abet a deadly denial that can serve neither human beings nor the planet well.

In this essay, I explore the connection between Robinson's narrators and the wildernesses that they inhabit to make sense of the role of the American West in making these characters who they are. In the process, we can come to understand why Robinson places so much value in the moral power of a sparsely settled wilderness—a frontier landscape where small groups of people live in human communities perched on the last edge of the vast unoccupied space that lies around them. I analyze why she thinks that the romance of these landscapes can both inspire and preserve us, but also why she thinks that this romance can be a dangerous and destructive force in human lives.

One might fear that Robinson's vision of a frontier democracy—one in which the great unoccupied space beyond offers the prospect of land, of freedom, and of a self-sustaining existence for each and every member of our democratic community—was always doomed to be a fleeting one. We might well conclude that the material conditions that made American democracy thrive in Robinson's beloved nineteenth century could not be sustained and that they were bound to end in the very tragic destruction of both wilderness and community. At times it seems that Robinson is devoted to chronicling this demise in truly heartrending fashion. Fingerbone, this little outpost of the great American wandering, can no longer tolerate wanderers; Gilead, another little outpost of a peculiarly American moral impulse, is being depopulated by people who have lost the faith that animated their forefathers, including the very group of people it was created to save.

Perhaps this is not surprising. After all, as Frederick Jackson Turner argued one hundred years ago, the American wilderness—vast as it was—was not inexhaustible, and the way of life that was born of homestead acts and injunctions to "go west, young man" could not be sustained forever. And yet, Robinson is not entirely pessimistic about the prospects for maintaining the moral character of our frontier democracy. She sees opportunities to sustain and build on the work of our pioneer forebears and to preserve the more vibrant and more open democracy they forged on the American frontier. Our relationships to the land and to others have become more mediated and more difficult to discern as we have moved into a more modern existence, but they are not entirely indecipherable for us. In her more optimistic voice, Robinson wistfully muses: "The real frontier need never close. Everything, for all purposes, still remains to be done."[5] In this regard, Robinson's theory of "mindfulness" as a fundamental element of democratic existence (articulated in Shannon Mariotti's contribution to this volume) still provides us access to the type of self-understanding of our place in the American landscape and the American community that Robinson thinks we need to survive as a people worthy of the name. Perhaps the hard press of a challenging life on the frontier made some realizations inescapable for "our" ancestors that are too easily lost in our foreshortened and insufficiently reflected upon inheritances of "their" America. Robinson, however, always reminds us that living in the landscape is, in the words of Hannah Arendt, "nothing more than to think what we are doing."

Life on the Frontier

Robinson's understanding of our imposition on the natural world invokes both modern environmentalist tropes and classic theories about the meaning of the "frontier" for American life and self-identity. Her first two novels, *Housekeeping* (1981) and *Gilead* (2004), both open with accounts of how their narrators' ancestors came to occupy the spaces on the North American continent where they landed.

Housekeeping begins with a long reflection on the life and death of Edmund Foster, a grandfather whom the narrator, Ruth, never knew. He had "grown up in the Middle West, in a house dug out of the ground, with windows just at earth level, so that from without the house was a mere mound, no more a human stronghold than a grave, and from within, the horizontality of the world in that place foreshortened the view so severely that the horizon seemed to circumscribe the sod house and nothing more."[6] One day, Edmund Foster simply "quit his subterraneous house, walked to the railroad, and took a train west. He told the ticket agent that he wanted to go to the mountains" (4). He had long dreamed of mountains, and he painted them for years in awkward compositions, "none of them identifiable, if any of them were real." Edward eventually "settled" (if never too firmly) in Fingerbone, where "there are mountains, uncountable mountains, and where there are not mountains there are hills" (4). Edmund's passage to this place, a tiny railroad town, hemmed in between towering mountains and a deep lake where the transcontinental line forces its passage through a treacherous and narrow gap in the Rockies, reenacts the western flight of both Robinson's own ancestors and hundreds of other young people who sought new lives in the West. That Edmund "stayed" in this place, while continuing to work the railroad, forever participating in the great ferrying of people and materials across our continent, speaks to how deeply his experience situated him within this American trope. That he ultimately was swallowed, with an entire trainload of his countrymen, speaks to how deeply he, like other American literary characters, was "sink[ing] down to the very bottom of the West."[7]

Ruth never names the state from which Edmund Foster embarked, but it sounds suspiciously like Iowa, the setting of Robinson's subsequent novels. The town of Gilead is named for a hill in the Bible, but in elevation at least, the name is ironic here because western Iowa has no hills and no mountains. It is, as Robinson brilliantly invokes in her description of Edmund's childhood home, perfectly circumscribed by the horizon. As *Gilead*'s narrator, the third Reverend John Ames, puts it, "Mountains would seem an impertinence from that point of view."[8] As we will see, the remarkable flatness of the plains in Iowa operates as both a description and a political metaphor in Robinson's Gilead novels. It comes to represent a certain type of egalitarian commitment that is central to understanding both why the plains were settled and what life on the plains might mean for us.

Thus, the third Reverend Ames begins his story by describing how—and more importantly *why*—his family came to the plains from whence Ruth's grandfather would escape. This John Ames's grandfather—also named John Ames—grew up in Maine. As a young man there, he had a vision that inspired him to join the struggle against slavery, and he came to Gilead in the 1850s with other abolitionists to fulfill a mission, to overcome the scourge of slavery by fighting against the slaveholding settlers who were seeking to control neighboring Kansas. Long passages of the work are devoted to explaining the intertwined history of the abolitionist cause and the Ames family. Only reference to that interrelationship can explain their comings and goings from Gilead—a history of loyalty and loss, of duty and desertion—as they were brought to that distant outpost for a war that scarred one generation and profoundly influenced those that would follow. Some of those descendants rejected the commitments of their fathers and others forgot them, but in the autobiography of Robinson's narrator John Ames, which is also the autobiography of a place, no one escaped the influence of the founding impulse: "Towns like ours were a conspiracy. Lots of people were only there to be antislavery by any means that came to hand" (182). The narrator John Ames reflects again and again on what this history reveals about both the town and the greater motion of which it was one part. The story is moved by the testing of principles and practices, "the same words that carry a good many people into the howling wilderness in one generation [and that] are irksome or meaningless in the next" (204).

It may seem odd to yoke Ruth Stone and the Reverend John Ames so closely together, but both of these narrators' stories are essentially defined by and extensions of major currents in the great human migrations that transformed the North American continent from wilderness into one of the most densely inhabited, and technologically transformed, places on our planet. Robinson's novels, then, must be understood as reflections on *why* this great resettlement and domestication took place and how it continues to define the children, and grandchildren, and great-grandchildren, of its pioneers.

As I have noted above, Robinson's essay "Wilderness" (1998) begins by situating the author herself in this defining march westward that structures both her first two novels and her understanding of the American experience. We came to be who we are by a history told in stories of our ancestors' encounters with the North American wilderness and our inheritance—both geographic and moral—of their experiences: "I am an American of the kind whose family sought out wilderness generation after generation. My great-grandparents settled in Idaho, much of which is wilderness now" (246). There is a "kind" of American who is born from this wilderness encounter, and although many Americans may have parents whose quest for the wilderness landed them in places quite transformed today from their original state, Robinson's introduction suggests that something of that pioneer spirit still inhabits them (and us). In this regard, she tends to speak of Americans' past in a somewhat misleading (and perhaps truly problematic) first-person plural: "We are the children of pioneers." Obviously this account of American identity does not literally include all Americans today, and there is an unmistakable and problematic tendency in Robinson's writing to group all Americans together with an Anglo-American experience of the nineteenth century as the defining experience for a wide range of peoples whose ancestors may have been through something very different—and perhaps were not here at that time at all.

But Robinson thinks that we are all influenced by that "kind" of American whom she describes, and she is not entirely incorrect. There is a sense in which the American people as a whole are the inheritors of a previous generation's encounters with the North American wilderness and the lessons that may be drawn from those encounters. Those lessons are, in Robinson's account, valuable, and she fears that they may be fading. "Perhaps it was a misfortune for us that so many interesting ideas were associated with access to a habitable wilderness," she writes (*Child,* 90). But her works provide that access for us. We might say that we receive from Robinson a doubly attenuated account of what might be learned on the frontier. We are the readers of the secondhand accounts of grandchildren who are haunted by the "mysterious, aloof, and rapturously gentle" spirits of their grandfathers' frontiers (*Child,* 91).

The central place that this perspective receives in both Robinson's fiction and essays suggests that she thinks that these are spirits that must be preserved and consulted. Robinson speaks of the older West as haunting the new West, and perhaps the country as a whole. The image of the ghosts of the frontier is sustained across both her fiction and nonfiction work. Of course, stories of the lost West may be commonplace in the American context, but Robinson's version of them is not as easily categorized. Generally speaking, stories of this sort are heroic tales in the American telling, stirring accounts of how through ingenuity, courage, and fortitude (perhaps we could say "true grit"), Americans have forged a road into and through a wilderness to make the world a better place for peoples otherwise consigned to the margins of older, more settled, and more traditional societies; "the hungry, the poor, and the huddled masses yearning to be free" would find food, riches, and space in the American wilderness, and they would make homes there. The idea of "homesteading," of crafting a home from the wilderness, is a uniquely American one that frames the lives of several of Robinson's characters and that plays a central role in her thought, but Robinson's traditionalist narratives generally culminate in rather untraditional conclusions. She forsakes the easier and more traditional way of telling these stories—the clichéd westerns about heroes of the frontier—in order to unveil retrospective views that place our wilderness experience in a longer context.

This is not to say that Robinson ignores the traditional tropes. She speaks of the American frontier narrative as "a very pure replication of our national myth" and a "potent allegory," and she speaks of this allegory in both mythological and biblical terms ("Wilderness," 248). She refers to the 1862 Homestead Act as a founding poem akin to Deuteronomy, associates "Lewis and Clark mapping the wilderness" with the *Aeneid,* and rhapsodizes the spirit of life on our western frontier as the "orphan child of a brilliant century" (*Child,* 94, 83). Robinson writes, "I think it is correct to regard the West as a moment in history much larger than its own" (*Child,* 90).

But Robinson is never fully converted to the American mythology that our Manifest Destiny was entirely a blessed event for both the peoples and the landscapes of the American West. She recognizes that, in many respects, our western expansion was a tragedy, much to be lamented: "At its simplest level, it amounted to no more than the movement of European-origin people into a part of the world where they had no business being. By the mid-nineteenth century, this was very old news" (*Child,* 88). She claims that her "governing assumption" in assessing this motion is "that history is a dialectic of bad and worse" and, therefore, that "the history of European civilization vis-à-vis the world from the fifteenth century to the present day is astounding and terrible" (*Child,* 88). In her essay "Wilderness," she laments that there are no longer any places in our nation where our imprint and influence are clearly in evidence, and she regrets that "we must surrender the idea of wilderness, accept the fact the consequence of human presence in the world are universal and ineluctable" (254). She leaves little doubt that we have done much violence and have a great deal to answer for.

And yet, in the same essays and often the same breath, she is quick to point out that she thinks the American experience of the frontier cannot be critiqued in the same register as the European "Great Game" of colonizing Africa and South Asia, where "penal colonies and pauper colonies and slash-and-burn raids on the wealth of the land . . . made the history of the most colonized places so unbelievably desolate" (*Child,* 89). Our experience was, she insists, vindicated by its "Utopian impulse" and the "considerable optimism about what people were and what they might become." "Our West" had its fair share of terrible abuses and environmental crimes to be sure, but it also generated "beautiful human society" amid the towering mountains and vast emptiness of the plains, and Robinson is dedicated to understanding and restoring the worthy parts of this motion to its proper place in the "national imagination" (*Child,* 91).

In this regard, Robinson might be read alongside and in dialogue with Frederick Jackson Turner. For all his faults, no other author so clearly articulated the common American assumption that the character of "our people" is born from and encapsulated in our western expansion, and yet Turner wrote about this unique character wistfully, as a relic of a recent but all too easily forgotten past. He delivered his groundbreaking essays on what he came to call "the idea of the frontier in American life" in the late nineteenth and early twentieth centuries as a historian's response to the "closing of the frontier," which was officially announced in the report of the 1890 census.

Recognizing himself in the anomalous role of both historian and participant in history, Turner notes that he collected and published his "frontier" essays in 1920 in part because "they may have some historical significance as contemporaneous attempts of a student of American history, at successive transitions in our development during the past quarter century to interpret the relations of the present to the past." In particular, he hoped to provide a firsthand but historically informed account of "America's contribution to the history of the human spirit" by tracing "the nation's peculiar experience in extending its type of frontier into new regions."[9]

I would suggest that Robinson also attempts to trace these "successive transitions" through fictional characters whose unique perspectives on these transitions she finds particularly worthy of note. As we have noted above, Ruth of *Housekeeping* and the third Reverend John Ames of *Gilead* stand at a very similar vantage from which to determine what the American engagement with the frontier meant in terms of "contribution to the history of the human spirit." Not only is each a grandchild of the frontier, but each is an inheritor of a strand of that spirit that Robinson thinks worth preserving—Ruth carries her grandfather's sense of individualism, love of the wilderness, and freedom from social convention, and the narrator Reverend John Ames carries his grandfather's commitment to the democratic dignity of the freedmen farmers who settled the small towns of the American Plains.

Although neither narrator has personal memories of the settlement of their outposts on the edge of the American wilderness, each knows people who did have such memories. Each is haunted by the spirit that brought a grandfather to what was — in their day— the farthest reaches of the American settlement. The abolitionism that brought the first Reverend John Ames to Iowa and the wanderlust that brought Edmund Foster to Fingerbone are characteristic of many others who sought the freedom and the opportunities of the American frontier, but they are particularly strongly felt by the grandchildren who find voice in Robinson's novels.

In fact, these narrators cannot let go of something that their grandfathers bequeathed them, and even as others seem to be moving on from the passions and purposes that informed their ancestors' westward adventure, Ruth and the narrator Reverend John Ames hold fast to, reflect on, and revisit (quite literally) the worlds that brought their families to particular places on the North American continent. Thus, Robinson provides a deep reading of the "human spirits" that settled this land and conquered this wilderness, and we should never lose sight of the many respects in which she sees this as a haunting. Her novels reveal that there are many ghosts in the wilderness and spirits to be found at the old frontiers. Through her narrators' voices, Robinson offers a chance for "the West to assert itself in the most interesting terms, so that the whole country must hear and be reanimated by dreams and passions it has too casually cast aside and too readily forgotten" (*Child,* 91). I am tempted to suggest that her novels are nothing less than an effort at reasserting the West in these "most interesting" terms by tying the experience of (some?) American's frontier ancestors to issues that continue to haunt us, to cast their struggles as indicative of and intimately related to, those that we face today.

Housekeeping in the Wilderness

In *When I Was a Child I Read Books,* Robinson identifies her first novel, *Housekeeping,* as a "western," a variation on the old genre that has so defined American film and literature. Her revision of the formula was to cast a female lead because "my one great objection to the American hero was that he was inevitably male—in decayed forms egregiously male. So I created a female hero, of sorts, also an outsider and a stranger" (90). In Robinson's vision, the essential elements of the western are the placement of the outsider, the loner, the wandering visionary in an outsize landscape in which human self-confidence is chastened by the sheer scope and grandeur of the encircling wilderness and in which setting we are to see "that human nature is replete with nameless possibilities and, by implication, that the world is accessible to new ways of understanding." She adds: "I must say too how beautiful human society seems to me, especially in those attenuated forms so characteristic of the West—isolated towns and single houses which sometimes offer only merest, barest amenities" (91).

The isolated town in which Edmund Foster eventually paused in his westward trek and in which his granddaughters, Ruth and Lucille, are eventually deposited is revealed in Robinson's rapturously evocative setting shots to be the most attenuated of settlements in the most sublime and intimidating of landscapes. Perched on a narrow shelf between a deep lake and soaring mountain peaks, Fingerbone "was never an impressive town." It literally clings to its existence, always on the verge of being swallowed by the landscape that surrounds it. "It was chastened by an outsized landscape and extravagant weather, and chastened again by an awareness that the whole of human history had occurred elsewhere" (62). In several passages in the novel, we are encouraged to look at the town from across the lake that enwraps it, and this perspective always emphasizes its ephemerality: "The town itself seemed a negligible thing from such a distance. Were it not for the clutter on the shore . . . it would have been possible not to notice the town at all. The mountains that stood up behind it were covered with snow and hidden in the white sky, and the lake was sealed and hidden yet their eclipse had not made the town more prominent" (34).

The name of Fingerbone itself and the purpose for which it exists in this most inhospitable of settings remind us that our ancestors did not go into the West simply for adventure and the possibility of discovering new dimensions of human existence. Fingerbone is a rail junction, a town created and maintained to manage a link in the transcontinental railway. Its name suggests that it is one of the smallest, and perhaps one of the most fragile, links in this engineered system of human conveyance and conquest, but we are never allowed to forget that Fingerbone is a through-station, a passage *through* the wilderness by which thousands of people—many of them anonymously stashed in freight cars—transit the unforgiving western landscape. It is an outpost of an aspiring civilization that has matched itself against the wilds and forged a passage through them. But it is also a place where few stop to set up housekeeping and where existence is fragile and always threatened. Most of the western passengers only see Fingerbone from a distance, a few lights in a great darkness that seems to engulf them.

The train itself serves as nothing less than a character in the novel. Its entrances and exits, and even its death, are essential to the work. Robinson's surprising and evocative use of the train as the civilizing force in this wilderness reminds us of a recurring trope of American literature and the western settlement, of the American engagement with wilderness and the tensions between continental aspirations and the landscapes we inhabit. In placing the train as a presence that is powerful and important and yet so easily and completely lost in this "outsized landscape," Robinson appropriates a familiar trope from American literature of the nineteenth century.

Leo Marx famously speaks of this "recurrence of a particular episode in the work of many canonical American writers—Emerson, Thoreau, Hawthorne, Melville, Mark Twain, Henry James, Henry Adams, Frank Norris, Ernest Hemingway, William Faulkner—in which a machine, or some other token of the new industrial power suddenly intrudes upon the serenity enjoyed by the writer, or a fictional protagonist, situated in a natural, perhaps idyllic, setting."[10] Building his analysis on an event in Thoreau's *Walden,* Marx suggests that the archetype of his "interrupted idyll" trope is the sudden sound of a steam engine in the wilderness, a scene replayed many times in both American literature and film. Marx suggests that our reaction to the appearance of the "machine in the garden" is often an ambivalent one. Although we are often enraptured by the sublime experience of being truly at one with nature, surrounded by wilderness and enthralled by its silent grandeur, we are also relieved and comforted to discover that we are not alone and that our power is not wholly inadequate to sustain the works of technology and civilization even in these intimidating landscapes.

Robinson both invokes and inverts this trope in *Housekeeping*. The single most important event in the entire history of Fingerbone appears to be a negative commentary on the solidity of our technology's hold on the wilderness. Here we find that a great herald of civilization and technological power—repeatedly described as the finest and most luxurious train on the entire line[11]—is engulfed by the surrounding scene. For reasons no one can identify, the famous Fireball slipped off the rails as it crossed the long trestle and disappeared into the lake; the deep and brooding center of this northwestern wilderness literally swallows the technological impertinence in a way that "was not, strictly speaking, spectacular because no one saw it happen"; "the engine nosed over towards the lake and then the rest of the train slid after it like a weasel sliding off a rock" (5). This image of the train, swallowed whole, silenced by the depth of the lake and the magnitude of the western wilderness, suggests that our settlement of the West is far from complete.

Throughout *Housekeeping*, it is the social, the technological, and the developed that it is always on the verge of being swallowed up by earth or water, and our hold on the great western wilderness that is tenuous and continually threatened. Robinson tells us that she was always struck by this omnipresent threatening "silence" that loomed around those who live in our western wilderness: "I knew that the mountains and the lakes and the woods brought people's lives to disastrous conclusions, often too frightening to repeat in the hearing of children."[12] *Housekeeping* may be understood as a long and solemn reflection on this feature of the western landscape and its influence on our social interactions. Civilization and the ways of life that it sustains are tenuous. Death is said to pervade the lake and the surrounding landscape.[13] In a memorable scene, Ruth and Lucille spend much of their first week under the care of Sylvie sequestered in the upstairs bedroom as early spring rains flood the town and threaten to swallow it in the lake. The high water casts the graves in the cemeteries as sunken pools, creates "vast gaps in the Dewey decimal system" in the town library, moves houses from one side of submerged streets to the other, and makes the still-frozen lake bellow and groan through the night like a ghost. It is in this setting, afloat in the little ark of the house and surrounded by a vast and mysterious flood, that Sylvie offers Ruth and Lucille her first discourse on the virtues of loneliness.[14]

We are reminded again and again that "we have colonized a hostile planet" and that those who wander off onto the water or into the mountains may never return" (*Child*, 90). Ruth herself nearly disappears into the mountains on two occasions before her final departure from Fingerbone. In the first, she wanders miles up the shore with her sister Lucille to fish and to watch the lake, eventually staying too late and spending the night in the woods. As they left town, they were accompanied by a local dog, long familiar in town, who was called "Crip." Ruth notes: "I describe her at such length because a mile or so from town she disappeared into the woods as if following a scent and never appeared again. She was a dog of no special consequence, and she passed from the world unlamented" (111). Clearly the disappearance of Crip serves in some respect as a reminder of what might have happened to the two girls.[15] Their adventure might have resulted in a similar ending, but they survived and returned from a night spent on the shores of the lake. They returned, however, as two very different people.

After an afternoon of fishing, Lucille makes the suggestion that they stay out for the night on a distant spit of land, a rocky peninsula extending far out into the surrounding lake. Together, they build a tiny cabin of rocks and driftwood there. Lucille enacts the claiming of a homestead by writing her name in pebbles on the sand at the door to their little outpost, but only Ruth experiences the night on the lake as a revelation. She imagines herself as one with the darkness and the shimmering reflections of the lake. Sitting in silence, listening to owls, coyotes, and loons, she experiences a vision of the world stripped of the veils that obscure its true workings and imagines herself among ghosts and in the presence of the whole of nature.

For Lucille, this ultimate act of setting out from society proves to be frightening and threatening. As Ruth notes, Lucille fretted and paced through the darkness, throwing stones when animals came down to the lake to drink. She was "never still, never accepting that all our human boundaries were overrun" (115).[16] At the first gray suggestion of light, Lucille returns to town resolved to transform herself into a person who is fit for society. She reforms her dress that very day, becomes obsessed with her appearance, and reaches out to new friends. As she tries desperately to bring Ruth along, she insists: "We have to *improve* ourselves. *Starting right now!*" (123). The sisters' separation, although it takes some time to culminate, proves to be grounded in that night on the lake, that brush with the vastness of a wilderness that might swallow us whole.

Ruth experiences the wilderness in the terms that Robinson herself remembers from her childhood: "My bond with my native landscape was an unnamable yearning, to be at home in it, to be chastened and acceptable, to be present in it as if I were not present at all" ("Wilderness," 246). Describing her sense of the wilderness in *When I Was a Child,* Robinson writes:

> Walking into the woods by myself and feeling the solitude around me build like electricity and pass through my body with a jolt that made my hair prickle. I remember kneeling by a creek that spilled and pooled among rocks and fallen trees with the unspeakably tender growth of small trees already sprouting from their backs and thinking, there is only one thing wrong here, which is my own presence, and that is the slightest imaginable intrusion—feeling that my solitude, my loneliness, made me almost acceptable in so sacred a space. (86)

Ruth is capable of feeling herself as part of the landscape, one citizen among many with equal or greater claims to be there as she has.

Lucille, conversely, experiences the wilderness as a threat to her humanity. If its song has any siren quality to her ear, it serves only as an alarm that some terrible boundary is about to be crossed and that some precious humanity is about to be lost. Lucille immediately sets out to firmly establish that both sisters belong in the little civilization of which Fingerbone is the tiny pocket, rather than in the vast surrounding wildness. It is hard to imagine the urgency with which Lucille sets about separating herself from what she saw on the lake. As Ruth sees it, "Lucille would busy herself forever, nudging, pushing, coaxing, as if she could supply the will I lacked, to pull myself into some seemly share and slip across the wide frontiers into that other world, where it seemed to me then I could never wish to go" (123).

Indeed, we now see that the frontier is a semipermeable barrier that is difficult to cross in either direction. Having passed through it, Ruth is as reluctant to cross that threshold "back" into society as Lucille is anxious to reestablish herself on the civilized side of the line. But for Ruth, "it seemed to me that nothing I had lost, or might lose, could be found there, or, to put it another way, it seemed that something I had lost might be found in Sylvie's house" (123). At this moment, the girls walked away in separate directions—one to a drugstore and one to a house that proves little more than a portal to a space that cannot be contained by walls.

Ruth's second night in the wilderness reveals even more fully the depth and vitality, the awesome and frightening force, of the world beyond our borders and our influence. Her second sailing comes with Sylvie, who takes her across the lake to "a little valley between two hills where someone built a house and planted an orchard and even started to dig a well. A long time ago" (137). Sylvie takes Ruth across the lake to this lost homestead. Sylvie is convinced that even though the homestead is long-abandoned, there are feral children nearby whom she might attract with the marshmallows she carries in her pocket. Ruth's reflections on this lost homestead—"a fallen house" that has collapsed into its own cellar, swallowed by the earth—tell us a great deal about how Ruth sees herself as a lost soul wandering in the wilderness and haunted by the ghosts of those who first settled there (150, 154). She reflects on the many ways in which the sad fate of this homestead fits into other stories of calamity that she has heard about the isolated homes in the mountains around Fingerbone: "The houses in the mountains of Fingerbone were generally built as this one had been. . . . If the house began to lean, the chinking sprang loose and the pine knots popped out and as often as not the windowpanes fell and the door could only be opened with increasing effort. . . . There were so many stories, in fact, that there must have been at some time a massive exodus or depopulation." (156). The fragility of these homesteads, the disturbing suggestion that the earth itself might swallow them whole, haunted the people of Fingerbone as "one cry of alarm is carried among birds through the whole of the woods and even the sky" (157).

Ruth imagines their house, whose "relative solidity" might be "deceptive." "For all the appearance these things gave of substance and solidity, they might better be considered a dangerous weight on a frail structure." She reflects on how it might all collapse, sending books and piano as well as Sylvie, Ruth, and Lucille "plummet[ing] disastrously through the dark, knowing no more perhaps than that our dreams were suddenly terrible and suddenly gone" (159). Later, after a harrowing and mysterious night spent on the lake with Sylvie waiting to watch a train pass over them as they floated immediately above the lost train that took her grandfather, Ruth dreams "that the bridge was a chute into the lake and that, one after another, handsome trains slid into the water without even troubling the surface" (174).

Ruth's dreams of the earth and water swallowing homesteads, trains, and families speak to a haunting that she comes to share with Sylvie. Sylvie lives among the ghosts of the frontier—the spectral families of feral children who were left to wander when their houses were swallowed by the earth and the spirits of the passengers (both paying and hitching) who anonymously descended into the depths of the lake (153, 167): "And below [the surface] is always the accumulated past, which vanishes but does not vanish, which perishes and remains" (172). These presences inhabit the wildernesses that have swallowed them, and they call to those who look back. And yet, most of us do not see them or appreciate the power that they exercise over our fates. The surface of the deep lake is "untroubled," and what lies beneath it is hidden from most people. Only those who "see" what is hidden in the deep are troubled by the immensity and implacability of the western wilderness. Where Lucille comes to see only threat, Ruth sees the possibility of a certain type of homeless belonging.

The sojourn to the lost homestead and the night on the lake ultimately leads to a legal attempt to remove Ruth from Sylvie's dubious care and thus to the novel's conclusion. While Robinson cannot be said to side with either the sheriff and his town or Sylvie and Ruth's desperate choice to risk the perils of the night-crossing of the bridge and a wandering life, she makes it clear that the line that separates the two is not very distinct. Indeed it is precisely because the town itself was born of wandering and "a diaspora threatened always": "There was not a soul there but knew how shallow-rooted the whole town was. It flooded yearly, and had burned once. Often enough the lumber mill shut down or burned down. There were reports that things were otherwise elsewhere, and anyone, on a melancholy evening, might feel that Fingerbone was a meager and difficult place" (177).

Fingerbone's existence itself is cast as an accident of the great American restlessness that pushed us across the continent and a monument to that diversity that this great wandering produced. Ruth speaks of it as an evolutionary accident that has produced a unique but threatened species that now is desperately clinging to its existence: "that creature will live on if it can" (177). That which created it now threatens it, and its ambivalence about policing the impulses from which it was spawned may be read in the sheriff's hesitation to perform his duty in removing Ruth from Sylvie and his discomfort in even speaking of what he thinks he must do.

Thus, in one sense, "the end to housekeeping" with which the novel concludes is a reenactment of an old drama from which the scattered towns like Fingerbone that dot our western landscapes were born and by which many of them have been abandoned and reclaimed by the wilderness. It is not unlike the dramatic abandonment of the earthen house on the plains that brought Edmund Foster to Fingerbone or that left behind the swallowed homestead where Sylvie scoured the hillsides for the phantasmal children. This is the story of the American West. It allows for, and even stimulates, the emergence of brilliant voices like Ruth Stone's and the respectability of eccentric collectors of nature's beauties like Edmund Foster. It produces a profusion of eclectic and unique little communities like Fingerbone. But it is tenuous, and these small communities are threatened always by both the grandiose nature in which they are set and the very impulses from which they are born. Their entire populations might, perhaps at any time, become unmoored and wander away into the surrounding hills.

In *When I Was a Child I Read Books,* Robinson notes, "The opposition frequently made between individualism on the one hand and responsibility to society on the other is a false opposition as we all know. Those who look at things from a little distance can never be valued sufficiently" (87). *Housekeeping* returns time and again to the idea that we must achieve and understand this perspective. The view from Fingerbone, or perhaps the view *of* Fingerbone, from the far side of the lake or from a train passing over the long bridge, allows us to understand this fundamental kinship between "that famous individualism associated with Western and American myth" and the settling impulses that have developed, perhaps all too inevitably, to challenge our western sensibilities. It is a vantage from which we can see "that the West has lost its place in the national imagination" and that "by some sad evolution, the idea of human nature has become the opposite of what it was when the myth of the West began" (*Child,* 91). This is not to say that *Housekeeping* is entirely an elegy. Robinson speaks of a hope that the West might "assert itself in the most interesting terms." But it is to say that she thinks she must redirect our vision to this perspective lest "the dreams and passions [that we have] too casually put aside [be] forgotten" (*Child,* 92). Robinson urges us to explore the West again as a guide to reestablishing a balance between the individual and the communal, a certain sense of appreciation of those around us as individuals, that she thinks is essential to well-functioning democracy. Failing this, she despairs for our polity and our souls.

Gilead on the Plains of Democracy

Thus, *Housekeeping* speaks to both the possibilities of radical individualism and nonconformism that may be essential to realizing the boundless potential of human expression. Paradoxically, in doing so, it also provides space for a rare sense of connection with nature's greater chorus in which humans provide only one small section among many voices that are too often overlooked, othered, or lost. The importance of remembering both the eclectic peoples and the very landscape of the lost West will figure prominently in the final section of this essay, but to make sense of her environmentalist critique of what we might do with the now depopulating Mountain West, we must make sense of another strand of Robinson's frontier vision of American life.

Robinson's second novel, *Gilead,* and to a lesser extent her subsequent novels, *Home* and *Lila,* speak to another strand of American identity that she associates with our western expansion, our experience of the frontier, and our transformation by, and in, the wilderness.[17] This is what she calls the "spirit of utopianism" that pervades many movements in America's march west into what she characterizes in *Gilead* as the "howling wilderness."

Robinson speaks of this "Utopian impulse" in our engagement with the West most directly in her discussion of the Homestead Act in *When I Was a Child I Read Books:* "It appears to me that the Homestead Act was designed to consolidate the North's victory in the Civil War by establishing an economy of smallholder farming, of the kind that prevailed in the North, as opposed to plantation farming on the Southern model" (89). She speaks of this act as "resembling Deuteronomy" and specifically cites the fifteenth chapter of that book as the benediction to her essay on Jonathan Edwards titled "Open Thy Hand Wide": "As God bestoweth his benefites on us, let us beware that wee acknowledge it towards him, by doing good to our neighbors whome he offereth unto us, so as wee neither exempt ourselves from their want, nor seclude them from our abundance, but gently make them partakers with us, as folke that are linked together in an inseperable bond" (82). Thus, her understanding of the purpose of the homesteading of the plains was clearly to establish a form of society in which the care of others might be practiced consistently with the freedom and relative self-sufficiency of all and the enslavement of none.

The family of *Gilead*'s narrator John Ames came, as we noted, to the plains of Iowa before the passage of the Homestead Act but for the purposes that act imagined. His ancestors were in many respects the act's precursors and its inspiration, and he clearly, in turn, speaks of himself as a sojourner of sorts in the plains, a man whose family must be identified both with where they live now and from whence they came. This perspective is so fundamental to his being that it colors even his view of the divine: "I suppose Calvin's God was a Frenchman, just as mine is a Middle Westerner of New England extraction. Well we all bring such light to bear on these great matters as we can" (142).

These "utopian" New England types came to the Middle West for a purpose that transcended simple wanderlust or some desire for economic opportunity. They came to set up farming communities that both modeled freehold farming and abetted the escape of the slaves that made the alternative—and far less democratic—mode of society on a plantation model possible: "Towns like ours were a conspiracy. Lots of people were only there to be antislavery by any means that came to hand" (180); "A stranger might ask why there is a town here at all. Our own children might ask. And who could answer them? It was just a dogged little outpost in the sand hills, within striking distance of Kansas. That's really all it was meant to be. It was a place John Brown and Jim Lane could fall back and rest. There must have been a hundred little towns like it, set up in the heat of an old urgency that is all forgotten now" (267).

The people of these towns were so committed to the cause that they located, and in some cases relocated, their towns specifically to better accomplish the goal of setting enslaved human beings on their road to freedom. In one hilarious but pointed vignette that Ames relates to his son, the people of one such town built a tunnel to hide escaping fugitives that became so large that it collapsed under the weight of a horse in the street. Forced to cover their activities, the town's people trade for the horse, spend untold labor trying to shore up and then to cover up the tunneling, and ultimately "moved the town, such as it was, half a mile down the road" to hide their conspiracy: "The tunnel became a kind of creek bed, a freshet in the spring, with nice grassy banks and flowers that had run wild from old gardens. People who did not know better would picnic beside it" (67–71). Thus, they moved and transformed the earth itself, created watercourses and seemingly "natural" garden spots, in their efforts to free the captives.

The metaphor is apt because they were transforming a land that Ames repeatedly characterizes as a "wilderness" in hopes of transforming the economic and human relations that define American democracy.[18] As the people of these radical towns siphoned away the labor force of slaveholding settlements in Missouri and Kansas, they were building a new nation on a far more egalitarian basis, one in which mutual aid was literally enacted in its foundations and embedded in the land they inhabited in the form of the tunnels, trapdoors, and hidden rooms that abolitionist frontier families constructed so others might make their way to freedom. They planted antislavery as surely as they planted crops.

Even though one might expect *Gilead* to celebrate the glorious victory of the North and its plans to establish a nation of freehold farmers, Robinson offers a more ambivalent narrative. Our narrator, the third Reverend John Ames, is trying to grapple with how this vision has proven to be "no more than dreams" (200). The utopian impulse that led to the settlement of *Gilead* and the other "ramparts" along the freedom front of western Iowa ultimately fizzled and failed—and what this failure says about the land and the people who now inhabit it—is revealed in imagery of the Fourth of July speech of the first Reverend Ames and his grandson's subsequent reflections on that sermon as well as in the trek into the Kansas wilderness in which two John Ameses seek the body of the first.

Perhaps the most central theme of the family story of the narrator John Ames is the disillusionment and disappearance of his grandfather. The first Reverend John Ames, the scion who brought our narrator's family to Gilead, grows old in the years following the Civil War, and as he grows old, he grows more and more deeply disappointed in the aftermath of this seminal event in his, and the nation's, life.[19] This disappointment culminates in a speech that he gives, at the request of Gilead's mayor, on the Fourth of July in the early 1890s. Elsewhere in this volume Christie Maloyed analyzes this speech as a particular example of the jeremiad, but for our purposes here, the connection with that genre is particularly salient insofar as jeremiads in general, and this speech in particular, often use the fallen state of the land as a metaphor for the moral failures or decline of the people who inhabit it. In the very first passages of Jeremiah, the failure of the people to live up to the destiny and the purpose for which God has brought them into the promised land is illustrated in terms that invoke images of pollution and neglect: "Where is the Lord that brought us up out of the land of Egypt, that led us through the wilderness, through a land of deserts and of pits, through a land of drought, and of the shadow of death, through a land that no man passed through, and where no man dwelt? And I brought you into a plentiful country, to eat the fruit thereof and the goodness thereof; but when ye entered, ye defiled my land, and made mine heritage an abomination."[20]

In the elder Ames's version of this story, it was the mission of God to bring people like himself to the plains to "free the captive. Preach good news to the poor. Proclaim liberty throughout the land." But he laments that this mission has been lost: "our dreams are forgotten long before we are." And he concludes that the land itself has been defiled or debased by the failures of the people who could not realize this vision: "But what is left here in Gilead? Dust. Dust and ashes. Scripture says the people perish, and they certainly do. It is remarkable" (200). The narrator John Ames's pondering on the utter lack of a response from the audience at his grandfather's attempt to rouse them is telling: "I have thought about that very often—how the times change, and the same words that carry a good many people into the howling wilderness in one generation are irksome or meaningless in the next" (201).

But the images of the land forgotten, ashes and dust, and the "howling wilderness" are not simply metaphors for the lost hope of the abolitionist grandfather's utopian impulses. For shortly after the Fourth of July jeremiad, John Ames the grandfather leaves his family behind and returns to Kansas, where he disappears from his family's life and eventually dies.

The grandfather John Ames's return to Kansas leads to the son John Ames and the grandson John Ames (our narrator, then aged twelve) embarking on their own adventure into the "howling wilderness" of a depopulated and drought-stricken Kansas that shapes a great deal of how John Ames views his grandfather's commitment to abolitionism, the relationship between the landscape of the plains and the character of the people who live there, and his own place in the vast sweep of American history and the American landscape. The importance of this journey into Kansas in search of his grandfather's body is underscored by its prominence in the text that our narrator produces for his son. He tells the story early and returns to it repeatedly. It is, he insists, an essential element of explaining who the Ames family is.

Thus, two John Ameses, father and son, left Gilead in 1892 and wandered into a depopulated and desolate area of eastern Kansas: "A drought had driven most of them away, those who had not already left for towns closer to the railroad. . . . I don't often use the expression 'godforsaken,' but when I think back to that place, that word does come to mind" (11). The journey proved to be much harder than expected: "There were times when I truly believed we might just wander off and die" (12). When they finally find the eldest John Ames's resting place, it is explicitly described in terms of the ashes and dust, the burned-over and deserted image—reminiscent of the opening chapters of Jeremiah—of the ground that he had invoked in his Fourth of July speech. As the narrator John Ames tries to describe this landscape for his own son, he struggles to find words adequate to describe its desiccation: "If I were to say it was going back to nature, you might get the idea that there was some sort of vitality about the place. But it was parched and sun-stricken. It was hard to imagine the grass had ever been green" (14).

And yet, the two younger John Ameses, father and son, expend every last ounce of energy trying to provide some semblance of order to this lost wilderness. They enact the rituals of the homesteaders in the service of the dead: clearing brush, erecting fences, marking property, and inscribing names. They plant flowers with seeds they had saved from their own garden and carried west to serve as the progenitors of a new blooming. Our narrator remarks that there were small graves—quite likely those of lost children—that were hard to even identify, but they took great care not to step on them and to leave intact the stones outlining them (14). Their solicitude for the ghosts of that lost frontier haunts our narrator into his old age.

Like Ruth Stone, whose nights in the little makeshift homestead on the peninsula and at the threshold of the lost homestead in the valley culminate in moments of insight and epiphany, our narrator John Ames is rewarded for his hardships with a vision of how he fits within this harsh and forbidding, but beautiful, landscape.

> I realized that what I saw was a full moon rising just as the sun was going down. Each of them was standing on its edge, with the most wonderful light between them. It seemed as if you could touch it, as if there were palpable currents of light passing back and forth, or as if there were great taut skeins of light suspended between them. . . . They seemed to float on the horizon for quite a long time, I suppose because they were both so bright you couldn't get a clear look at them. And that grave, and my father and I, were exactly between them, which seemed amazing to me at the time, since I hadn't given much thought to the nature of the horizon. (16)

This image of the horizon on the plains, this inescapable fact that we are always at the center of a cosmic drama and that our actions in the land are always framed by the greater motions of nature, proves to be a defining moment in the youngest John Ames's life much as the realization that "all our human boundaries were overrun" transformed Ruth Stone's life (*Housekeeping*, 115). When we can find the beauty and the larger meaning beyond human purposes in our connection with nature, our human existence is enriched, rather than diminished, by that realization. On the frontier, we can find ourselves in the whole.

Even in his old age, our narrator speaks of this journey, "our desert wanderings," as the metaphor that defines his understanding of what it means to be human and what it means to be lost (18): "That is how life goes—we send our children into the wilderness. Some of them on the day they are born, it seems, for all the help we can give them. Some of them seem to be a kind of wilderness unto themselves. But there must be angels there, too, and a spring of water. Even that wilderness, the very habitation of jackals, is the Lord's" (135). For Ames, to set out on a journey into the wilderness is to confront the moral confusion and despair of our condition, but it is a journey that might end in hope if we are willing to make it: "I have wandered to the limits of my understanding any number of times, out into that desolation, that Horeb, that Kansas, and I've scared myself, too, a good many times, leaving all landmarks behind me" (217). But even in his deepest moral confusion, he finds in the "ongoingness of the world" the insight that "it is remarkable" (217). These insights all seem to underscore our narrator's often repeated mantra about the importance of the phenomena around us: "This is an interesting planet. It deserves all the attention you can give it" (33).

We can now see that the parallels and disjunctions between the odysseys in *Gilead* and *Housekeeping* are even more striking than they might first appear. Edmund Foster wanders away from his home on the plains and never, so far as we can tell, looks back, but the eldest John Ames wanders off to return to his roots, to the place where he had felt committed to a cause and involved in good work. Each perishes, buried in the wilderness they sought out and forever lost to their grandchildren. Each becomes a source of a questioning and longing—Edmund lost in the lake haunts Ruth Stone as his grandfather's frightening commitment haunts our narrator John Ames. Both narrators suffer through wanderings in the wilderness that culminate in an epiphany as they hover or float above their lost grandfather's resting place—Ruth as she rocks in the small boat with Sylvie under the bridge awaiting the train above but contemplating the train below, and John Ames as he is suspended in the "taut skeins of light" contemplating the character of the horizon, himself marking the point of confluence between the setting sun and the rising moon beside his grandfather's grave. Each finds in that epiphanic moment a sense of connection both forward and backward in time, to the land and to the water, and to a sense of the cosmic motions that mark our passage through time and space with the earth and all its passengers. Robinson's narrators thus both lead us to contemplation of what it means to live in the land and particularly in the lands of the American West. These are both stories about a new generation finding meaning in the ghosts of the American frontier.

Ames's struggles with his father (the second John Ames) turn in fact on this boundedness, or groundedness, that defines ways of life. The second John Ames relocated with his older living son to the Gulf Coast, to the South, the land of slavery and segregation that the elder Ames had so despised, and he returned to Gilead only twice.[21] The second occasion leads to the tense parting of the father and the son: "When I mentioned the history we had here, he laughed. . . . 'I have become aware that we here lived within the limits of notions that were very old and even very local. I want you to understand that you do not have to be loyal to them.'" This patronizing statement provokes the narrator's angriest reaction in the entire book: "He thought he could excuse me from my loyalty, as if it were loyalty to him, as if it were just some well-intended mistake he could correct for me, as if it were not loyalty to myself at the very least" (268).

John Ames's loyalty to the mission that brought his grandfather to the plains—however passé or forgotten it might be now—merges in the end with his love of and loyalty to the land itself: "I love the prairie! So often I have seen the dawn come and the light flood over the land and everything turn radiant at once, that word 'good' so profoundly affirmed in my soul that I am amazed I should be allowed to witness such a thing. . . . Here on the prairie there is nothing to distract attention from the evening and the morning, nothing on the horizon to abbreviate or to delay. Mountains would seem an impertinence from that point of view" (282). The egalitarian character of this passage is striking. The glory of the plains is the sense that everyone can be bathed in the light simultaneously. Radiance touches each equally, and no one is left in another's shadow.

This passage, situated in Ames's last reflections in *Gilead,* serves as the most astonishing marker of the evolution of his thought over a long lifetime of reflection. Suspended between setting sun and rising moon at his grandfather's grave, when he first experienced the remarkable character of a landscape unobscured by "eminences" (human or geographical), Ames thought he was experiencing a special dispensation from the divinity—an augur of a "manifest destiny" or special calling. He is surprised, and perhaps a little disappointed, when his father seems to dismiss the power of the moment: "You know, everybody in Kansas saw the same thing that we saw" (56). Reminding us that he was twelve at the time, our narrator continues to insist that what others would have seen was the special and providential sign that he witnessed, but later, having contemplated "the nature of the horizon," the aged narrator John Ames seems ready to accept that "the sun and moon aligned themselves as they did with no special reference to the two of us" (56).

However, this insight does not undermine his confidence in the special character of his grandfather's mission. Quite the contrary, it strengthens his commitment to holding his place at the "center" of this most egalitarian of landscapes. Perhaps, it is this sensibility—this understanding of a horizon that allows each human being to stand in some sense at the center of the miraculously self-conscious center of the surrounding creation—that allows John Ames to see the light in others in a way that might be too often missed. Where his grandfather had interpreted the drought-stricken expanses of "ashes and dust" as a sign that the plains had fallen from divine favor or failed to live up to their divine promise, it is his grandson who, in the midst of so much sad evidence that his grandfather's vision had not been realized, still sees hope in the sunrise over the wide expanses of the American Middle West.

Conclusion: Wilderness Out of Sight and Out of Mind

We have seen that "wilderness" is a key concept in Robinson's writing. It has deep resonances for her both in a literal and an allegorical sense, and those senses often merge and intertwine in her complex portraits of the individuals who give American democracy its unique shape and character. Even though we can safely proclaim Robinson to be an "advocate" in some sense for the "wilderness," it would be difficult, and perhaps an imposition, to characterize either Ruth Stone or our narrator John Ames—or their author—as an "environmentalist." Robinson does not appear to be concerned with the preservation of a landscape for its own sake, nor does she offer us narrators who are committed to identifiable public policies of any sort, let alone the Clean Air Act, Clean Water Act, or Wilderness Act.[22] And yet, these narrators do articulate affinities with Robinson's own environmentalist leanings that are born out of an appreciation of nature and of humanity's relationship with it, a relationship that I have suggested is particularly available to us at the boundaries where civilization meets wilderness on the American frontiers. The character of these relationships—how and why Ruth Stone and John Ames celebrate the landscapes in which they are embedded—proves to be essential to understanding Robinson's own works on her avowed environmentalism.

At first glance, environmentalism may appear to be an afterthought in Robinson's work. She has explicitly dedicated only one essay and one nonfiction book (probably the least widely read of her books) to the topic, and although she has referred to that book—*Mother Country*—as her most important book, she has not spoken as often, or as vehemently, about environmental issues as about austerity politics or democratic theory or Calvinism. Her sustained focus on the historical dimensions of abolitionism, which is so in evidence in *Gilead* as well as in the essays collected in *The Death of Adam* and *When I Was a Child I Read Books,* appears to cast her attention to modern environmentalist issues in a very minor light.

And yet, Robinson clearly establishes the link between the abolitionists and modern environmentalism in her essay "Wilderness":

> Those who are concerned about the world environment are, in my view, the abolitionists of this era, struggling to make an enlightened public aware that environmental depredation is an axe at the root of every culture, every freedom, every value. There is no group in history I admire more than the abolitionists, but from their example I conclude that there are two questions we must always ask ourselves—what do we choose not to know, and what do we fail to anticipate? The ultimate success of the abolitionists so very much resembled failure that it requires charity, even more than discernment, to discover the difference. We must do better. Much more is at stake. (251)

Thus, Robinson associates preservation of "wilderness," of some semblance of the organic environment that would exist before or without our interferences, to be an essential element of human survival and flourishing. As the abolitionists recognized that no one could be free or live in democratic autonomy while some were enslaved and refused to ignore ("to choose not to know") the suffering of the slaves, so we must not ignore, or place out of mind, the damages that our ways of life are doing to the earth on which we live. Indifference of this sort is equally fatal to democracy as an ideal, which in Robinson's view is fundamentally premised upon attention to the least among us.

Robinson thinks of the environmental movement as a sort of replaying of the abolitionist movement. She clearly celebrates what *Gilead's* narrator John Ames referred to as his grandfather's "strenuousness in ethical matters that was to be admired finally" in the attitudes of environmentalists, but she also cautions that much of this "strenuousness" might be misplaced or misapplied (*Gilead*, 103). And she fears that those who care about the world's environment might win significant, but ultimately isolated, victories while losing the war and its aftermath. Just as the narrator John Ames is left to sort through a country and a town in which the aftermath of the Civil War had left the purported success of his grandfather's abolitionism very much in doubt, Robinson wonders whether we might celebrate saving the whales only to discover that we have lost the sea ("Wilderness," 251).

Robinson's concept of "mindfulness" is essential here because her arguments in both "Wilderness" and *Mother Country* focus on raising awareness of actions that might be happening "out of sight" and "out of mind" in areas of our countries where few are present to see and report the consequences. Thus, in "Wilderness," Robinson laments that the greatest problem associated with the "closing" of the American frontier and the depopulation of large chunks of our less productive territories (in this essay, the Mountain West) is that these places are now severed from the popular view—a place where things can be dumped or landscapes destroyed without any consequential indignation or protest. The most damaging "permission apparently implied by empty spaces" is the permission to do with them what we will. They become, like the sea, "a place where actions would not have consequences" (247). She sees the efforts of environmentalists as too often too selective—focused on "the outdoor pleasures of cherishing exotica" rather than on the deeper and more systemic problems that threaten every life and every culture on the planet: "I think the peril of the whole world is very extreme, and that the dolphins and koalas are finally threatened by the same potentialities that threaten every thing that creeps on the face of the earth" (252–53).

Among the virtues of the small pockets of democracy that Robinson finds on the western frontier, we might focus on the immediacy of the decision maker and the consequences of their decision. She can imagine the sheriff in *Housekeeping* suffering considerable discomfort in his meetings with Sylvie—not because his concerns about Ruth's well-being are entirely displaced but because he recognizes for all her eccentricity that Sylvie cares for the girl in her own fashion and will be injured by losing her.[23] The distant governments making decisions about the deposition of radioactive wastes in the Irish Sea and Yucca Mountain have no direct contact with the people or places they endanger and consequently no discomfort in destroying that which they do not see and do not understand.

Robinson argues, or at least imagines, that the appreciation of nature is intimately tied to the experience of it, and thus, she sees the demise of the little pockets of frontier democracy that she celebrates in *When I Was a Child I Read Books* as an invitation to a certain heedlessness. She fears that the mediating influence of a nature that we once knew up close and personally marks a turn toward a certain indifference that she saw in Thatcher's England and fears may be coming in the United States as well. By engaging the wilderness, we access that uniqueness and specialness in ourselves that are too easily lost in the impress of society and its pressures to conform. Wandering in the wilderness, both Ruth Stone and John Ames find a new sense of themselves and their purpose. Each experiences revelations that speak to both what makes them unique and what makes them part of a larger whole.

Robinson's narrators—and one is tempted to suggest Robinson herself—are haunted by the ghosts of the American frontier who faced the great western expanses of our nation as a challenge and a source of personal exploration and transformation. As Ruth Stone proclaims, echoing Thoreau, we are forced to recognize that "all our human boundaries are overrun" (*Housekeeping,* 115). In this regard, our commitments are tested. The American wilderness provided space for wandering and nonconformism, for utopian experiments, and terrible contests of ethical principle that spilled blood and transformed a nation. It is the connection with these ghosts and some sense of the dangers they traversed, the wonders they witnessed, and the insights they gained that she fears we might lose if we allow the West to "lose its place in the national imagination" (*Child,* 91).

As we noted above, she speaks of a "sad evolution" that has brought us an "idea of human nature [that] has become the opposite of what it was when the myth of the West began" (*Child,* 91). She fears we have lost some deep optimism that "human nature is replete with nameless possibilities and, by implication, that the world is accessible to new ways of understanding" (*Child,* 90). If the voice of Ruth Stone and the narrator John Ames rekindle memory of "so many interesting ideas [that] were associated with access to a habitable wilderness, the real frontier need never close" (*Child,* 90). There is hope for a certain type of democratic experimentation and human diversity to be found even in the *memory* of the western wilderness.

And yet landscape, for all its allegorical power and metaphorical import, matters in a much more literal sense. We live in the land, and Robinson reasserts that we are dependent upon it and lost without it. As our frontier access to the wilderness is foreclosed by the development of our continent, we risk losing far more than the memory of the impulses that made our ancestors adventurous, tolerant, eclectic, insightful, or democratic. We risk so othering the vast expanses of [nearly] empty spaces that we no longer see the damages that we are inflicting on parts of our planet with implications for all of us. She warns that we cannot tolerate the abuse of purported wildernesses as a sink into which we will dump the toxic detritus of our cities and our economic engines. Ironically, the depopulating of parts of our western interior and the partitioning of areas that are declared to be the wilderness "invite[s] denial in every form" ("Wilderness," 249). When we no longer "seek out wilderness," we place out of mind both pollutants and peoples who fall into expandable spaces far from the attention of urban powers who "have fairly ransacked the world for ornaments and privileges and we all know it" ("Wilderness," 251).

Robinson's solicitude for the margins of modern society—the remote, the archaic, the forgotten, and the eccentric—encompasses a sensibility both environmentalist and democratic. She finds in this ethic a concern for the "least of these" that includes both human and nonhuman others, and she writes in a spirit of reminding us that our culture and its values once considered these people and these spaces to be of the most vital importance. John Ames's dictum echoes across her writing: "This is an interesting planet. It deserves all the attention you can give it" (*Gilead,* 33). Robinson asks us to reflect on nothing so much as what we are doing here.

Notes

1. Michael Lewis, "American Wilderness: An Introduction," in *American Wilderness: A New History,* ed. Lewis (Oxford: Oxford University Press, 2007), 7.

2. Among the secondary works that have explored Marilynne Robinson's work as particularly focused on the "West" and America as a nation defined by the West, consider Andrew Delbanco, "Her Calling," *New York Times Sunday Book Review,* April 20, 2012; Charles Peterson, "West Towards Home: Tracking Marilynne Robinson's Intellectual Pilgrimage," *Book Forum,* February/March 2012, www.bookforum.com/inprint/018_05/8874; Maureen Ryan, "Marilynne Robinson's *Housekeeping:* The Subversive Narrative and the New American Eve," *South Atlantic Review* 56, no. 1 (January 1991): 79–86; and Thomas Schaub and Marilynne Robinson, "An Interview with Marilynne Robinson," *Contemporary Literature* 35, no. 2 (Summer 1994): 231–51.

3. Marilynne Robinson, "Wilderness," in *The Death of Adam: Essays on Modern Thought* (1998; New York: Picador, 2005), 254. Hereafter cited parenthetically.

4. See Joseph Sax, *Mountains Without Handrails* (Ann Arbor: University of Michigan Press, 1980).

5. Marilynne Robinson, *When I Was a Child I Read Books: Essays* (New York: Farrar, Straus and Giroux, 2012), 90. Hereafter cited parenthetically.

6. Marilynne Robinson, *Housekeeping* (New York: Farrar, Straus and Giroux, 1981), 3–4. Hereafter cited parenthetically.

7. See Robert Penn Warren, *All the King's Men* (Orlando: Harcourt, 1974), 248.

8. Marilynne Robinson, *Gilead* (New York: Farrar, Straus and Giroux, 2004), 282. Hereafter cited parenthetically.

9. All of my citations to Turner reference the 2010 Kindle edition of the 1920 collection of his essays *The Frontier in American History* (Digireads.com, 2010). The quotes above are both from loc. 23.

10. *The Machine in the Garden: Technology and the Pastoral Ideal in America,* Thirtieth Anniversary Edition (1964; Oxford: Oxford University Press, 2000), 374–75. The close connections between Marx's list of "canonical authors" and Robinson's own account of the authors who most shaped her thinking is worth noting.

11. For just a few examples, see *Housekeeping* 5, 39, and 168.

12. *Death of Adam,* 236.

13. See *Housekeeping* 161–162, 172, and 190–93.

14. Compare *Housekeeping,* 66, with *When I Was a Child I Read Books,* 86–88.

15. Lorraine Krall McCrary reveals other dimensions of this fascinating vignette in her essay in this volume.

16. Ruth's language here suggests Thoreau's final passages in *Walden:* "We need

to witness our own limits transgressed, and some life pasturing freely where we never wander" (*The Portable Thoreau*, ed. Carl Bode [1947; New York: Penguin, 1982], 557). Bob Pepperman Taylor offers an extended reflection on this passage in the preface to his *Our Limits Transgressed: Environmental Political Thoughts in America* (Lawrence: University Press of Kansas, 1992). This phrase seems to be one that resonates in Robinson's thought. She clearly uses it in a somewhat different context in *When I Was a Child* (87) to speak of her grandparents' western sensibilities.

17. As we note in the introduction and we also reference in the preface to our interview with Marilynne Robinson, *Lila* arrived literally as we were putting the finishing touches on this volume, and therefore we were unable to incorporate discussion of that work here other than in our brief discussion in the introduction.

18. References in *Gilead* to the empty spaces of Iowa and Kansas as "wilderness" or close cognates include 11, 55, 135–36, 146, 201, and 217.

19. It is perhaps worth noting in situating our narrator John Ames's life relative to that of others that it appears that the narrator is seventy-six while he is writing *Gilead* and that the year is 1956. Therefore, the narrator appears to have been born in 1880—fifteen years after the Civil War.

20. Jeremiah 1:6–7, King James Version.

21. In *Lila,* we learn that Edward(s) and the narrator John Ames are in fact the youngest sons of a much larger family of siblings who passed away in a diphtheria outbreak. One of those "lost children" was an older "John Ames" who died as a child and whose name was reused, purportedly to ensure that the first Reverend John Ames would have a living namesake, and this is a charge that our narrator himself apparently takes quite seriously in appointing himself the conservator of his grandfather's church and his grandfather's memory. Although *Lila* arrived too late for sustained analysis in this book, it would be a worthy question for future work to explore what this revelation (and John Ames's silence on the subject in *Gilead*) might add to Robinson's reflections on life on the American frontier and the themes of hardship, loyalty, community, and abandonment.

22. Ames does note that if he lives into the fall, he will vote for Eisenhower (*Gilead,* 172), but exactly what policy commitments this implies are hard to concern. He reads the *Nation* (*Gilead,* 269), and he discusses politics with Broughton, but it is hard to say just what positions he takes. Ruth, conversely, reads novels and *National Geographic* (*Housekeeping,* 118, 132).

23. See *Housekeeping,* 176–78, 190, and 204–8.

CHAPTER 3

Gilead's Two Models of Action against Racial Injustice

Alex Zamalin and Daniel Skinner

Marilynne Robinson's *Gilead* helps theorize how citizens should act against racial injustice. This is unveiled in exquisite detail through the perspective of a dying septuagenarian preacher, John Ames, as a memoir directed to his seven-year-old son about his relationships in the fictional town of Gilead, Iowa, known for its abolitionism in the nineteenth century. Two men are at the center of the Ames's narrative: his grandfather, John Ames, a radical abolitionist who fought with John Brown and was deeply involved in the violent struggle in Kansas in the 1850s, and John Ames (Jack) Boughton, the troubled son of his close friend, who returns to Gilead. The bulk of the narrative consists of the narrator's attempt to make sense of the utility of his grandfather's abolitionism, which is still memorialized by Gilead's citizens, even as this memorialization haunts. The narrator eventually recognizes that what makes the elder Ames's abolitionism especially important is its firm—and exceptional—ethical commitment to emancipating slaves by any means necessary and convincing others through a public performance of this commitment. Yet, at the novel's conclusion, the narrator is briefly exposed to Jack's racially egalitarian attitudes toward his African American wife, Della, and his willingness to accept her father's wish that he terminate their relationship in a still-segregated society with deeply entrenched antimiscegenation laws.[1] Recognizing this reframes the narrator's view of Jack. Ames no longer reduces Jack's character to his shameful and cavalier decision to father a child with a poor—and very young—woman, only to then have his family watch the child die from poverty. For the narrator, Jack's unacknowledged and ordinary actions toward Della and her African American family constitute an ethical commitment, which he hopes to transmit to his own son. Implicitly juxtaposing his abolitionist grandfather's commitment to action against racial injustice with that of Jack Boughton, the narrator concludes *Gilead* with the hope that his seven-year-old son might learn how to act courageously and purposefully in his life: "This whole town does look like whatever hope becomes after it begins to weary a little, then weary a little more. But hope deferred is still hope. I love this town. I think sometimes of going into the ground as a last wild gesture of love—I too will smolder away the time until the great and general incandescence. . . . I'll pray that you grow up a brave man in a brave country. I will pray you find a way to be useful. . . . I'll pray, and then I'll sleep."[2]

This dramatic context underscores our argument that Robinson's *Gilead* contributes to the theorization of struggles against racial exclusion, racism, and unequal freedom between blacks and whites. In what follows we explain in greater detail how this theoretical contribution works by contrasting the political possibilities and limitations of what we call a romantic-heroic model of action with a more tragic-everyday model. Robinson shows how the rich possibilities of Grandfather Ames's abolitionism, as an example of romantic-heroic action, also contain rich possibilities for effecting—and convincing others to effect—large-scale changes to unjust racial institutions. But this kind of action also works against his ability to focus on his own racially counterproductive commitments. In contrast, Robinson underscores the unnoticed potential of Jack Boughton's rejection of racial paternalism in his personal worldview and the acceptance of his white-skin privilege as an instance of tragic-everyday action. Such action is limited in terms of effecting changes to large-scale racial orders, but its focus on examining one's deeply held racial convictions and enactment of critical listening and generosity toward African Americans can contribute to the larger project of racial justice within American society. This is the case even if such action is exceedingly difficult and lonely and often fails to achieve its desired results.

Our argument unfolds in three parts. First, we identify Robinson's theorization of the various components of a romantic-heroic model, which are always already intertwined in *Gilead*. We label this mode of action "romantic-heroic" because it rests on the belief that single individuals can themselves, almost single-handedly, transform unjust institutions through exceptional actions. Likewise, we call it "romantic" because it rests on the assumption that one's passionate commitment to and embodiment of ethical principles (as opposed to its outcomes) is precisely what makes such action successful. Notably, Robinson shows that what makes such action useful for racial justice is that it is rooted in (1) attacks on official unjust institutions, (2) absolutist commitments to ethical principles, and (3) acting and persuading others to act through the public sacrificing and the risking of one's life. However, she also shows that such an approach to action is limited for racial justice because it does not demand that one reconstruct one's personal (racial) commitments. To this extent, her tone is one of solemn resignation even as she helps readers see the way forward.

Second, we identify Robinson's theorization of the various components of a tragic-everyday model of action. We call it "everyday" because it is rooted in practices that individuals take up on a daily basis and are not necessarily guaranteed by epic or macro-level theoretical commitments. This theme runs throughout Robinson's works, as when, in her essay "Austerity as Ideology," she praises "Western society" for its "serene sort of courage that allows us to grant one another real safety, real autonomy, the means to think and act as judgment and conscience dictate" and the assumption that "this great mutual courtesy will bear its best fruit if we respect, educate, inform, and trust one another."[3] The most admirable values of such a society, she suggests, are also usually the most fragile, the least certain.

Furthermore, we call it "tragic" precisely because its solitary nature makes it difficult to sustain and because it makes life increasingly difficult for the actor. Although such action does not have the capacity to alone transform unjust racial institutions because it neither attends to public persuasion nor directly attacks the institutions themselves, it does establish an important set of lived, egalitarian counterstandards that themselves model a racially just society. Unlike the romantic-heroic, the tragic (1) is focused on ensuring that one's personal racial attitudes are ethical, (2) is based in a strategic, pragmatic negotiation of the exigencies of circumstances, and (3) exemplifies a form of sacrifice that requires a receptive listening.

Third, we argue that Robinson's argument can contribute to a larger theoretical conversation between prominent political theorists of racial justice. Whereas many theorists illuminate what citizens must know about racial reality in order to better confront it, we suggest that *Gilead* illuminates the political possibilities and limitations of different ways of acting to change it.

John Ames and the Romantic-Heroic

John Ames's abolitionism exemplifies a mode of romantic-heroic action that seeks to topple official laws and institutions that impede racial justice. First, the target of his action is not one's personal contradictions, inconsistencies, or unexamined racial attitudes but is, rather, the external, large-scale political institution of slavery. The narrator explains that Ames's grandfather "had preached his people into the war, saying while there was slavery there was no peace, but only a war of the armed and powerful against the captive and defenseless. He would say, Peace will come only when that war ends, so the God of peace calls upon us to end it. He said all this with that gun in his belt. And everyone there always shouted amen, even the littlest children" (100–101).

Grandfather Ames recasts slavery as a national, rather than parochial, problem for which all Americans are morally responsible. He transforms slavery into a distinct political problem, which must be tackled, irrespective of whether individual citizens support it or themselves harbor racist attitudes. Slavery is not a benign cultural relic of the past but a form of warfare, which actively denigrates human beings; it is not mutually beneficial to all but creates a sharp distinction between those with power and those without it. The very existence of slavery makes everyday life constitutively immoral. Grandfather Ames's revision of peace as possible only with the abolition of slavery makes resistance neither optional nor avoidable. The audience's enthusiasm for Ames's message points to its far-reaching effect; confronted with such a revision of their de facto moral complicity for injustice, the congregation in Gilead moves from passivity to direct action, from moral slumber to moral awakening.[4]

Second, Grandfather Ames's action is based on a deep-seated commitment to the principle that injustice must be abolished because it is decidedly immoral instead of impractical, politically problematic, or illegal.[5] This becomes clear in a speech toward the end of his life in which he berates the post–Civil War generation for lacking commitment to the radical struggle against injustice. Grandfather Ames asserts there that his commitment to abolitionism comes from a vision he had as young man:

> When I was a young man the Lord came to me and put his hand just here on my right shoulder. I can feel it still. And He spoke to me, very clearly. The words went right through me. He said, Free the captive.

> Preach good news to the poor. Proclaim liberty throughout the land. That is all Scripture, of course, and the words were already familiar to me at the time. But it is clear enough why He would feel they needed special emphasis. No one lives by them, unless the Lord takes him in hand. Certainly I did not, until the day He stood beside me and spoke those words to me. (175)

Ames's invocation of God's name suggests spiritual dimensions, but this spiritualism itself extends to a conception of action rooted in ethical precepts that transcend corporeal constraints, pragmatic considerations, or legality.[6] His abolitionism, like Lincoln's, neither is based on the strategic worry that slavery is politically divisive nor problematically perpetuates an unsustainable cycle of hostility and animosity. Instead, it is based around a commitment to freeing those in captivity, assisting the poor, and promoting freedom generally. It is not insignificant that these practices are themselves organized around the substantive principles of equality and freedom, both of which have been conceptualized as conditions for justice. Yet what is more significant is that they become religious in their non-negotiability and fixedness.[7] That they come as a direct revelation from God makes them transcendental, their authority vested not in fragile citizens or the always already corrupt laws they instantiate. That they are guided by a higher authority engenders faith in moments of faithlessness, resilience amid impossible circumstances.

Of course, it is precisely this fundamentalist faith in justice over the law that gives Ames's action its ambiguous moral status, as it justifies his involvement with John Brown and the related "violence in Kansas before the war" (85). To perform the legitimacy of such violence to his congregation, Grandfather Ames preaches immediately after he mortally injures and then abandons a U.S. Army soldier who comes to Kansas in search of John Brown. The narrator's father recalls:

> My father stood us from his chair. He said, "I remember when you walked to the pulpit in that shot-up, bloody shirt with that pistol in your belt. And I had a thought as powerful and clear as any revelation. And it was, This has nothing to do with Jesus. Nothing. Nothing. And I was, and I am, as certain of that as anyone could ever be of any so-called vision. I defer to no one in this. Not to you, not to Paul the Apostle, not to John the Divine. Reverend."

> My grandfather said, "So-called vision. The Lord, standing there beside me, had one hundred times the reality for me that you have standing here now!" (85)

Grandfather Ames's response to his son's suggestion that violence has little to do with the pacifist teachings of Jesus interprets violence as an acceptable, even if problematic, means to achieve peace. The elder Ames subsumes all action under the higher principle of justice, which becomes an end in itself. Violence becomes nothing more than an amoral instrument, which leads to the death of others. Laws, conventions, or the mere words of Gospel, Grandfather Ames implies, fail to capture a reality that is much more truthful and foundational and that violence only helps secure.

Yet even in this passage it is clear that the transformative political potential of this commitment to justice stems from how moral authority is, in this case, self-directed. Grandfather Ames's suggestion that his own reality exceeds that of scripture itself makes clear that he acts from individual conscience, which reflects a personal attempt to live ethically, not governed by conventions, external institutions, or the larger community. For Ames, such conscientious existence demands absolute fidelity and personal perseverance and diligence. This is what makes him reduce his body and mind into an instrument of usefulness to achieve it. The narrator writes:

> My grandfather told me once about a vision he'd had when he was still living in Maine, not yet sixteen. He had fallen asleep by the fire, worn out from a day helping his father pull stumps. Someone has touched him on the shoulder, and when he looked up, there was the Lord, holding out His arms to him, which were bound in chains. My grandfather said, "Those irons had rankled right down to His Bones." He told me that as the saddest fact, and eyed me with the one seraph eye he had, the old grief fresh in it. He said he knew then that he had to come to Kansas and make himself useful to the cause of abolition. To be useful was the best thing the old men ever hoped for themselves, and to be aimless was their worst fear. I have a lot of respect for that view. (49)

Jesus's captivity, suffering, and pain does not immobilize Grandfather Ames but testifies to the importance of converting himself into an instrument of use-value, in the Marxian sense, for the ideal of sacrificing himself for a greater end. Making oneself useful, he suggests, amounts to complete, almost irrational deference of oneself to a higher end. His action thus escapes the liberal principle of self-preservation and the modern logic of self-interest. Yet it is not directly predicated upon a concern for concrete human beings with specific needs, complexities, and ambiguities, as much as the ethical principle of responding to injustice. This is made clear through Grandfather Ames's description of his wish to be useful to the general movement of abolition rather than the specific black subjects of slavery.

Third, Grandfather Ames's action is ultimately rooted in public performance as a mechanism through which to convince others to support his cause.[8] The Sunday after he kills the U.S soldier, Ames's son recalls:

> "It was the very next Sunday the old devil preached in one of those shirts, with that gun in his belt. And you would not have believed how the people responded, all the weeping there was, and the shouting." And after that, he said, his father would be gone for days sometimes. There were Sundays when he would ride his horse right up to the church steps just when it was time for service to begin and fire that gun in the air to let the people know he was back. They'd find him standing in the pulpit, with his eyes red and his face pale and dust in his beard, all ready to preach on judgment and grace. (110)

The bloody shirt symbolizes Ames's physical commitment to the struggle, a commitment that is also performed in his participation in the Civil War, in which he is badly wounded and loses one eye, "even though he'd have been well into his forties. And he lost that eye, and came back finally with it as healed as it was going to be" (88). Likewise, his gun symbolizes his willingness to act directly for the sake of his beliefs rather than remain a passive bystander and thus an accomplice of injustice. The shirt and gun, along with his red eyes expressing a mixture of fury and passion, function as nonlinguistic forms of rhetoric that seek to persuade through dramatizing the difference between words and deeds, quietism and engagement, apathy and commitment, cowardice and courage.[9]

Centrally embedded in this spectacle of bloodiness, however, is Grandfather Ames's willingness to sacrifice his own life. This is brought into relief when he interprets his wounds as necessary but unfortunate outcomes of the pursuit of justice—wounds that give meaning to his life:

> When my father found his father at Mount Pleasant after the war ended, he was shocked at first to see how he had been wounded. In fact, he was speechless. So my grandfather's first words to his son were, "I am confident that I will find great blessing in it." And that is what he said about everything that happened to him for the rest of his life, all of which tended to be more or less drastic. I remember at least two sprained wrists and a cracked rib. He told me once that being blessed meant being bloodied, and that is true etymologically, in English—but not in Greek or Hebrew. So whatever understanding might be based on that derivation has no scriptural authority behind it. It was unlike him to strain interpretation that way. He did it in order to make an account of himself, I suppose, as most of us do. (36)[10]

Ames interprets as an end in itself the bodily sacrifice that emerges from a transformation of his body into an instrument for justice. This, along with his equation of bloodiness with blessedness, foregrounds his understanding that self-sacrifice enriches one's own sense of self, whether or not it achieves the desired political outcomes. Ames's strategic etymology enables him to give an account of himself, but the etymology makes clear his perspective on bodily deformations as deepening, rather than attenuating, his own self-conception of morally exemplary behavior and as outward markers of his courage rather than defeat.

The power of Grandfather Ames's romantic-heroic action becomes clear through the way it is memorialized years later when radicalism is no longer entertained or considered viable. That his action is recalled by people as intellectually and politically diverse as John Ames, Jack Boughton, his father Robert Boughton, as well his Jack's black father-in-law confirms Hannah Arendt's thesis that action in the public sphere itself leaves a legacy that speaks volumes to future generations. The character's divergent memories and interpretations also remind us that memory is often constituted within distinct channels and historical lineages, underscoring the power of storytelling itself as a political act. As Arendt writes, "[action] 'produces' stories with or without intention as naturally as fabrication produces tangible things."[11]

Yet Gilead also dramatizes how Grandfather Ames's preoccupation with and direct action against larger-scale state institutions that perpetuate slavery direct his attention away from examining the potentially counterproductive racial commitments he and the citizens of Gilead harbor. There is no evidence that Grandfather Ames himself harbors racist sentiments, but there is equally no evidence that he is deeply critical of white supremacy, white paternalism, or the myriad myths of inferiority associated with black skin. What is instead made apparent through the burning of the black church in Gilead, which forces the remaining black families in the town to move to Chicago, is that Gilead's current citizens harbor at least some of these beliefs. As the narrator describes it: "It wasn't a big fire—someone heaped brush against the back wall and put a match to it, and someone else saw the smoke and put the flames out with a shovel. . . . That church sold up some years ago, and what was left of the congregation moved to Chicago. By then it was down to three or four families" (36).

Similarly, Grandfather Ames's decision to leave Gilead for Kansas ostensibly represents his own antiracism and disappointment over the townspeople's refusal to fulfill the radical legacy of abolitionism. Upon hearing that the preacher of the razed black church preached a sermon on brotherly love rather than vengeance and retribution, the elder Ames tells his son, himself a pacifist preacher: "Reverend, no words could be bitter enough, no day could be long enough. There is just no end to it. I eat and drink it. I wake and sleep it" (84). Although Ames himself is not responsible for the fire, his last written words acknowledge and express disappointment over the deep entrenchment of racism in Gilead. As he describes it in a letter outlining his decision to leave: "No good has come, no evil ended. That is your peace. Without vision the people perish. The Lord bless you and keep you" (85).

Acknowledging that "no evil" has ended in Gilead is an admission that his abolitionist efforts were only partly successful, but his assertion that the people of Gilead are visionless is not without irony. Indeed, Grandfather Ames's own vision, so outwardly focused on "free[ing] the captive," prevents him from performing a set of inward, racially egalitarian counterstandards in everyday life (175). Of course, he does engage in everyday acts of generosity. Indeed, a commitment to the principle of justice over law compels him to help the less fortunate and poor citizens of his community. In the words of his grandson: "My grandfather never kept anything that was worth giving away, or let us keep it, either, so mother said. He would take laundry right off the line" (31). Yet it is equally striking that this generosity is never translated into a form of critical respect of or receptive listening toward African American citizens. To the contrary, Grandfather Ames's own distorted vision—both metaphorically, as well as literally, having lost his right eye in battle[12]—prevents him from providing an antiracist or racially egalitarian vision for how people could change the way they live their everyday lives. His myopic focus on toppling slavery by any means necessary precludes the kind of individual reconstruction that might have prevented the fire in the black church. Central to this myopic focus is also a failure to acknowledge the deficiencies and potential shortcomings of his action. Grandfather Ames is too focused on following through on his commitment at the expense of any deeper self-reflection. He confidently asserts the intrinsic value of his participation in the Civil War, even if it leads to great personal loss and does not accomplish its intended objective. Arguing that abolition is a necessary condition for peace illustrates his belief that racial justice is ultimately measured through eradicating laws and policies that perpetuate racial injustice rather than changing the habits of everyday life.

The result is a clear articulation of the limitations of the romantic-heroic model.[13] Ultimately, the thickness of Gilead's culture serves to hedge against the potentials that the great deeds of particular individuals might have. On the one hand, therefore, we are introduced to exemplars who serve as models for commitment in the face of racial justice. On the other hand, we come to appreciate the scale and cultural reach of racial injustice itself. Like John Brown, whose actions at Harpers Ferry may be said to have abetted and gestured toward the end of slavery,[14] Ames's actions were necessary but ultimately insufficient to the attainment of his principled ends.

Jack Boughton and the Tragic-Everyday

Gilead's counterpoint to Grandfather Ames's romantic-heroic model of action is a tragic-everyday model embodied by Jack Boughton. Jack's maintenance of an interracial relationship amid the antimiscegenation laws of the racially segregated and white-supremacist Jim Crow south of the 1950s itself reflects courage, risk, and greater personal cost. Jack describes these difficulties to the narrator, again with a nod to the question of impaired vision: "But of course we couldn't find respectable accommodations, and the hotel clerk where we got a room charged me a good deal extra for turning a blind eye, or words to the effect. He had a phrase for the law we were breaking—'pernicious cohabitation?,' 'lascivious cohabitation'? Lewd.

For some reason I always forget that word. You can't imagine how many ways they make things difficult" (226). Yet Jack's actions toward his African American wife, Della, and her unnamed father ultimately reflect a kind of self-oriented and everyday action that models behavior necessary for a racially just society.

Robinson unfolds these complexities in several ways. First, unlike the elder Ames's action, which is outwardly directed toward unjust racial institutions, Jack's action is rooted in the construction of a personal worldview that rejects white supremacy and embraces racial egalitarianism. This is captured through Jack's description of his relationship to his wife, Della:

> "You see, I met Della during a fairly low point in my life. I won't go into that. Della was very nice to me, very pleasant. So I found myself now and then walking down that street at the hour, and sometimes I saw her and we spoke. I swear I had no intentions at all, honorable or otherwise. It was just pleasant to see her face." He laughed. "She would always say, 'Good afternoon, Reverend.' I was not at that time accustomed to being treated like a respectable man. I must say I enjoyed it. It got so that I would walk along her street with no thought of seeing her, just because there was a kind of comfort in being reminded of her." (222)

White skin affords Jack no bulwark against personal frailty, depression, and loneliness. Likewise, it does not grant him superiority over black women. Instead, it is a black woman, Della, who provides him a feeling of comfort, dignity, and self-respect at one of the lowest points in his life.[15] Jack recognizes that generosity and kindness trump racial identification. Della's presence (her speech and face) and deeds rather than her physical appearance as black define her identity. If anything, Jack reverses the traditional power dynamic between blacks and whites as he assumes Della to be in a position of power to alleviate his suffering and grant him respect. In Della, Jack sees a complex, equal human being who does not conform to the racial myth of black deviance or excessive piety. She is a sentient agent capable of giving as well as withdrawing compassion, not an object of a desire to which his white male privilege grants him absolute and unqualified access. Della is not to be manipulated for Jack's personal gain; instead, he recognizes that her generosity—a product of her own volition, desire, and agency—is something over which he has no control and without which he would continue to suffer.

Second, unlike Grandfather Ames's action, driven as it is by a rigid adherence to ethical principles, Jack is driven by a pragmatic consideration of his circumstances:

> But I still made myself speak to him at the door. I said, "I only want to assure you that my friendship with your daughter has been entirely honorable." And he said, "If you were an honorable man, you would leave her alone."
>
> I said, "Yes, I will do that. I came here to assure you of that." Which was a lie, of course. I did intend to stop seeing her, but it was an intention I had formed in his church that very morning. I thought that Della's standing with her family might be helped if I impressed him as a plausibly decent man, and my only chance of doing that was by going away. And I could see what a very good life she had. I'm not sure what my intentions had been in going there. Certainly I never thought I would leave without saying even one word to her. But I did. I left for St. Louis that same evening. (224–25)

Strict adherence to Grandfather Ames's advice might have led Jack to unequivocally reject Della's father's wish because it would simply perpetuate unjust antimiscegenation laws in a still-segregated society. But, understanding the importance of outcomes over principles, Jack accepts her father's wishes and overrides this principle. His shift in thinking occurs unexpectedly as conditions change; Della's father's concrete desires, themselves productive of his lived experience, militate against Jack's own. An unwavering commitment to truth might have forced Jack to divulge the honorable reason of love that drove him to persuade Della's father of accepting him. Instead, Jack's pragmatic decision to lie reflects his understanding of truth as a process, an outcome of improvisation, where what works comes not from strict adherence to rules but from the negotiation of exigencies. Lying about his initial intentions becomes necessary when Jack recognizes that the support of Della's family is crucial to her own flourishing. Yet his lie reflects his understanding of a much more important truth concerning African Americans' equal capability to articulate, judge, and deliberate over the conditions that might enable this.

Third, unlike the elder Ames's action, which is rooted in courage and personal sacrifice in public for the purpose of persuading others, Jack's pragmatic modification of his approach is itself based in receptively listening to the needs and experiences of others. His decision echoes what William Connolly understands as a crucial "ethos" of democratic citizenship: "Critical responsiveness takes the form of careful listening and presumptive generosity to constituencies struggling to move from an obscure or degraded subsistence below the field of recognition, justice, obligation, rights, or legitimacy to a place on one or more of those registers."[16] Specifically, in the passage immediately prior to the one quoted above, we learn that Jack's decision to accept Della's father's wish is prompted by his own tacit understanding that her father's concerns about white supremacy are legitimate: "The church was full and I sat near the back, but I was the only white man there, and people noticed me. Della's sister was in the choir, so of course she saw me. And I could tell her father suspected who I was, by the way he watched me. He preached about those who come among you in sheep's clothing but inwardly are ravening wolves. He also spoke about whited tombs, which inwardly are full of dead men's bones and all uncleanness. Looking at me the whole time, of course" (224).

Hearing Della's father warn his black congregation to beware of people who outwardly profess good and pure intentions but are inwardly filled with exploitative and distorted ones informs, in part, Jack's decision to leave Della. As the only white man present, Jack recognizes that these words speak to a genuine concern that a latent—even if unacknowledged—belief in white supremacy lies hidden beneath his outward expression of goodwill. His refusal to interrupt the sermon, become bitter, or leave the church exemplify his prioritization of the needs and particular experiences of African Americans. Jack neither seeks to assuage, falsify, or render illegitimate Della's father's fears; he does not speak truth to what he might see as parochial ignorance; he does not suppose that his experiences are correct or should ever trump Della's father's. Indeed, Jack's legitimation of this opposing perspective comes not because it is necessarily factual or incontestable but because of its experiential reality for another. That Della's father deeply believes this is reason enough for Jack to honor it as only one legitimate belief among many, especially since it is reasonable for black Americans to distrust their white compatriots in a racially segregated society.

Yet Jack's resistance to racial paternalism, pragmatic consideration of the sociopolitical reality of racism, and desire to reformulate his own activities through a consideration of others' viewpoints itself plunges him into a tragic condition of loneliness, despair, and personal unhappiness. Deep fidelity to ethical principles ensures Grandfather Ames a feeling of personal satisfaction, whether or not his actions successfully accomplish their intended goals. Yet Jack's prioritization of concrete others rather than principles renders him unable to live in peace with his wife and interracial child, Robert Miles.

Such personal decisions cannot themselves challenge the order of white supremacy or African American distrust, reminding us of the destructive psychological effects that follow from coming to terms with the destructive external world with which one is faced.[17] As the narrator explains, "If I had to choose one word to describe him as he is now, it might be 'lonely,' though 'weary' and 'angry' certainly come to mind also" (184). The efficacy of Jack's self-oriented activities for effecting change to race relations is limited because his activities do not directly seek to undermine antimiscegenation laws or to persuade others to live their lives according to his principles. Jack's failure to accomplish this is made vivid through the narrator: "I believe I saw in young Boughton's face, as we were walking along, a sense of irony at having invested hope in this sad old place, and also the cost of him of relinquishing it" (224). Yet it is perhaps in *Home* where Robinson most clearly illuminates the political limitations of this action.

Set at the same time as *Gilead,* the novel highlights Jack's increasing recognition that his own father's racist assertions make Gilead an unsafe haven for him and his family. For example, Jack fails to confront his father after he implicitly endorses racial segregation by saying "so much bad blood. I think we had all better just keep to ourselves."[18] Furthermore, Jack issues no serious response to his father's assertion that police violence against African American civil rights protestors should not disturb him. At best, Jack expresses indignation at his racism when he responds "Jesus Christ!" to his father's assertion that "there's no reason to let that sort of trouble upset you" (98). Yet this feeling of deep frustration amounts to nothing more than a feeling; it not the inspiration for critique.

The irony is that Jack's father assumes the position of moral educator when he chastises his son for saying Christ's name in vain. Jack's father holds that offense should be taken at Jack's profane, blasphemous utterance rather than at his own racism. This radical difference in perspective can provide the impetus for honest conversation, predicated on a genuine attempt at mutual understanding. Yet it is only filled with deafening silence, as Jack's fragile attempt at saying something ends with an apology, which inadvertently affirms his father's truth: "Jack said, 'I—' as if he had been about to say more. But he stopped himself. 'Sorry'" (98).

Just as she shows this, however, Robinson also shows that the rhetoric and practice of everyday self-work can actually play a role in the preservation of racial injustice. Indeed, Jack's father uses the rhetoric of self-work to displace blame from whites and place responsibility on African Americans for their social marginalization, noting, "I do think they're going to need to improve themselves, though, if they want to be accepted" (155). When Jack tries to point to the fallacy of this thinking by drawing attention to the brutal murder of a fourteen-year-old African American boy, Emmett Till, Jack's father does two things to dismiss it as an example that points to a rule. First, he assumes the position of perspectivalism and resistance to orthodoxy, suggesting, "I think there must have been more to it" since he "had another memory of it." Second, he reads the murder as a consequence—at least in part—of abrogated parental responsibility: "Still, parents have a responsibility. . . . They bring children into a dangerous world, and they should keep them safe" (156).

But here as elsewhere Jack's willingness to change the topic shows that perhaps the tragedy of his everyday action is not only that it makes it harder for those who enact it to live in an oppressive society but also that its deeply personal nature offers no strong imperative to persuade others to live like oneself (155). At the same time, what makes it tragic is that the commitment to listen to others and validate their different experiences and perspectives can lead to the perpetuation of the unjust status quo. In *Gilead,* such a practice works as a disruptive force against racism, paternalism, and white supremacy, enacted as it is by a white man (Jack) toward two black citizens (Della and her father). In *Home,* however, it helps keep such things intact.

Gilead's final pages nonetheless highlight the power and importance of self-directed, everyday action for racial justice, beyond its limitations. Moved as he is by Jack's courage, sacrifice, and generosity, the narrator Ames no longer sees in him a misguided adolescent but one who lives an exemplary conscientious existence:

> Here I was supposed to be a second father to him. I wanted to say something to him to that effect, but it seemed complicated, and I was too tired to think through its possible implications. It might sound as if

> I were trying to establish some sort of equivalency between his failings and mine, when in fact I would have meant he was a better man than I ever thought he could be. So I said, "you are a good man," and he gave me a look, purely appraising, and laughed and said, "You can take my word for it, Reverend, there are worse." (231)

There is no compelling evidence to definitively say whether the narrator's recognition represents Robinson's favoring of Jack's action over Grandfather Ames's. Yet this concluding encounter strongly implies that Jack's private action, which is otherwise easy to ignore, marginalize, or see as nonpolitical, should not be overlooked or jettisoned, especially by future citizens. The narrator's final description of Jack to his son supports such a reading: "You might wonder about my pastoral discretion, writing this all out. Well, on one hand it is the way I have of considering things. On the other hand, he is a man about whom you may never hear one good word, and I just don't know another way to let you see the beauty in him" (232). The narrator's insistence that his son see the beauty in Jack insists that the memory of past deeds is crucial for orienting future action. Yet the focus here is not on the epic and grandiose but on the everyday and quotidian.[19] To this extent, for every "I have a dream" speech the scholar of racial justice is well advised to inquire instead (or as well) into the multitude of lesser minor literatures that move the needle, on the one hand, and weigh it down, on the other. This claim echoes Arendt's argument that "without remembrance . . . the living activities of action, speech, and thought would lose their reality at the end of each process and disappear as though they have never been."[20]

Action, Political Theory, and Racial Justice

Racial politics concerned with the pursuit of justice must concern itself with chronicling the everyday. Whereas Arendt valorizes the remembrance of heroic and publicly witnessed deeds carried out in clear "spaces of appearance," Robinson points out the importance of remembering everyday ones, many of which are performed in the shadows and even homes of sometimes unknown actors. The power of the political, it is possible, may arise from the interaction of the two spheres. After all, as Robinson notes in "Imagination and Community," "The shrinking of imaginative identification which allows such things as shared humanity to be forgotten always begins at home."[21] Ultimately, though Arendt doesn't seem to see it, the germination of the political may *begin* at home. It is there, after all, that we either steel ourselves for the challenges of public life and the civic, collective pursuit of justice or are disengaged in such a way that we studiously avoid ever leaving the confines of home, thereby eschewing critical aspects of political and even human existence. Rather than distance the political from home, as Arendt does, Robinson warns against "the sad tendency of domesticity—as of piety—to contract and of grace to decay into rigor and peace into tedium."[22] But this is only a tendency—a failure of imagination—not a fait accompli. Accordingly, though we may not need to jettison the idea of "home" altogether to engage in politics,[23] we must take care to interrogate the relationship between these two spaces and understand how they either facilitate or stunt the pursuit of political aims.

It is in this spirit that we suggest that *Gilead*'s insights offer an important contribution to contemporary political theoretical discussions about racial justice. Given the depth and breadth of American racism, it risks platitude to note that racial equality is far from a reality in American life. De facto residential segregation significantly impacts black education and labor opportunities, "hyper-incarceration" disproportionately disciplines and punishes black men, while regulating their access to work and citizenship and inequities in economic wealth, housing, and education all continue to foreclose social mobility for black citizens.[24] Over the past two decades, political theorists have argued that action against such a condition becomes more likely only insofar as Americans bridge the gap between the sociological facts of racial reality and the idea of a postracial society. Some scholars argue that widespread opposition to monetary reparations for slavery and Jim Crow, mass-scale affirmative action, and programs aimed at social and economic redistribution can be successfully reversed if American citizens recognize that still, today, "race matters" and continues to shape African American access to education, housing, employment, and wealth.[25] Others maintain that action against racial inequality requires the incorporation of the memory of slavery and Jim Crow into American public consciousness—a crucial practice that strategically exposes how current patterns of structural inequality are not products of a pathological culture but a result of a complex and accumulated network of oppression for which all Americans are collectively responsible. As Thomas McCarthy contends, "the greater the public familiarity with and knowledge of that history, the greater are the chances of effectively interpreting current problems as belonging to its accumulated effects and thus of publicly framing them as moral issues or issues of justice."[26]

But what still remains inadequately examined in these accounts is not only what citizens must know, but how should they act. Robinson's *Gilead* and its perspective shift in *Home* remind us that the Arendtian call to action—rooted in positions taken freely and articulated in public spaces—must be central to our fictionalized depictions of American racial history to adequately provide readers of those fictionalizations with an operationalizable sense of "what is to be done." Hence, in "Puritans and Prigs," Robinson underscores the importance of working through and directly encountering the past in a way that bridges to the future: "In great things as in small, we are forever in a process of recovery from a past that is always being reinterpreted to account for present pathologies." Doing so, however, requires considerable dedication and willingness to rebuild critical parts of American culture since the "assumption of present responsibility for the present state of things was a ritual feature of life in this culture for two and a half centuries, and is entirely forgotten by us now."[27]

A central normative question becomes: Should citizens simply seek to convince others of the pervasiveness and immorality of racial injustice, or should they work to excise their own problematic racial assumptions and treat African Americans with respect and presumptive generosity? Not only does this question still deserve further elaboration, but citizens must decide for themselves whether they should invest themselves in action to move from passivity to engagement. *Gilead*'s final lines, comprised of the narrator's final words to his son, might reflect Robinson's own hope that her readers will take on this project: "I'll pray that you grow up a brave man in a brave country. I will pray you find a way to be useful" (247).

Notes

1. This mark of Jack's love for his family, which transcends antimiscegenation laws, both brings the family together and breaks them apart. In engaging the close relationship between justice and familial bonds and traditions, Robinson reasserts the political dimension of the family and casts the formation and dissolution of families as political acts. This theoretical move is not without disagreement. Most famously, Hannah Arendt distinguished the political nature of the public sphere

of action from, among other things, the "social" and unpolitical world of laboring, which she regards as endemic to family and other forms of nonpolitical life (Arendt, *The Human Condition* [1958; Chicago: University of Chicago Press, 1989]). While many feminist theorists have criticized this position (see, e.g., Wendy Brown, *Manhood and Politics: A Feminist Reading in Political Theory* [Totowa: Rowman and Littlefield, 1988]), the breakdown of such categories—and the attendant rethinking of the political such breakdowns initiate—is one of the most important roles fiction can play in political theorizing. The interrelationship of family life and American politics is clear in classic works as different as William Faulkner's *Go Down, Moses* and Toni Morrison's *Beloved*. The breakdown, it seems, often flows logically from close engagements with the everyday (as opposed to "epic" theory).

2. Marilynne Robinson, *Gilead* (New York: Farrar, Straus and Giroux, 2004), 247. Hereafter cited parenthetically.

3. Marilynne Robinson, "Austerity as Ideology," in *When I Was a Child I Read Books: Essays* (New York: Farrar, Straus and Giroux, 2012), 44–45.

4. At the same time, such moments stand in contrast to those that led the narrator to burn his only Great War–era sermon. Thus we are reminded that Gilead is a place of ambiguity and limits. As he notes, "I knew the only people at church would be a few old women who were already about as sad and apprehensive as they could be and no more approving of the war than I was." In Gilead, as elsewhere, presumably, the power of language had dimmed and moved away from social engagement and toward scripture: "I seemed ridiculous to myself for imagining I could thunder from the pulpit in those circumstances, and I dropped that sermon in the stove and preached on the Parable of the Lost Sheep" (48).

5. As Friedrich Nietzsche notes, by way of a critique of the often utilitarian relationship between truth and social power, "One must have become indifferent, one must never ask whether the truth is useful or a fatality" (Nietzsche, *Twilight of the Idols* [London: Penguin, 2003], 125).

6. Perhaps the most famous articulation of this distinction in more recent American political history is Martin Luther King Jr.'s "Letter from a Birmingham Jail," archived at the King Center, www.thekingcenter.org/archive/document/letter-birmingham-city-jail-1.

7. Not to mention of questionable political value. For a critical reading of these rhetorical modes, see George Shulman, *American Prophecy* (Minneapolis: University of Minnesota Press, 2008).

8. Here, for Robinson, publicness takes on an important political dimension. Gilead—the town—is notable for its resistance to the privatization of the conversations concerning race that Robinson recounts. To this extent, Gilead presents an opportunity for thinking through the Arendtian notion of "spaces of appearance" as central to politics. The flip side of this coin, of course, is the role that

shame plays in ejecting "immoral" actors from the public sphere—especially John Ames Boughton in the wake of his miscegenation. While Arendt might be the ideal, Michel Foucault's "Order of Discourse" seems more to the point because of its emphasis on power's ability to constrain the terms of discourse (see Arendt, *The Human Condition*; and Michel Foucault, "The Order of Discourse," in *The Archeology of Knowledge*, trans. A. M. Sheridan Smith [New York: Pantheon, 1972]).

9. It is for this reason that Ames is productively compared and contrasted with John Brown. For a particularly fruitful textual comparison, see Russell Banks's *Cloudsplitter* (New York: HarperFlamingo, 1998), in which Banks—similarly to Robinson—uses a fictional vehicle in the form of letters from one of John Brown's sons, Owen, to bring out the complexities of action in resistance to slavery. For Brown, of course, a key factor was his allegiance to God.

10. It is possible that Robinson wants us to think of Luke 10:25–29: "And behold a lawyer stood up to put him to the test, saying, 'Teacher, what shall I do to inherit eternal life?' He said to him, 'What is written in the law? How do you read?' And he answered, 'You shall love the Lord your God with all your heart, and with all your soul, and with all your strength, and with all your mind; and your neighbor as yourself.' And He said to him, 'You have answered right; do this, and you will live.' But the lawyer, desiring to justify himself, said to Jesus, 'And who is my neighbor?'" Jesus answers the lawyer with the telling of the parable of the Good Samaritan. Who is our neighbor and whether we all answer that question "desiring to justify ourselves" is at the heart of *Gilead* (and perhaps *Home* as well). Appreciation to Joseph Lane for pointing us to this possible connection.

11. Arendt, *The Human Condition*, 184.

12. Here Robinson evokes the double-edged imagery of Oedipus, whose stubbornness mars his ability to see what is obvious to the audience—which has the benefit of hindsight and even theoretical reflection—and leads to his physically ripping out his own eyes. The prevalence of vision metaphors reminds us of the etymological linkage between theory and vision, dating back to the classical Greeks. For an important discussion of this connection, see Sheldon S. Wolin, *Politics and Vision: Continuity and Innovation in Western Political Thought* (Princeton, NJ: Princeton University Press, 2004).

13. Especially because it merely topples unjust institutions but does not exterminate latent racist attitudes in citizens or construct laws and public policies to ensure that justice is maintained.

14. See, for example, the perspective taken by David S. Reynolds in *John Brown, Abolitionist* (New York: Vintage, 2005).

15. Joan C. Tronto has argued that care is best understood to be relational, not hierarchical (see Tronto, *Caring Democracy: Markets, Equality, and Justice* [New York: New York University Press, 2013]).

16. William Connolly, *Pluralism* (Durham, NC: Duke University Press, 2005), 126.

17. Sigmund Freud, *Civilization and Its Discontents,* trans. James Strachey (New York: Norton, 1968).

18. Marilynne Robinson, *Home* (New York: Picador, 2008), 147. Hereafter cited parenthetically. In *Cloudsplitter,* Russell Banks similarly characterizes Frederick Douglass as unwilling to act. Douglass, as is well known, deeply respected John Brown yet was unwilling to support the Harpers Ferry invasion, about which he prophesied total disaster. In a critical passage, Brown peels back history to undo the part of the project that Washington did help complete, to underscore the necessary risk involved in the Harpers Ferry plan: "I'm glad you weren't around to advise our Revolutionary forebears," he tells Douglass. "We'd all still be British subjects" (734).

19. In "McGuffey and the Abolitionists," Robinson highlights the tendency for New England abolitionists to fail to account for slavery itself (Marilynne Robinson, *The Death of Adam: Essays on Modern Thought* [New York: Picador, 2005], esp. 144–46).

20. Arendt, *The Human Condition,* 95.

21. Marilynne Robinson, "Imagination and Community," in *When I Was a Child I Read Books,* 31.

22. Marilynne Robinson, "When I Was a Child," in *When I Was a Child, I Read Books,* 93.

23. For a more detailed engagement with the concept of "home" in Robinson's works—especially her essays—see Shannon Mariotti's essay in this collection.

24. On residential segregation, see Douglas S. Massey and Nancy A. Denton, *American Apartheid: Segregation and the Making of the Underclass* (Cambridge: Harvard University Press, 1993). On mass incarceration, see Loïc J. D. Wacquant, *Prisons of Poverty,* expanded ed. (Minneapolis: University of Minnesota Press, 2009). See also Melvin L. Oliver and Thomas M. Shapiro, *Black Wealth, White Wealth: A New Perspective on Racial Inequality* (New York: Routledge, 2006).

25. Cornel West, *Race Matters* (New York: Vintage, 2001); David Theo Goldberg, *The Racial State* (Malden, MA: Blackwell, 2002); David Theo Goldberg, *The Threat of Race: Reflections on Racial Neoliberalism* (Malden, MA: Wiley-Blackwell, 2009); Imani Perry, *More Beautiful and More Terrible* (New York: New York University Press, 2011).

26. Thomas McCarthy, "Vergangenheitsbewältigung in the USA: On the Politics of the Memory of Slavery," *Political Theory* 30 (2002): 640.

27. Marilynne Robinson, "Puritans and Prigs," In *The Death of Adam,* 155.

CHAPTER 4

"In Those Old Days"

The Old and the Aging in Marilynne Robinson's Gilead *and* Home

Emily C. Nacol

In her novels *Gilead* and *Home,* Marilynne Robinson explores the meaning of oldness as a quality of persons, places, and objects. As interpreters have noted, the "old" holds a significant place in Robinson's work, and she infuses it with an array of meanings and possibilities. Especially in these two novels, which A. O. Scott aptly characterizes as "twinned portraits of . . . the godly, elderly patriarchs" John Ames and Robert Boughton, Robinson considers the potential of the old and familiar to comfort and soothe, as well as to oppress and harm. But perhaps most interestingly, she finds newness in aging and the discovery of oldness, a capacity to unsettle the everyday and introduce a space for introspection and even novelty.[1] In this chapter, I will also suggest that in Robinson's complex account of oldness and the richly detailed portraits of old people themselves that we encounter *Gilead* and *Home,* we can find a particular democratic ethos.

In many respects, the Reverend John Ames, *Gilead*'s narrator, articulates Robinson's treatment of the old in a brief personal reflection. In the letter to his young son, Robby, that constitutes the novel, he remarks: "I am . . . inclined to overuse the word 'old,' which actually has less to do with age, as it seems to me, than it does with familiarity. It sets a thing apart as something regarded with a modest, habitual affection. Sometimes it suggests haplessness or vulnerability. I say 'old Boughton,' I say 'this shabby old town,' and I mean that they are very near my heart."[2] Robinson's own use of the word "old," which marks so many pages of both *Gilead* and especially *Home,* frequently connotes this tenderness for the well-known and well-worn, but it also captures the fearsome human confrontation with time and mortality.

In the first section of this chapter, before turning to Robinson's character portraits of old men, I will explore some other loci of oldness in her novels. Certainly Gilead, Iowa, the fictional setting for both novels, is the "shabby old town" that the Reverends Ames and Boughton call home, but my interest particularly rests with two of its old homes and their contents. The old Boughton home with its myriad collections of old things is a particularly important and complicated site of identity and memory in *Home.* Likewise, *Gilead's* narrator is troubled by the collection of old papers in the parsonage attic that constitute the record of his life. As Ames points out, these "material things are so vulnerable to the humiliations of decay," reminding those who dwell among them of the fragility and sorrow that often comes with aging (100). But they also are treasured sites of meaning and continuity, carrying with them what Iris Young calls "a sedimented history which is the story of [a] life, and the story of . . . shared lives."[3] While the inner lives of Robinson's characters constitute the deeper story about oldness and aging in *Gilead* and *Home,* she notably situates them in a material context of objects marked by decay and memory. They are old people living in old homes with old things, even as the world around them changes.

The constellation of old things and places that form the context for Robinson's characters constitutes one part of her story about the materiality of aging. The second part of this chapter will focus primarily on a trio of embodied, aging selves—two lifelong friends, Ames and Boughton, who are facing their mortality, as well as the long-dead patriarch who lives in their memory as the fieriest of old men, Ames's grandfather. Robinson significantly presents all three as embodied subjects, and Ames and Boughton daily encounter the new fragility and material decay of their bodies with grief, anger, wry humor, and wonder. As Simone de Beauvoir ruminates in *The Coming of Age:* "Old age is particularly difficult to assume because we have always regarded it as something alien, a foreign species: 'Can I have become a different being while I still remain myself?'"[4] De Beauvoir voices here a central question that Ames and Boughton have about themselves as they simultaneously look forward to a life after death and back on their earthly pasts: Who am I *now*, as an old man?[5] In the contrasts between these two old ministers, whose decaying bodies and steadfast religious devotion demand a looking-forward and a looking-back that do not sit easily together, Robinson suggests that the difficult process of aging can sometimes generate a love of the present, a heightened and poignant willingness to appreciate daily life as it comes.[6]

The third part of this chapter interprets this simultaneously painful and joyful encounter with past, present, and future that Robinson's elderly characters experience as the basis for one kind of democratic ethos. In *Democracy and Tradition*, Jeffrey Stout embarks on a recovery of three virtues associated with the American democratic project, virtues that are "commonly interpreted in religious terms."[7] These are piety, hope, and generosity, three components of democratic character that Stout recasts in temporal terms:

> The first of these, piety, looks toward the past. It concerns proper acknowledgement of the sources of our existence and progress through life. The second, hope, looks toward the future. It concerns our capacity for ethical and political striving when success appears uncertain or unlikely. The third, love or generosity, can be directed to past, future, and distant objects, but it mainly binds us to those with whom we share our time and place. It concerns our capacity to respond appropriately to our fellows, as no less worthy of being cared for and cared about than we are ourselves.[8]

Together, *Gilead* and *Home* form an account of how a democratic character may be cultivated through attention to and struggle with the challenges of maintaining piety, hope, and generosity in the face of the suffering and decline that come with aging. These two novels also suggest that these virtues are the work of a lifetime, developed through habit and practice, and hence we might well look for them first in the very old among us, who often by necessity undertake the ruminations on present, past, and future that these virtues require.[9] Thus I argue that *Gilead* and *Home* offer not only a sustained meditation on the joy and pain of being and getting old but suggest there is a democratic ethos that can be forged in the aging process.

"Both Strange and Familiar": Old Things and Old Spaces in *Gilead* and *Home*

The old men of *Gilead* and *Home* find themselves immersed in material contexts that also bear the marks of age. Nowhere is this more evident than in *Home,* a novel about—among other things—an old house and its objects. For the house's owner, the elderly widower Reverend Robert Boughton, it is a space of well-being, worthy of tender affection: "He spoke of the house as if it were an old wife, beautiful for every comfort it offered, every grace, through all the long years."[10] But, significantly, the reader rarely sees this house from Reverend Boughton's perspective, instead encountering it from the point of view of two middle-aged Boughton children who have returned home, Glory and Jack.

Glory, living with her father again after the collapse of her personal and professional life, especially feels the weight of the house's history and of all of its things. She notes that its "furniture and the damage done to it in the course of the old robust domestic life were all still there. And the old books" (58). While Glory allows herself the occasional reverie about how she might make the old house look new or different, its "immutable" character persistently overwhelms her (40).[11] Like her father, she is not immune to its comforts—its reminders of old family events, treasured habits, and familiar routines. One Sunday, as she comes back into the house from the garden, she notices "the house had already begun to smell like Sunday. It brought tears to her eyes. That old orderliness, aloof from all disruption" (39). For Glory, the house and every old thing in it are what James Krasner calls "materialized memory," and even as they soothe her when she returns to Gilead after a string of disappointments, they ultimately disarm her, too.[12] As William James Booth writes, "We wonder what to make of memory and its gifts, though sometimes we are hardly even certain that they are gifts"—an apt description of Glory's ambivalent encounter with her old home and its things as repositories of memory.[13] Glory seems all too uneasy about the sense in which her identity is bound up with the old house and its dusty books, worn furniture, and attic teeming with "things that had been displaced from current use but were not in the strict sense useless" (93).[14] Glory's perspective on her old home, understood as the materialization of both her identity and memory, is colored by her suspicion that it might become her permanent dwelling and thus the context for the rest of her life. Hence she ultimately finds herself in a very different position from her father, who finds comfort at the end of his life in the home's meaningful objects and how they convey his life story.[15] Glory, while she experiences fleeting moments of happiness or comfort like her father's, also feels oppressed by the house and its memories, due to her worry that she will have to live among them forever: "The past was a very fine thing, in its place. But her returning now . . . had turned memory portentous. To have it overrun its bounds this way and become present and possible future, too—they all knew this was a thing to be regretted" (8). The old Boughton home and its contents are the material embodiment of the past's unwanted creep into Glory's present and future, and a representation of her dread that she, too, might be "displaced from current use" while not "in the strict sense useless" and consigned to her old home forever.[16]

Across town in Gilead lies the literary twin of the Boughton home, the Ames parsonage. While the parsonage is also very old and has an old resident in John Ames, both have been "transformed without being changed" by the unexpected arrival of a youthful wife and young son, Lila and Robby Ames (*Home,* 25). For decades after the death of his first wife and young daughter, Ames lived alone in the parsonage, and like the Boughton home, the house itself holds the memory of that difficult time intact for its only longtime inhabitant. In his letter to Robby, Ames remarks on how, in the house, the past sometimes reappears as present: "When I'm up here in my study with the radio on and some old book in my hands and it's nighttime and the wind blows and the house creaks, I forget where I am, and it's as though I'm back in hard times for a minute or two, and there's a sweetness in the experience which I don't understand. But that only enhances the value of it. My point here is that you never do know the actual nature of even your own experience. Or perhaps it has no fixed and certain nature" (*Gilead,* 95). The house's materials (creaky boards) and its objects (radio, old book) conjure what might be called a sweet and easy "motion between past and present" facilitated by Ames's old home, understood as a space of things bearing "sedimented life meanings" for him.[17] Notably, here an old house and its objects do not exactly create continuity or stability for Ames, as they do for his friend Boughton. Rather, Ames has a brush with the same sense of the uncanny that rattles Glory during her homecoming, only he registers it as wonder rather than dread, a welcome reminder that even our own experiences are hard for us to interpret with seamless progression and must sometimes be accepted simply as they are and were.

The encroachment of the past on the present is not always something to be marveled at, however, and Ames's uneasy cohabitation with one particular set of old material objects in the parsonage reflects the darker side of home as a space of memory and identity. Ames's old sermons, boxed and settled in his attic, are a persistent source of reflection for him, bordering on consternation. Even as he attempts to write down his memories and impressions for Robby, he remains keenly aware that one version of a material record of his life *already* exists, in the form of these sermons. The presence of decades of collected ephemera unsettles him, and thus he frequently writes to Robby (and himself) about the problem of what do with them. On the one hand, he expresses interest in preserving them as precious objects, a life's work made manifest on paper. On the other hand, he considers destroying them to spare himself a humiliating confrontation with what he fears might turn out to be a record of his spiritual shortcomings. As he explains to Robby:

> I think every day about going through those old sermons of mine to see if there are one or two I might want you to read sometime, but there are so many, and I'm afraid, first of all, that most of them might seem foolish or dull to me. It might be best to burn them, but that would upset your mother, who thinks a great deal more of them than I do—for their sheer mass, I suppose, since she hasn't read them. . . .
>
> It would be worth my life to try to get those big boxes down on my own. It's humiliating to have written as much as Augustine, and then to have to find a way to dispose of it. There is not a word in any of those sermons I didn't mean when I wrote it. If I had the time, I could read my way through fifty years of my innermost life. What a terrible thought. If I don't burn them then someone else will sometime, and that's another humiliation. (*Gilead,* 40)

In this first mention of the sermons to Robby, Ames articulates his contradictory feelings about what he calls "a record of [his] life, after all, a sort of foretaste of the Last Judgment" (41). He identifies them as the materialization of fifty years of work, notable not only for its impressive bulk but also for what he knows to be its sincere spiritual content. And yet, the temptation to burn the boxes of sermons nags Ames, who is motivated by a fear of disappointment and perhaps also some trepidation about reading his way through his "innermost thoughts," a prospect he deems "terrible."[18] Ames's infirmity stops him from physically confronting the aging record of his life, as does his younger wife, who wants to keep them. The latter prospect even prompts a moment of vanity that opens into a broader expression of doubt about the value of his life's work beyond its material record—he confides to Robby that he might get one box of sermons down from the attic and sort them for Lila. He tells his son: "It would put my mind at ease to feel I was leaving a better impression. So often I have known, right there in the pulpit, even as I read the words, how far they fell short of any hopes I had for them. And they were the major work of my life, from a certain point of view. I have to wonder how I have lived with that" (69). The heavy boxes in Ames's attic and the question of what to do with their contents are the objects of some anguish for him; as he notes, he has dwelled with these sermons for a long time and aged alongside them, and as with Glory and the objects of her home, he may find them both a comfort and a disturbance, old things both familiar and strange.

By the end of his letter, Ames has reached some resolution about the sermons, which he plans to ask Lila to burn after his death. He allows that she can keep the ones she might want, but he concludes that in their own time they "mattered or they didn't and that's the end of it" (244). Here he appears to follow his own compassionate intuition that human beings can never really know the nature of their own experiences, and so he turns away from his vexing curiosity about the sermons as artifacts of his past, to be read and interpreted for clues about the meaning of his life. He returns his sermons to their own present moment in past time, concluding that it will be impossible to know with certainty what his words did or did not do for his congregation. Moreover, he lets go of any worry about how they might be read and understood in the future.

Home and especially *Gilead* are foremost accounts of the aging and oldness of human beings, but as I have suggested in this section, Robinson's careful attention to the old spaces people inhabit and the old objects they dwell alongside are integral to the novels' telling of what it can mean for a person to grow old. It is difficult to imagine the elderly ministers Boughton and Ames outside the material contexts of their old homes, which tell their stories. Likewise, we witness Glory's struggle to come to terms with the idea that she might age in her old home, too, living uncomfortably among the relics of her past. In fact, Glory's query, "Home. What kinder place could there be on earth, and why did it seem . . . like exile?," reflects most aptly the dual character of old homes. These spaces and their things are treasured repositories of memory and identity, a place where inhabitants can fall easily into well-loved habits, but they can also pose moments of strangeness, alienation, and wonder.[19] Living a life both strange and familiar is also a feature of aging itself, as I will suggest in the next section of this chapter, which focuses on the struggle with old age enacted by three old men in Gilead past and present.

Expected but Unforeseen: Growing Old in Gilead

Gilead and *Home* provide vivid depictions of aging as a phenomenon that all humans expect but can never imagine, a process that warrants various and sometimes contradictory responses—wry humor, rage, grief, and even, at moments, a touch of serenity.[20] In Ames's letter to Robby in *Gilead,* we find meditations on his own age and infirmity juxtaposed with those of his grandfather, the eldest John Ames. In *Home,* we see the difficulties of Ames's old friend Boughton, struggling with both a failing body and old anxieties and pangs of conscience, reflected through the eyes of his children Glory and Jack. In rendering the differences and commonalities of the aging and oldness of these three men, Robinson explores the meaning of growing old along multiple dimensions—the material, the spiritual, and the political.

Old age in *Gilead* and *Home* is a decidedly embodied experience. From Ames's memories of the piercing stare of his one-eyed, grizzled old grandfather, to his attentive and often humorous recording of his own achy joints, *Gilead* underscores the idea that "age has a tendency to make one's sense of oneself harder to maintain," and that this problem begins with the surprises dealt to the spirit by a changing, decaying body on its way to death. This physical decline is a source of both disappointment and wonder for Boughton and Ames, and something about it seems sudden and thus startling to both of them. In *Home,* Glory observes the last phase of the lifelong friendship of her father and Ames and notices that the two old men frequently find some kind of humor in what the passage of time has done to them: "The joke seemed to be that once they were very young and now they were very old, and that they had been the same day after day and were somehow at the end of it all so utterly changed" (28). The end result of what always looked like continuity turns out to be something of a rupture, a mutual and sudden discovery of their old bodies.

This rupture is a source of sorrow as well as wry amusement for both men, and thus Robinson's novels register the idea that the surprise of old age is frequently cause for grief. Two moments in *Home* reflect the sadness and despair that may come with finding oneself old. Upon the return of his prodigal son, Jack, old Boughton finds himself struggling to cope with the arrival of the son he has prayed for years to see again. In his confession to one of his other sons, Teddy, he registers that his oldness has made this longed-for encounter even more difficult than he anticipated: "The old man put his arms around [Teddy], rested his head on his shoulder, and wept. 'I'm so glad you're here, Teddy!' he said. He tried to speak in his reasonable, fatherly voice, but it was broken by sobs. 'It's been hard, Teddy. I knew it would be. But it's been very hard!' And he wept. 'I'm so old!' he said." (259).

Boughton's oldness forces something of a role reversal on him in this moment, as Glory notes earlier that her "sad old papa" is the person "upon whose shoulder much of Presbyterian Gilead above the age of twenty had at some time wept" (7). At the end of his life, he seeks solace on the shoulder of his son Teddy, unable to counsel himself through a final confrontation with a loved but distant son. As Jack experiences his own spiritual crisis and prepares to leave home again, Boughton's body degenerates further still, and he articulates his own decline in terms of bewilderment and uncertainty, remarking, "Jesus never had to be old" (313). Old age is, for Boughton, uncharted territory, and not even the most beloved old book of wisdom in his home has much to say to him about the experience.

Ames, too, finds grief in the discovery that he is old, and attempts to make peace with corresponding feelings of bitterness and sorrow. We once again find him counseling himself in his letter to Robby, just as he works through the problem of what to do with his old sermons: "The fact is, I don't want to be old. And I certainly don't want to be dead. I don't want to be the tremulous old coot you barely remember. I bitterly wish you could know me as a young man" (*Gilead,* 141; see also 94). Ames struggles to make sense of his increasing slowness and the finitude of his body, remarking that to be old and dying is like being "some straggler and people can't quite remember to stay back for me" (142).[21] Ames attempts to show himself some compassion for his futile resistance to aging and dying, as he has to the many old and dying people he has counseled over the years, commenting to himself and Robby: "I don't have to fault myself for feeling this way. The Lord wept in the Garden on the night He was betrayed, as I have said to people in my situation many times" (141). Unlike Boughton, Ames finds some guidance in the "strange old book," but his model is a grieving Christ in Gethsemane, who openly prays and struggles to find peace in the midst of betrayal and the promise of violent death.

While Ames and Boughton give voice to the grief and loss that comes with aging, they also find wonder and mystery in the strange familiarity of their old bodies. Characteristically, Ames in particular reads his old body as a novelty in itself, drawing on the poetry of George Herbert to find a link between aging, preservation, and creation. He considers his own body as a storied material object, lovingly preserved by a Creator, and he wonders at the mystery of this idea of the old as a space for creativity and newness:

> There's a mystery in the thought of the re-creation of an old man as an old man, with all the defects and injuries of what is called long life faithfully preserved in him, and all their claims and all their tendencies honored, too, as in the steady progress of arthritis in my left knee. I have thought sometimes that the Lord must hold the whole of our lives in memory, so to speak. Of course He does. And "memory" is the wrong word, no doubt. But the finger I broke sliding into second base when I was twenty-two years old is crookeder than ever, and I can interpret that fact as an intimate attention. (115)

Ames finds in the assorted aches and pains of his present body not only the story of his long life but also new marks of the re-creation of his body by an attentive divine maker. Much as the damaged and worn objects of Boughton's old home provide him with the story of his life, the pangs of arthritis in Ames's old joints are trappings of the home his body provides for his spirit—a source of memory and identity, and a reminder of the mysteries of a life lived in earthly time. *Gilead* thus reveals a complicated story about growing old—an experience full of sorrow and wonder—through Ames's uneasy dwelling between his past youth and his anticipation of a life after death.[22]

Boughton and Ames are not, however, the only or even the most vivid old men in the novels. In *Gilead*, Ames also probes the challenges of old age by recalling in detail the last years of his grandfather, an abolitionist preacher also named John Ames. The eldest Ames was known only to his grandson as part of a cohort of radical old men who once fought for the abolition of slavery alongside John Brown in Kansas. Ames's memories of his grandfather and this group of "bodacious old men" now battling the passage of time characterize them as "unreposeful," but in a different way from him and Boughton (50). Unlike the gentle bewilderment and bereavement that mark Boughton's and the younger Ames's confrontations with aging and the end of life, the elder Ames and his friends harbor a barely suppressed wild grief. Memories of these restless old men prompt the younger Ames to ponder a different dimension of the sorrows of getting old, beyond the problem of a failing, slow body. Of his grandfather, Ames remembers: "He was just afire with old certainties, and he couldn't bear all the patience that was required of him by the peace and by the aging of his body and by the forgetfulness that had settled over everything. He thought we should be living at a dead run. I don't say he was wrong. That would be like contradicting John the Baptist" (36).

The eldest John Ames chafed against the quiet expected of him in final years, losing patience with his old body and with the expectations brought on by the conclusion of the Civil War and the public turn away from political radicalism. Instead, he wanted to "live at a dead run," to struggle openly for social and political justice as he did when a younger man, a desire that ultimately motivated him to flee back to Kansas to preach and wander until he died. In his letter to Robby, Ames remembers his grandfather as simultaneously a peculiar man of a long-past time and a model for a vital if unsettled old age. Of those "bodacious old men" like his grandfather, he comments that their hope was always to do something useful, and their fear was to have no purpose, no cause, a view he respects.[23] But he also notices that time did not wait for these men: "Those saints got old and the times changed and they just seemed like eccentrics and nuisances, and no one wanted to listen to their fearsome old sermons or hear their wild old stories. . . . I have thought about that very often—how the times change, and the same words that carry a good many people into the howling wilderness in one generation are irksome or meaningless in the next" (174, 176).[24]

Ames's reflections on his grandfather as a man out-of-time, a wild and fiery old man become a minor eccentric, parallel his own worry of being a tedious "straggler" left behind by the young and the new.[25] At the same time, however, there is a marked difference between these two old men. Ames the narrator is physically unable to keep up with his young family and worries at his slowness, whereas he remembers his grandfather as too restless and wild for the family and society in which he found himself growing old.

Robinson's memorable renderings of old men—especially the eldest Reverend Ames, his grandson John Ames, and Ames's best friend Robert Boughton—provide a multifaceted account of the experiences of aging and dying. All three feel the surprise of finding their spirits residing in bodies marked by decline and decay, and their respective confrontations with what de Beauvoir calls "the most expected" event of any person's life inform and reflect the shape of their characters in their last years. In the older abolitionist Ames, we find restless grief and anger; in his grandson, an uneasy mix of bitterness, wonder, and joy; and in old Boughton, mostly sorrow tempered by the tiniest bit of amusement, the occasional shared joke with his old friend Ames. In the next section of this chapter, I will draw out three particular virtues that we can also find in Robinson's finely drawn portraits of the old—piety, hope, and generosity. Although these virtues are certainly grounded in the individual sensibilities of the old men of Robinson's novels, they are also habits of character that are enhanced by the reflections on time, memory, and experience that old age invites. As such, while *Gilead* and *Home* are novels about old men, I will argue that they also offer up rich possibilities for a democratic ethos understood in terms of tradition.

Old Virtues and Democratic Renewal

In *Democracy as Tradition,* Jeffrey Stout contests what he identifies as a democratic commonplace—that democratic politics is inherently resistant to tradition, understood as the hierarchies and ethical habits of the past. Instead, he investigates whether democracy, with its commitment to citizen power, freedom, and equality, might be a tradition itself. Stout answers in the affirmative, largely by unpacking the idea of "tradition" and arguing for its connection with culture and an ethical life as something worth saving. He notes that "there is much to be gained by abandoning the image of democracy as essentially opposed to tradition, as a negative force that tends by its nature to undermine culture and the cultivation of virtue. Democracy is a culture, a tradition, in its own right. It has an ethical life of its own, which philosophers would do well to articulate."[26] Stout suggests that the ethical culture of democracy understood *as* tradition is the point at which resistance to hierarchies of power can be at home with care for the development of virtue and character.[27] The three virtues of interest to Stout are old religious ones that would not have been out of place in nineteenth- and early twentieth-century Gilead—piety, hope, and generosity. In many respects, this triad of interwoven democratic virtues—in their religious sense—was for a long time the bedrock of individual, family, and town life in Gilead. In this section, I argue that we can interpret *Gilead* and *Home* as literary representations and reflections of Stout's vision of American democratic culture, one saturated in religious spirit, and aged and developed by the passing of time and its hardships. While these three virtues may seem to be on the decline in mid-twentieth-century Gilead, the setting for *Gilead* and *Home,* we still find exemplars of piety and hope there. But, perhaps what emerges most clearly from the confrontation with aging depicted in *Gilead* in particular is a hard-earned generosity, a virtue that enhances and strengthens the other two. Importantly, we also find difficult examples of the absence of these virtues, or passionate disagreement about how they ought to be practiced, which further points to their significance as qualities worth conversation and cultivation in democratic politics.

Stout devotes the most attention to piety in *Democracy as Tradition* because it poses the most difficulty for his argument. If democracy is predicated on newness and resistance to old ways and old forms, how can we claim piety as a virtue for democracy? As Stout points out:

> Democracy will appear intrinsically *impious,* and thus vicious to its foes in part because they see it as an all-out attack on the social structures that have long been taken to be among the sources of our existence and progress through life. Piety, if understood as deference to a hierarchy of powers on which social life depends, seems simply to be washed away in a tidal wave of democratic self-assertion. In deferential respect, common people once bowed down in gratitude and humility to everything higher than themselves in the chain of being.[28]

By this account of piety, democracy's suspicion of hierarchy should disqualify it as a pious form of ethical life or mode of political action; conversely, piety should be of little use to democrats. As Sheldon Wolin argues, "Democracy was born in transgressive acts, for the demos could not participate in power without shattering the class, status, and value systems by which it was excluded."[29] Hence democracy has a reputation for a particular kind of wildness and disorder that is antithetical to traditional forms of piety, which demand homage to structure, order, and hierarchy.

Stout, however, wishes to unseat older, more traditionalist conceptions of piety in favor of a piety that is distinctly democratic in character. "From a democratic point of view," he argues, "the only piety worth praising as a virtue is that which concerns itself with *just* or *fitting* acknowledgement of the sources of our existence and progress through life."[30] In Stout's reworking of the virtue of piety, it remains a backward-looking social and political virtue, but it bears a critical posture toward the past that concerns it. As such, piety *may* affirm orders and structures as sources of human existence and progress, or it *may not*.

Robinson models forms of democratic engagement that challenge traditionalist notions of piety in *Gilead* especially, through the figures of the eldest Ames, his son the second Reverend Ames, and his grandson, the John Ames who narrates *Gilead*. In the latter's recollection of his grandfather's dedication to the cause of abolition and his willingness to ride into Kansas with John Brown, we find the kind of radical political action that Stout links to the traditionalist critique of democracy as an inherently *impious* mode of life.[31] On the heels of a vision of Jesus in chains, Ames's grandfather, then a young man, went to Kansas to devote himself to the cause of abolition, finding a purpose in resisting state-sanctioned slavery through small-scale acts of resistance and violence. Eventually, he participated in larger-scale efforts to unseat slavery, by fighting for the Union side in the Civil War. The youngest Ames recalls his grandfather as an old fighter bitter with disappointment, physically ill at ease in a peacetime America still teeming with racial injustice well past the outlawing of slavery. He lived in restless discomfort right up to the day he ran back to Kansas to wander until death, a discomfort heightened by his son's antiwar position. Tellingly, Grandfather Ames left the following note for his son, daughter-in-law, and grandchildren: "No good has come, no evil is ended. *That is your peace.* Without vision the people perish. The Lord bless you and keep you" (85, emphasis added). The post–Civil War peace, and his son's repeated moral justifications of it, set the old man on edge until he was able to leave and return to the place where he began his active resistance to the injustices of slavery. His grandson remembers him as a kind of peculiar saint, suggesting that his resistance to injustice corresponded to a kind of piety in short supply.

Ames also remembers his own father's struggles with Grandfather Ames's violent past. After also going away to fight for the Union at the end of the Civil War, Ames's father returned with a different perspective. He ultimately rejected the eldest Ames's penchant for the most active modes of political resistance, casting them as fundamentally impious for their violence. While he found no fault with his father's resistance to unjust hierarchy and orders, the second Reverend Ames was troubled by the bloodshed his father was willing to brook in service of justice. In response, he turned to a life of pacifism, beginning by frequently avoiding his father's church and joining the Quakers on Sundays after he came home from the war. This embrace of a different kind of piety—one fundamentally formed in reaction to the horrors of war—carried through to the end of his life. In his middle age, he preached pacifism from the pulpit, in direct opposition to his father's hope that political redemption could come through war. As he said to his father the abolitionist: "I know you placed great hope in that war. My hopes are in peace, and I am not disappointed. Because peace is its own reward. Peace is its own justification" (84). Holding this view put him at odds with his father and inflected his choices about what to teach his congregation, and the youngest Ames records the personal costs of these decisions. Although we know little of the second Reverend Ames's political activities beyond his own brief and presumably horrifying service in the Union army, his pacifist views after the war frequently cut against the political tide, as he witnessed wars and violent solutions to political conflicts as the norm, well into his own old age. Thus he bore an old age almost as unreposeful as his father's. As the youngest Ames remembers: "My father did hate war. He nearly died in 1914, from pneumonia, the doctors said, but I have no doubt it was mainly from rage and exasperation" at the start of the biggest global conflict of his age (86). His restless old age was also a consequence of a critical piety. The second Reverend Ames's was a less overtly political piety than his father's, as it translated into few public actions that we learn about in the narrative. However, like his father, the middle Ames personally resisted some of the orders and structures of an unjust society as he identified them, although he found himself directly opposed to his father's commitments in the process.

In the youngest Ames, who records these memories of the conflict between his father and grandfather for his own son, we find perhaps a more capacious piety tempered by sympathy. Even as a small boy, he sides with both his father and grandfather, taking a critical view of both the problems of racial injustice and the human tendency to war and violence as a means of settling disputes. He understands the perspective of each older man and shows fellow feeling for both points of view and their bearers, suggesting that there is earnest if imperfect piety in both men, who seek "just and fitting" responses to the structures and orders of their societies (85–86).[32] In the oldest Ames, that response was active resistance and fighting to overthrow unjust orders, and in the middle Ames, the response was a turn away to a sometimes unpopular pacifism.[33] In the youngest Ames's retelling of the struggles of each man, and their interpersonal and political conflicts, we find the idea that piety is an essential political virtue, but a contested one that can issue in different perspectives and actions.

The youngest John Ames himself also shows a capacity for democratic piety in his critical reflections on contemporary racial injustice in Gilead and Jim Crow America, as he offers sympathy and support for his prodigal namesake Jack Boughton, who eventually entrusts him with the knowledge that he has an African American wife and biracial son. Like his father and unlike his grandfather, Ames does not hold a particularly martial view on what is to be done in response to the social ills he identifies, but neither is his approach wholly deferential to authority. Instead, he ponders the ethical connections between human beings in the world as a potential source of reconciliation, a critical, spiritual act of contemplation that frames his pious efforts to know and acknowledge the sources of human existence and progress. As such, his piety is intertwined with a commitment to generosity, the third in Stout's triad of democratic virtues. And, in the context of his letter/autobiography in *Gilead*, this generosity and piety are clearly the work of his old age, understood as an accumulation of experience that can never be fully known but that still guides action.

This combination of generosity and piety is, significantly, specific to old Ames as the story of Jack Boughton unfolds across *Gilead* and *Home*. In the character of Ames's best friend, Robert Boughton, we find the older, traditionalist sense of piety that Stout aims to unsettle in favor of the more critical approaches embodied in the Ames men. Nowhere is this more evident than in old Boughton's reactions to the civil rights struggles that he and his children witness on the evening news. As Boughton, Jack, and Glory watch white policemen with riot sticks, dogs, and fire hoses push back a protesting black crowd in Montgomery, Jack swears in dismay only to be reprimanded by his father for cursing. Old Boughton comments in favor of the police action that so distresses Jack: "I do believe it is necessary to enforce the law. The Apostle Paul says we should do everything 'decently and in order.' You can't have people running around in the streets like that" (*Home*, 98). In a later conversation about the murder of Emmett Till, old Boughton comments to Jack that there is "no reason for all [the] trouble" regarding race relations and the struggle for civil rights in midcentury America and expresses faith in the notion that the best solution to the problem is for black Americans to "improve themselves . . . if they want to be accepted" (*Home,* 156, 155). Boughton's orientation to the civil rights struggle conforms to the kind of traditionalist piety that Stout wants to unseat: "deference to a hierarchy of powers on which social life depends," an order in danger of being "washed away in a tidal wave of democratic self-assertion."[34] Old Boughton's deference to law and long-standing racial and social hierarchies reflects what we might think of as an antidemocratic piety, in contrast to the piety Stout endorses and that is expressed, in varying degrees, by the Reverends Ames. Moreover, old Boughton's unreflective piety also depletes the political hopes of his son Jack, who seeks a Gilead hospitable to his interracial family as well as a more integrated and just America.

While piety is effectively a backward-looking virtue predicated on knowing and evaluating the sources of the contemporary condition, hope is its forward-looking democratic counterpart. It demands that we continue to strive for ethical and political progress even when outcomes are uncertain or in grave doubt, as we have already seen in the clashes between the bellicose Grandfather Ames and his pacifist son, who place their hopes in different political methods. While *Gilead* is a reflection on different modes of piety, *Home* is, among other things, a meditation on the difficulties of maintaining hope. In some respects, it is a story of dashed hopes—Jack's disappointed search for a home for his family, Glory's initially hopeless return after a series of personal and professional devastations—but in the figure of Reverend Robert Boughton, we find an old man who has lived on hope for decades. It is an intensely personal hope for him, as he waits patiently for his son Jack to return. While they do not readily extend into a depiction of political hope, Boughton's struggles gives the reader a keen sense of the challenges of hope as an ethical orientation in relationship with God and family.

Robert Boughton is, his daughter Glory notices, hope embodied. In a vivid scene in which Glory grooms her father for a family dinner, she takes inventory of his decaying body and sees the marks of years of patience, hope, and waiting for a son who might never return home: "At the end of so much effort, the neck seemed frail, but the head was still lifted up, and the ears stood there, still shaped for attention, soft as they were. She'd have left all the lovely hair, which looked like gentle bewilderment, just as the lifted head and ears looked like waiting grown old, like trust grown old" (169). Boughton has patiently waited for twenty years for his son Jack to return in the wake of a family tragedy, and even his body has been shaped by the trust that this uncertain hope has required.

We find the fullest expression of Boughton's daily practice of hope for his family in a complicated prayer that he offers at his first meal in decades with his children Jack and Glory:

> "Holy Father," the old man said. "I have rehearsed this prayer in my mind a thousand times, this prayer of gratitude and rejoicing, as I waited for an evening like this one. Because I always knew the time would come. And now I find that words fail me. They do. Because while I was waiting I got old. I don't remember those prayers now, but I remember the joy they gave me at the time, which was the confidence that someday I would say one or another of them here at this table. If I lived. I thought my good wife might be here, too. We do miss her. Well, I thank you for that joy, which helped through the hard times. It helped very much." (41)

Boughton's prayer maps the contours of his hope for reunion with his son, vacillating between joy and grief, confidence and uncertainty, past and present. In his words and body, Boughton exemplifies the challenges of hope as an ethical orientation, which demands learning to live with the strains of uncertainty and giving in to the difficult vulnerabilities of trust (in Boughton's case, trust in God, but also trust in other people). It is clear from the example of Boughton that hope is perhaps even more ethically strenuous and thus more meaningful for the old, who have perhaps waited too long and seen too much. Moreover, they are haunted by the knowledge that their time is growing shorter.

We see a variation on this theme in *Gilead,* when Ames reflects on being an old father to a young son and reframes the relevant biblical story of Abraham and Isaac as a meditation on trust and hope for old fathers. As Boughton waited in hope for Jack for two decades, only to eventually drive him back into the world, Ames will need hope and trust when he considers Robby's future without him, noting that "any father, particularly an old father, must finally give his child up to the wilderness and trust in the Providence of God" (129). Hope, and as I am suggesting here, trust, are critical facets of character in the face of an unknown and unsettling future. We find hope in the bittersweet father-son relations of *Gilead* and *Home,* on a small and private scale, whereas the hope Stout conceptualizes in *Democracy as Tradition* is surely more a feature of fragile democratic alliances and coalitions, binding together citizens undertaking common causes with no promise of success. But, as I have argued, in the old men of Gilead, we find some of what we need to know about hope as a crucial element of democratic ethics, as it engenders a generous trust in the face of uncertainty and encourages a steady optimism with little to go on, as so many democratic projects require. Again, as with piety, we see the measure of hope not only in the sensibilities of individuals but also in the long passing of time that comes with age.

Home simultaneously offers a less sanguine take on political hope, one that mirrors some of the sufferings of the first two Reverends Ames in *Gilead.* Any glimmers we get of an overtly political hope in *Home* come from young Jack Boughton, who nervously watches and waits for news of the civil rights struggle from Montgomery and who clandestinely investigates whether his old home of Gilead might be a hospitable place for his interracial family. As already mentioned, old Boughton inadvertently dashes the intertwined political and personal hopes harbored by his son, as he registers little sympathy for the civil rights struggle and apologizes for the segregationist and unequal status quo of midcentury America.[35] Jack's destroyed hope leads him to depart Gilead again, having determined that it is no home for his family, only to miss the arrival of his wife and son, who come to find him and instead encounter Glory. However, this encounter reshapes Glory's hoped-for future, as *Home* ends with a prayer for her old age—that when she is an old woman, Jack's son will return as a man to Gilead and find a welcome place and family there. Just as *Gilead*'s and *Home*'s accounts of piety present the complexities of the virtue and its multiple manifestations, their story of hope is also a tangle, in this case of the personal and political dimensions of hope. Like democratic piety, democratic hope is also helped forward by generosity of spirit and moral imagination, and it dies in their absence.

This brings us to the third of Stout's democratic virtues. As noted in this essay's introduction, generosity—unlike hope and piety—is often temporally situated in the present. While "love or generosity can be directed to past, future, and distant objects, it mainly binds us to those with whom we share our time and place. It concerns our capacity to respond appropriately to our fellows, as no less worthy of being cared for and cared about than we are ourselves."[36] As with piety and hope, generosity lends itself to religious interpretation. In her essay "Imagination and Community," Robinson captures its character as a religious imperative with democratic implications: "In the first Epistle of Peter we are told to honor everyone, and I have never been in a situation where I felt this instruction was inappropriate. When we accept dismissive judgments of our community we stop having generous hopes for it. We cease to be capable of serving its best interests."[37] Generosity bears a family resemblance to notions of respect or compassion, which also push us to recognize the humanity in others and honor it in our treatment of them, especially in the here and now. As I have suggested, this generosity—understood as an imperative to act on fellow feeling—informs other democratic virtues of piety and hope, or at least ought to inform them.

As *Home* is in part the story of one old man's hope, *Gilead* follows another old man's quest for generosity. Like piety and hope and all other virtues that are a matter of time and habit, it would be a mistake to think that generosity comes easily, and we see this clearly in the struggle between Ames and his godson, John Ames "Jack" Boughton. Repeatedly in *Gilead,* Ames mentions to his son Robby that he struggles mightily even to accept his namesake, much less to love him. He struggles with fear and resentment, and the letter to Robby is partly the story of how he manages to work through these dark sentiments and find his way to generosity with Jack, blessing him and carrying back the story of the blessing to the old Reverend Boughton who lies dying.

While the story that emerges in the pages of Ames's letter to Robby is one of a valiant struggle to honor Jack's humanity with generosity, it is all the more remarkable because Ames is himself typically such a generous character. The character sketch that forms the backdrop of Ames's encounter with Jack is one of a generous old man full of love for the world and its people. The reader finds it in Ames's recorded sense of awe at the very fact of human existence, which is foremost in his mind as he finds himself old and in failing health, and he repeatedly characterizes even the most ordinary human experience as something to be treasured.[38] Although some of *Gilead*'s loveliest moments are expressions of Ames's wonder at the family of his old age—young wife, young son, and patient old cat Soapy—the clearest account he gives of what it means to be generous are in the reflections on baptism and the blessing of children that he writes down for Robby. Most poignant are his memories of holding his first child, who died shortly after being born. He writes to Robby: "Now, in my present situation, now that I am about to leave this world, I realize there is nothing more astonishing than a human face. . . . It has something to do with incarnation. You feel your obligation to a child when you have seen it and held it. *Any human face is a claim on you,* because you can't help but understand the singularity of it, the courage and the loneliness of it" (*Gilead,* 76, emphasis added).[39] Ames's assertion that looking into another human face elicits an ethical claim, an obligation, is a clear expression of what generosity requires—recognizing both the individuality and common humanity of others with whom we share a world.

In this sense, and as I have already suggested, generosity is the democratic virtue that informs all others. It is both accessible to all but also difficult to achieve. For Ames, who is about to leave the world, generosity is grounded in the simple experience of seeing the face of another person. In Ames's reflections, this simplicity is not straightforward but is in fact mysterious. In one of the most important pieces of wisdom he imparts to Robby, Ames writes: "In every important way we are such secrets from each other, and I do believe there is a separate language in each of us, also a separate aesthetics and a separate jurisprudence. Every single one of us is a little civilization built on the ruins of any number of preceding civilizations, but with our own variant notions of what is beautiful and what is acceptable—which, I hasten to add, we generally do not satisfy and by which we struggle to live" (*Gilead,* 197).

Generosity as a virtue is thus strongly connected to the experience of wonder at the complexity of other human beings, figured here by Ames as "little civilizations," continuous with a past but specific to the present. This generous respect for commonality and difference is born of both Ames's ministerial temperament and his sense that, as a sick old man, he is about to leave and miss the world and its precious and mysterious inhabitants. It reflects the democratic experience of living with others who may be opaque to us, and who for that reason are deserving of compassion and generosity.

Robinson's depictions of piety, hope, and generosity, both present and absent, in the lives of her aging characters do not always directly bear on their participation in democratic self-rule. Her literary representations of the complexity of these three virtues of character show, however, why they are vital to self-directing communities engaged in collective political and ethical projects, and how they add meaning and purpose to the lives of individuals within these communities. When taken together, all three point to what it would mean to partake of a democratic culture, to live in communities built on mutual sympathy, trust, and respect, communities that are attentive to the demands of justice at home and elsewhere. A long view on the sources of human progress and development is critical to the cultivation of a piety that knows when to resist oppressive structures and knows when to honor those that promote human dignity and flourishing; that the patience and waiting that come with hope and trust in a better future are a function of time; and that generosity may depend on the sense of wonder that a keen sense of mortality produces.

Notes

1. A. O. Scott, "Return of the Prodigal Son," *New York Times*, September 21, 2008,www.nytimes.com/2008/09/21/books/review/Scott-t.html?pagewanted=all&_r=0.

2. Marilynne Robinson, *Gilead* (New York: Picador, 2004), 28. Hereafter cited parenthetically.

3. Iris Marion Young, "A Room of One's Own: Old Age, Extended Care, and Privacy," in *On Female Body Experience: "Throwing Like a Girl" and Other Essays* (Oxford: Oxford University Press, 2005), 158.

4. Simone de Beauvoir, *The Coming of Age*, trans. Patrick O'Brian (New York: G. P. Putnam's Sons, 1972), 283.

5. While beyond the scope of this essay, it is worth noting here that both Ames and Boughton are steeped in the doctrine of the covenant of grace, which informs their views on life after death and changes their perspective on earthly time, if not their attachment to the world. For further development of this theme, see Christie L. Maloyed's essay in this volume, "The Death of Jeremiah? Marilynne Robinson and Covenant Theology."

6. This is Christopher Leise's account of Ames's point of view in *Gilead*; he describes Ames's letter to his son Robby as having the "strange effect of looking back as well as looking forward" (Leise, "'That Little Incandescence': Reading the Fragmentary and John Calvin in Marilynne Robinson's *Gilead*," *Studies in the Novel* 41, no. 3 [Fall 2009]: 348).

7. Jeffrey Stout, *Democracy as Tradition* (Princeton, NJ: Princeton University Press, 2004), 9.

8. Ibid.

9. It is worth noting, however, that the novels do not imply that these virtues are an inevitable by-product of aging; in fact, as I will suggest later in this essay, *Home* in particular illustrates the contrary possibility.

10. Marilynne Robinson, *Home* (New York: Picador, 2008), 3. Hereafter cited parenthetically.

11. Jack, unlike his sister, who largely preserves the home in the state she finds it, engages in housekeeping projects that are either restorative or out of step with the house's traditional look.

12. James Krasner, "Accumulated Lives: Metaphor, Materiality, and the Homes of the Elderly," *Literature and Medicine* 24, no. 2 (Fall 2005): 221.

13. William James Booth, *Communities of Memory: On Witness, Identity, and Justice* (Ithaca, NY: Cornell University Press, 2006), ix.

14. Krasner is also sensitive to the "delicate intertwining of identity and environment that occurs in the home" as part of his analysis of why elderly people are so reluctant to leave their homes (Krasner, "Accumulated Lives," 209, 211). Similarly, Iris Young's definition of "home" emphasizes this link between identity and material environment, as part of her argument for respect for the private, personal spaces of the old (see Young, "A Room of One's Own," 156).

15. Krasner notes that the "elderly home is more like a fictional world than most spaces, because every path and every object is likely to be 'storied'" (Krasner, "Accumulated Lives," 218).

16. The present and future are never quite like the past, though, even in the context of the same old house and its things. The aging and deterioration of the house's inhabitants add something uncanny to a familiar, unchanged setting. A simple evening at home, for example, conjures up a forlorn contrast between past and present for Glory: it was "a little like the old times. Graying children, ancient father. If they could have looked forward from those old times, when even a game of checkers around that table was so rambunctious it would have driven [Boughton] off to parse his Hebrew in the stricken quiet of the Ames house—if they could now look in the door of the kitchen at the three of them there, would they believe what they saw?" (*Home,* 78).

17. Krasner, "Accumulated Lives," 209; Young, "A Room of One's Own," 258.

18. The question of what "terrible" means here is worth pondering. Elsewhere in *Gilead,* Ames recalls that his mother said his grandfather attracted "terrible friendship," taking care to point out that this was "terrible in the old sense, of course, and meaning only respect" (47). It is possible that the confrontation with hundreds of his old sermons might warrant Ames's use of "terrible" in this old sense, too—a prospect worthy of awe and respect, and not simply dread or fear.

19. See also Shannon Mariotti's essay in this volume, "The Housekeeper of Homelessness: The Democratic Ethos of Marilynne Robinson's Novels and Essays."

20. This comes from Simone de Beauvoir's reflections on Proust in *The Coming of Age,* leading her to comment that "nothing should be more expected than old age: nothing is more unforeseen" (4).

21. As Laura Tanner writes of Ames's discomfort: "For Ames, the anticipation of his own absence renders him incapable of dwelling in the present with ease; his position both within and without undercuts his attempts—perceptual and representational—to steady his hold on experience. As he propels himself forward into a future he will not inhabit, Ames also pulls the anticipated experience of loss back into the present, where it disrupts his ability to cohabit in a world with others in the 'usual companionable way'" (Tanner, "'Looking Back from the Grave': Sensory Perception and the Anticipation of Absence in Marilynne Robinson's *Gilead,*" Contemporary *Literature,* 48, no. 2 [Summer 2007]: 249).

22. Tanner suggests that this uneasy dwelling is the source of his attachment to present experience, that it is a feature not only of his character but also of his age: "Although Ames's sensibility clearly accounts in part for his attentiveness to the world, the journal that he creates in *Gilead* also reflects the heightened self-consciousness of an aging, ailing individual whose awareness of his imminent death shapes both consciousness and perception" (ibid., 232).

23. In her work on oppression, Iris Young identifies the old as a marginalized social group, and she pinpoints loss of agency and purpose as a key facet of the oppression suffered by elderly populations. Even when old people have their material needs satisfied, she argues that "injustices of marginality would remain in the form of uselessness, boredom, and lack of self-respect" (Young, *Justice and the Politics of Difference* [Princeton, NJ: Princeton University Press, 2000], 55). In some respects, this parallels Glory's encounter with the old items in the Boughton attic, which occupy a weird liminal status between usefulness and uselessness.

24. For an analysis of the eldest Ames that focuses on his relationship to the jeremiad, see, again, Christie Maloyed's essay in this volume.

25. This may, however, be a matter of self-perception on the parts of Ames and Boughton, who focus on their own frailty. Other characters in the novels hold a different perspective on the two men. As Jack says to Glory after a particularly tense encounter with Ames: "Ah, little sister, these old fellows play rough. They look so harmless, and the next thing you know, you're counting broken bones again." While Ames and Boughton cannot muster the "old certainties" of their grandfathers, they may yet retain some of the moral purpose and spiritual fire they saw in those old men, if not their political inclinations (*Home,* 206).

26. Stout, *Democracy as Tradition,* 13.

27. For Stout, this democratic culture looks like philosophical pragmatism,

which he identifies as a tradition that matches resistance to power and hierarchy with the cultivation of democratic character (see Stout, *Democracy as Tradition*, 9). It is likely not a coincidence that Robinson's novels are, in my view, compatible with the kind of democratic tradition that Stout endorses; both Stout and Robinson draw on some of the same sources in the American religious, philosophical, and political democratic canons—Walt Whitman, most obviously, but others as well.

28. Ibid., 25, emphasis added.

29. Sheldon Wolin, "Fugitive Democracy," in *Democracy and Difference: Contesting the Boundaries of the Political*, ed. Seyla Benhabib (Princeton, NJ: Princeton University Press, 1996), 37.

30. Stout, *Democracy as Tradition*, 30.

31. Alex Zamalin and Daniel Skinner consider the status of the oldest Ames as a romantic-heroic figure in their essay for this volume, "*Gilead*'s Two Models of Action against Racial Injustice."

32. This is, perhaps, less obvious in the case of the middle Ames, the father of *Gilead*'s narrator, as we are not shown very many of his activities beyond his pastoral and family obligations. We mostly learn of his political views through Ames's recorded memories of the moral and political clashes between his father and grandfather, in which the middle Reverend Ames voiced disagreement with violent solutions to political problems.

33. Again, see the Zamalin and Skinner piece in this volume, which focuses helpfully on the distinctive models for combating racial injustice presented in *Gilead*.

34. Stout, *Democracy as Tradition*, 25.

35. This account of Jack's lost hope also appears—as told by Ames—in *Gilead* (see 242).

36. Stout, *Democracy as Tradition*, 25.

37. Marilynne Robinson, *When I Was a Child I Read Books: Essays* (New York: Farrar, Straus and Giroux, 2012), 27.

38. Tanner, "'Looking Back from the Grave,'" 231.

39. This passage in particular is resonant with the ethics of Emmanuel Levinas, which take root in the face-to-face encounter between humans (see esp. Levinas, *Totality and Infinity: An Essay on Exteriority*, trans. Alphonso Lingis [Pittsburgh, PA: Duquesne University Press, 1969]). Thanks to Joe Lane for pointing out this parallel.

CHAPTER 5

"Disabled and Dangerous"

The Individual and Society in Marilynne Robinson's Housekeeping

Lorraine Krall McCrary

In Marilynne Robinson's *Housekeeping*, the character Sylvie is portrayed as eccentric to the degree that the reader is left wondering about her sanity. Yet the topic of mental illness and the broader category of disability has been neglected by the novel's readers. This lacuna causes us to miss one of Robinson's central themes of the novel—that Sylvie's difference, perceived by the townspeople as mental illness—is potentially beneficial to the town, as well as potentially dangerous to it. Robinson gives a fair and even-handed articulation of a conflict to which there is no easy solution. She admits that the town has an interest in permanence and stability but also that Sylvie's instability has a role to play in the life of the community: Sylvie is a critic, a mystic, proclaiming the possibility of an alternative way of life centered on a valuable kind of individuality and loneliness. Robinson articulates this conflict in terms of disability—the townspeople call Sylvie disabled and dangerous as an attempt to shut down difference. But, ironically, this "disables" their own community. *Housekeeping* is admirable for staging this conflict in all its complexity and turning the reader away from easy judgment.

This essay will begin with a description of Sylvie's eccentricities, which Robinson presents in such a way as to require the reader to grapple with whether or not she is dangerous, and whether or not she is disabled. Next, it will turn to the secondary literature on *Housekeeping*, showing that disability has been almost entirely overlooked with reference to this novel, before explaining why the disability is an appropriate lens through which to analyze *Housekeeping*. Viewing the novel in light of disability both allows for the possibility that Sylvie has an impairment as well as critiques the townspeople for categorizing and excluding her. Then the essay will turn to what can be gained by understanding *Housekeeping* in light of disability: Robinson gives us a polyphonic novel, one in which different voices are presented fully and the author does not come down entirely in favor of one or the other. Robinson finds validity in both the position of the townspeople, as well as in Sylvie. Sylvie functions as a prophet and is also a potential danger to herself and her wards. The townspeople, likewise, have a legitimate responsibility to care for the good of the town, but in exercising this legitimate responsibility, they problematically create the category of disability and through it exclude Sylvie from their town. Later, the essay will turn to other voices that are part of this polyphonic presentation in the novel and in its precursor, a short story entitled "Connie Bronson," in order to further develop both the tension between individual difference and the town, as well as the benefits of difference to the town and the problems with excluding that difference.

Sylvie's Instability

Through the character of Sylvie, Robinson gives a sympathetic and yet brutally honest voice to someone who prefers a transient lifestyle and who may be mentally ill, at least if we accept the categories that society normally applies. Sylvie comes to care for her niece Ruth, the narrator, and her sister, Lucille. Ruth and Lucille are first left in the care of their grandmother after their mother commits suicide; after their grandmother dies, her sisters Lily and Nona come to care for them. The great-aunts quickly find the task daunting and send for Sylvie. In fact, their response to Sylvie's arrival is an early indication of her eccentricity—they want to leave Ruth and Lucille in her care, so they are determined to reassure themselves that Sylvie is an appropriate caregiver. Ruth recounts, "So when Lily said, with a glance at Nona, 'What a lovely dress,' it was as if to say, 'She seems rather sane! She seems rather normal!'"[1]

Robinson portrays Sylvie as a drifter who prefers to hang out on trains and buses: "Even when she slept, her body retained the formality of posture one learns when one sleeps on park benches, and as often as not she kept her shoes on" (138). She spends a lot of time by the nearby lake and loves to visit an island in the middle of it. She has odd housekeeping habits, welcoming nature into her house rather than trying to expel it as the townspeople do. As a result of her transience, Sylvie's child-rearing capabilities are questionable. She just leaves the house when the urge strikes her; the girls she is supposed to care for do not know if or when she'll return (71). She does not make the girls attend school; they skip classes for weeks at a time with no repercussions (77). She does not respect private property: she takes Ruth with her on a boat trip on a boat that she's borrowed without asking for permission. They have made few (and odd) provisions for food on the trip, including marshmallows, with which they might lure out the children that Sylvie believes inhabit the island (148, 151).

Parts of Robinson's description of Sylvie seem to go beyond the characteristics of a transient. Robinson describes Sylvie as a hoarder of useless things; the family's parlor gets overtaken with them (180). There are different ways to read this propensity to accumulate. On the one hand, a person with a previously transient lifestyle might be used to keeping and using things that others perceive to be worthless. On the other hand, the cans and magazines and brown paper bags that filled the rooms might be seen as an indication of something more than unusual habits. In addition, she claims to see people who clearly do not exist living in the hills of the island she visits. This might be an indication of a strong spiritual awareness or of a disconnection from earthly reality, or both.

Sylvie also walks out onto a railroad bridge over the lake just to see what it is like. Even Ruth, who is devoted to her aunt, says after watching her, "Clearly our aunt was not a stable person" (82). Ruth imagines Sylvie committing suicide, just to see what it is like, indicating that she is using "stable" to mean emotionally or mentally stable. Yet it is an interesting word choice, since "stable" has other meanings that also bear on the picture of Sylvie that Robinson is drawing. "Stable" can refer to being rooted, which contrasts with transience; it can refer to the place where horses are kept, which implies external restraint, control, and being caged. Moreover, Ruth's judgment of Sylvie's instability changes over the course of the novel. At the end, Sylvie and Ruth run away together, pushed out of Fingerbone when the townspeople threaten to separate them from each other. They embrace a truly transient lifestyle, dangerously crossing the same long railroad bridge over the lake after attempting to burn down their own house (211). This embrace of loneliness and individuality, while admirable in some ways, is not unmitigatedly good. Robinson portrays Sylvie as so introspective that she may be a danger to both herself and her niece. In so doing, Robinson admits that the townspeople's concerns are legitimate, particularly with regard to the safety of children.

There are several moments in the book where Robinson plays with the theme of mental illness with regard to Sylvie. It is ironic that Sylvie suggests a game of Crazy Eights during the flood, since her own "craziness" is a subject of the townspeople's concern (66). Likewise, when Sylvie takes Ruth for a trip in a boat that does not belong to them and the boat's owner chases them, Sylvie counters Ruth's suggestion that it is his boat by offering the alternate possibility that perhaps he is a lunatic (147).[2] Of course, this is likely precisely how the boat's owner views her. Later, while looking for hidden children in the mountains, Sylvie says to Ruth, "You'll probably think I'm crazy" (148). Sylvie's words resonate, if not for Ruth, then for the people of Fingerbone, as well as for the reader. Robinson's portrayal of Sylvie simultaneously critiques the townspeople's marginalization of Sylvie and leaves the question of her own sanity open.

Sylvie in the Literature

Scholars identify Sylvie as transient—even spiritually transient—and are helpfully attentive to the ways in which transience intersects with gender. Yet they do so almost entirely without reference to disability, whether in terms of the disabling effect of the community's exclusion of Sylvie or the possibility that Sylvie has a mental illness.[3] The literature's insights into Sylvie's transience, both physical and spiritual, become even more significant when put into the context of social rejections of difference, including through the creation of categories of disability.

Although Sylvie is not considered in the literature in terms of disability, Maggie Galehouse does consider Sylvie in terms of the phenomenon of transience in America in the 1930s and 1940s, particularly with regard to the junction between transience and gender. She cites "Box-Car Bertha, a political radical who hoboed during the 1920s and 1930s" and observes: "Whether it is promiscuity, or class, or both, female hoboes threaten the status quo by reminding the nontransient population that women can and do exist outside the polarities of prostitution and domesticity, and that many women might find themselves, given a certain set of circumstances, sleeping in boxcars. Bertha goes on to note that half of the women on the road in the twenties and thirties were from broken homes, while roughly 5 percent were mentally ill. The rest—and this is the category into which Sylvie falls—were somehow drawn to the hobo 'jungle.'"[4] Galehouse too quickly dismisses the possibility that Sylvie's transience is related to either a mental illness or to the townspeople's perception of her as disabled and her consequent exclusion. Sylvie's transience seems chosen rather than necessarily enforced by economic realities (as much of the transience of her day was). It is simultaneously not an entirely free choice: the townspeople's attempt to separate the family at the end of *Housekeeping* forces Sylvie to return to a transient lifestyle and take Ruth with her in order for them to stay together. Galehouse's explanation does not capture the social exclusion that contributes to her transience.

However, Galehouse rightly turns our attention to the fact that because Sylvie is both a woman and a transient, she is particularly marginalized. When Sylvie and Ruth try to burn down their house, they leave the place that is socially acceptable for them to inhabit.[5] As women they are sent to the home, and as socially incomprehensible and feared, they are sent away from it—the intersection of these two exclusions is a particularly invisible, voiceless place to be, as is indicated by the novel's ending, where communication between the transients, Ruth and Sylvie, and the stable Fingerbone and Lucille seems to be cut off permanently. Christine Caver describes Ruth as having lost "the ability to communicate with those around her. . . . Ruthie escapes the forces of conventionality but at the cost of a silenced voice and a disappearing body. Only the reader has access to her thoughts."[6]

William Burke talks about Sylvie's and Ruth's transience in terms of border crossings, both spiritual and perceptual.[7] He considers the novel's ending as hinting at a border crossing:

> At the least we are invited to understand the journey across the lake as a description of that ultimate border crossing from life to death. The story that Ruth narrates may be coming from and may constitute a verification of the mysterious realm of ghosts, spirits, and the place of the perished of the earth. If such speculation is too romantic or unscientifically realistic, we can still read this deliberate ambiguity as an attempt to convey a perception that Ruth acquires in her transience. It affirms a consciousness that accounts for the past and the present, the living and the dead, in a vision of wholeness and harmony.[8]

If Robinson indeed hints at a final border crossing between life and death, then Sylvie's transience is even more profound. Sylvie seeing children on the island becomes a foreshadowing of the insight into the afterlife that may be gained through death. Not only is her rejection of the townspeople's lifestyles threatening to them, but so are her spiritual insights, and her acceptance of the natural order of life and death that they seek to control: "Self-declared drifters like her threaten the community because they expose what others try not to see, namely that 'every soul is put out of house' . . . , that perishability, not permanence, is the distinguishing attribute of the human condition."[9] She lives out Augustine's insight that humans are pilgrims on earth, separate from their true home. The transience that Sylvie chooses is, in some sense, inescapable, no matter how hard the townspeople work to deny that reality. Sylvie's profound transience and the truth about being human that it points to make the townspeople's perception of her as mentally ill and their consequent exclusion of her even more harmful.

Why Disability?

Disability draws attention to the way that society creates categories as an attempt to control those who act outside of its conventions. According to Robinson, control or rejection of disability is one aspect of a larger societal intolerance of difference. Identifying and medicalizing aberrance in an attempt to shut down difference is a move that Robinson critiques as profoundly antidemocratic. At the same time, Robinson takes seriously the townspeople's concerns about Sylvie, allowing that she might have a mental impairment, perhaps one that threatens society and her nieces. Ultimately, Robinson asks us to view difference, including disabling difference, as something from which we might learn. As we will see, Robinson uses the term "disability" in her essays and articulates the phenomenon in *Housekeeping* in such a way as to deconstruct and undermine society's understanding of disability and mental illness.[10]

Robinson's deconstruction of the term "disability" points to larger, ongoing difficulties involved in conceptualizing disability and its relationship to impairment, as well as the relations between the individual and community that give rise to disability. Contrasting conceptions include the medical model, which finds the disability located in the body of the individual, and the social model, which finds the disability located in social exclusion.

Neither model is sufficient for understanding disability. The difficulty in theorizing disability is reflected in legislation: the Americans with Disabilities Act of 1990 identifies disability as "a physical or mental impairment that substantially limits one or more major life activities of such individual." The 2008 amendment identifies major life activities as including, but not limited to, "caring for oneself, performing manual tasks, seeing, hearing, eating, sleeping, walking, standing, lifting, bending, speaking, breathing, learning, reading, concentrating, thinking, communicating, and working."[11] While the ADA focuses on bodily impairments and the corresponding limitation on life activities, the World Health Organization proposes a more complex biopsychosocial model:

> Disability and functioning are viewed as outcomes of interactions between health conditions (diseases, disorders and injuries) and contextual factors. . . . Among contextual factors are external environmental factors (for example, social attitudes, architectural characteristics, legal and social structures, as well as climate, terrain and so forth); and internal personal factors, which include gender, age, coping styles, social background, education, profession, past and current experience, overall behaviour pattern, character and other factors that influence how disability is experienced by the individual. [The model] identifies the three levels of human functioning . . . : functioning at the level of body or body part, the whole person, and the whole person in a social context.[12]

Here we see disability not solely in the mind or body of the individual but rather in the complicated and multidimensional interaction between the individual and the community. Ongoing and developing ideas about the existence of disability show that the concept is far from settled. Robinson's own articulation of disability is complicated: she acknowledges the possibility that Sylvie is mentally ill (a sort of impairment) but critiques the townspeople for categorizing her as disabled and excluding her. In fact, she suggests that attention be paid to the positive aspects of what society sees as impairments.

Throughout her writing, Robinson describes the contemporary suppression of individualism and of loneliness using the language of disability. She maintains that our culture attempts to medically treat individualism and loneliness rather than accepting that they can teach us something that is true about the human condition: "In modern culture these are seen as pathologies—alienation and inauthenticity in Europe, maladjustment and depression in the United States" (*Child,* 89). In her essay, "Facing Reality," she identifies this as one element of our overmedicalization: "illness for us has overspilled definition and is now to be discovered everywhere, in everyone."[13] This is dangerous because it can cause us to ignore aspects of our human condition, which inescapably involves anxiety and loneliness. Robinson gives one particularly striking example of the suffering that can be caused by mistreatment, and then medicalization:

> Antebellum doctors described an illness typical of enslaved people sold away from their families, which anyone can recognize as rage and grief. By medicalizing their condition, the culture was able to refuse the meaning of their suffering. . . . It may be necessary to offer ourselves palliatives, but it is drastically wrong to offer or to accept a palliative as if it were a cure. . . . It may be that we cannot bear to undermine . . . our belief—consistent with the medicalization of our sorrows and in general with our ceasing to value inward experience—that they were indeed aberrant, that they say nothing meaningful to us or for us. (*Adam,* 83–84)

Rather than attempt to bring justice to the enslaved people, the doctors were trying to force them to adapt to their condition. Similarly, medicalizing individual difference, particularly difference that violates societal norms, may be a human attempt to refuse the meaning of the suffering of others, as well as of our own suffering. It may be an attempt to ignore something that is true about another's experience and perhaps about the human experience as a whole. For example, by marginalizing disability, society pretends that it is filled with independent, self-sufficient individuals rather than admitting that over their lifespan, each person experiences periods of extreme dependence. Likewise, marginalizing Sylvie's transience may be part of the townspeople's overall attempt to ignore their own transience.

Not only do the antebellum doctors of Robinson's example downplay the suffering of their patients, but their medicalization of suffering was also an instance of attempted social control: "To say that behavior is aberrant is much more powerfully coercive among us than to say an action is wrong. It implies that behavior is not really willed or controlled, and this undermines the self-confidence of the offending person" (*Adam*, 82). Another example relevant to our consideration of Sylvie the transient is Robinson's identification of England's Poor Laws as an attempt to control laborers, including through the "criminalization of idleness. If 'the vagabonds who were unprofitable members, or rather enemies of the commonwealth, were punished by death . . . it were not without their deserts.'"[14] Social control in all these instances identifies certain behaviors as aberrant—either as a result of disability or criminality, and sometimes eliding the two—and seeks to force the individuals to follow social norms.

Intolerance of impairments is one instance of a wider intolerance of difference that Robinson sees as a threat in contemporary America. In the title essay of her most recent collection, *When I Was a Child I Read Books*, Robinson describes *Housekeeping* as an attempt to reanimate the western ethos, seeing individualism that affirms loneliness as a good (89). She argues that what is needed in contemporary America is a reassertion of individualism over the pressure to conform to society. Such an individualism is not altogether at cross purposes with community; rather, it is oriented toward developing good communities, communities that encourage their citizens to grow as individuals, communities that have space for and draw upon the resources offered by difference. At the same time, Sylvie manifests a unique instance of individualism and difference: she is not simply a nonconformist, intentionally choosing to follow Thoreau into the woods while forsaking society. This would imply that just as easily she could choose to conform, even for a time and for the benefit of her nieces. Rather, Robinson has chosen a more complicated heroine: it is not clear whether Sylvie has chosen her difference, or whether it is something that is given about her, though certainly she accepts the difference that exists. Robinson is primarily concerned with asking how, given Sylvie's character, she can relate to the town and to her family.

The rejection of disability and the corresponding rejection of individualism have profound political consequences; they can lead to social stagnation and to the tyranny of the majority. Robinson writes that, contrary to the idea of human nature encapsulated in the myth of the American West, in which individualism is praiseworthy, "now people who are less shaped and constrained by society are assumed to be disabled and dangerous. This is bad news for the American psyche, a fearful and antidemocratic idea, which threatens to close down change" (*Child*, 93). A democratic political culture ought to include and learn from the differences of its citizens; instead, we attempt to assimilate difference, declaring those who resist to be "disabled and dangerous." Identifying as disabled those who do not conform to social mores is part of society's attempt to control and regulate its members. In Robinson's telling, society's label of disability goes hand in hand with a label of danger. Not only does society stigmatize difference, but by articulating difference in terms of safety, it encourages fear in its members.

In Robinson's analysis, contemporary society is exactly wrong—it is really the "tightly knit communities in which members look to one another for identity, and to establish meaning and value, [that] are disabled and often dangerous, however polished their veneer."[15] She turns the category of disability on its head: now "disabled and dangerous" refers not to those who buck social conventions but to the society that attempts to colonize and assimilate them into a cohesive and inflexible identity. For Robinson, a healthy democratic society is one that not only allows for difference (both chosen and unchosen) among its members but positively encourages and benefits from that difference. Difference provides a point for critique: it allows a space from which to evaluate and question societal norms. This does not mean Robinson naively ignores or wishes away the tensions between individual and the community, nor does she think that the cultivation of difference is the only social good. By portraying *Housekeeping*'s Sylvie as simultaneously potentially dangerous and insightful, Robinson both critiques common ways of approaching disability and imaginatively enacts an alternative.

The Polyphonic Novel

Disability is the key point of tension between Sylvie and the townspeople. Sylvie's difference, perceived by the townspeople as mental illness, is the reason that the townspeople attempt to break up Sylvie and Ruth's family, and the reason that they flee Fingerbone at the end of the novel (209). Robinson portrays Sylvie as both choosing a lifestyle that eschews society and possibly being mentally impaired; she deftly shows the reasons for Fingerbone's reaction to Sylvie while also problematizing it. In this way, Robinson captures what Mikhail Bakhtin finds in Dostoevsky—polyphony. Polyphony is "[a] plurality of independent and unmerged voices and consciousnesses, a genuine polyphony of fully valid voices."[16] He continues: "A character's word about himself and his world is just as fully weighted as the author's word usually is. . . . It possesses extraordinary independence in the structure of the work; it sounds, as it were, *alongside* the author's word and in a special way combines both with it and with the full and equally valid voices of other characters."[17]

Robinson allows Sylvie space to be a subject, albeit through Ruth's narration, in a way that the townspeople do not. Yet she does not shut down the townspeople's perspective but rather articulates it as fully valid also. Robinson does not offer us a neat resolution; rather, she lays out the problem for us in all of its complexities. Her polyphonic novel is consistent with Robinson's democratic politics: Robinson maintains that our political problems stem from the scorn that people feel for their fellows. She writes in an essay that deals with political fiction, "I fear it may not be a very long step from this secular *contemptus mundi* to the excesses of modern European history—which, having their origins in the violent rejections of the modern world, have, perversely, disgraced it and made it a terror to us all."[18] It is when we begin to see our political opponents as our fellows and when we begin to acknowledge their voice that we stop rejecting the world and begin to accept it. That is the solution that Robinson offers. She advocates a form of democracy that encourages our fellows to come along with us in the process of questioning our political premises and developing alternatives to them. Through her portrayals—of Sylvie, the people of Fingerbone, the family, a lonely dog in *Housekeeping*, and Connie Bronson in her short story of that name—Robinson models for the reader her polyphonic approach, honestly showing the strengths and weaknesses of each character.

Sylvie, the Prophet

Robinson's polyphonic method comes through in her portrayal of Sylvie. Although she acknowledges Sylvie's eccentricities and that they may be dangerous to herself or to Ruth, she also highlights the truths that Sylvie contributes to the community, such as the importance of beauty, nature, and being alone, as well as the ubiquity of death. The fact that her differences are insightful and valuable make Fingerbone's attempt to exert social control over Sylvie and Ruth particularly dangerous and disabling. First, Sylvie delights in what is fanciful and pretty. Ruth describes "the velvet bows and plastic belts, the atomizers and gilt dresser sets, the scalloped nylon gloves and angora-trimmed anklets, Sylvie always brought us treasures" (94). When Sylvie arrived in Fingerbone, she was wearing a "deep green [dress], with a satiny shine. It had short sleeves and a large round collar on which there was a brooch, a little bunch of lilies of the valley" (45). In these descriptions, it is possible to read in Sylvie a questionable interest in cheap, inappropriate, useless things. At the same time, it is possible to find in Sylvie an appreciation of beauty, albeit inexpensive, transitory beauty. This is a striking contrast to the dry practicality of the town.

Second, Sylvie is acutely aware of the reality of death, whereas the people in the town go out of their way to distance themselves from it (164). This is perhaps most obvious when Sylvie walks fearlessly out over the lake on the railroad bridge; even the hoboes under the bridge assume that she is going to kill herself (81). But this is not a death wish as much as a familiarity and friendliness with danger. Ruth and Lucille's great-aunts, on the other hand, were "terrified of all signs of transience, the flush on a cheek that might mean a fever, a cough, or the outgrowing of shoes, which would signal their inevitable growth and decay."[19] Sylvie recognizes and is at peace with one of the fundamental truths of the human condition: we all die.

Moreover, Sylvie and Ruth live lives that are permeable and attentive to nature in a way that the townspeople's are not. This corresponds to their openness to being alone—the lake is a good place to escape society, and the island that Sylvie finds is even more remote. It also corresponds to their embrace of transience—the lake and the island are also places to get away from their home and from housekeeping. Housekeeping is what the aunts, as well as the townspeople, cling to against nature and transience.[20] In contrast, Sylvie reimagines housekeeping: she keeps house in such a way that welcomes nature into it and erodes the boundaries between them. For instance, she and the girls often eat dinner in the dark, more attuned than the townspeople to natural rhythms; Sylvie cleans by opening up the doors to the air and by scattering nicely the leaves that gather in the house (85–86). Sylvie's embrace of nature critiques the townspeople's avoidance of it. The town is frightened of transients because they remind the town of what it is—a little civilization barely holding on in the face of natural forces: "So the transients wandered through Fingerbone like ghosts, terrifying as ghosts are because they were not very different from us" (178).

Most importantly, Sylvie is comfortable with being alone; she is unconcerned with conformity to social expectations. She recognizes the human condition of loneliness, not as something to be fought and avoided but as something to be embraced. In celebrating loneliness, Sylvie, and later Ruth, are not rejecting tradition altogether. Rather, they are locating themselves in an alternative American tradition: in the vein of the western, it sees being alone not as something to be avoided but as providing a space for reflection on society and the cultivation of individual identity. Robinson said of Ruth in an interview: "There are things that she wishes to reconcile herself to that are bitterly difficult for her to do, to reconcile herself to. At the same time, she's speaking from an old, old tradition, of an attempt to establish an equilibrium, or to establish a sort of freedom through renunciation of the world, in effect. It's what every prophet in the Bible does. It's the monastic tradition. If you want to go outside this culture, it's what Buddhist monks do. She's not inventing anything."[21] Robinson is talking about a separation from society that nevertheless sees itself as contributing in some way to that society, even if it is simply by the witness of living a different sort of life. The example of the biblical prophets is perhaps the most politically engaged—these prophets have to be separate and different in order to first critique and then lead the Israelites.

The characters of Sylvie and Ruth reveal problems with limiting our ideas of human community and human nature and being closed to their expansive and creative possibilities. Robinson's thought problematizes the dismissal of difference by labeling it as "disabled and dangerous." Difference that might be considered a mental disability should not be excluded from social and political communities but ought to be engaged with openness and attentiveness to what it could teach us about being human and living in community. "So I created a female hero, of sorts, also an outsider and a stranger," Robinson writes. "And while Sylvie obviously has her own history, to the degree that she has not taken the impress of society she expresses the fact that human nature is replete with nameless possibilities and, by implication, that the world is accessible to new ways of understanding" (*Child,* 92). Robinson's outsider and stranger is both the disabled person and the person who embraces difference; it is the critic of society, and it is potentially every person. Robinson provides a basis for rethinking both the categorization of disability and the ways that it is used to control individuals, as well as the societal contributions by some who are considered to be disabled. She brings to the reader "the rumor of a life lived otherwise" (*Child,* 92–93).

There is one problem with Robinson's identification of Sylvie with the prophet, however. In Robinson's telling, Sylvie seems different from others, possibly due to mental illness and/or Fingerbone's exclusion of her. She embraces this difference, though it seems to have emerged from something that was given about her and maybe even her family—Sylvie's grandfather is considered unusual in the previous generation, and Sylvie's sister, Helen, commits suicide. This is a problematic model for disability if people are forced into the role of prophet who do not choose or desire it. Perhaps they do not want to be critics of society but simply want to be accepted and welcomed as members of society. Perhaps they do not want to live, like Sylvie, on the edges of society; perhaps they do not want to live a transient life, nor do they have special spiritual knowledge, nor are they more attuned to nature. Society has often approached disability with one of two models—the model of the victim or the model of the hero. Disabled people are often painted as very long-suffering and tragic or as overcoming difficulty in the face of great odds. Either model oversimplifies the experience of disability, and the individual person is lost in a constructed category. It does not take into account the vastly different responses to disability that individual's experience. It may also assume that disability and difference are the controlling facet of an individual's identity, which may or may not be consistent with how a disabled person experiences her disability. Perhaps identifying and praising Sylvie as prophet is not as radical a critique as Robinson thinks it is. Perhaps in some sense it buys into the same sort of categorizing that she problematizes.

The People of Fingerbone

In addition to fully developing Sylvie's voice and being attentive to the ways in which she offers an implicit critique of the townspeople, Robinson also takes the people of Fingerbone seriously. She not only criticizes them for the way in which they attempt to control and exclude Sylvie but also polyphonically presents them as having a legitimate perspective—it is reasonable for the townspeople to be concerned for the other members of the town. In an interview with Tace Hendrick, Robinson clearly articulates her evaluation that the townspeople are, in some sense, right to be critical of Sylvia:

> TH: Well, this Sylvie-like experience seems dangerous to the people of the town. They do seem to want to make her stay put.

MR: She's threatening to them in the way that someone who tempts you is threatening. That's the way I see it. At the same time the townspeople acknowledge her and Ruth as a family even though they're obviously not suited to being one; and by virtue of having some expectations of Sylvie, they're acknowledging the legitimacy of her relationship with the child, her responsibility for the child. The book is supposed to operate on the level of reality to the extent that people might actually think that Ruth was in danger. For all that people know at the end of the book, the worst possible thing might have happened. So it's not wrong for them to be anxious. When I write in general I try not to create oppositions. What I've tried to do whenever there are conflicts is to make both sides as equal as possible.

TH: Most readers want to be on the side of Ruth and Sylvie, but that's not how you see it.

MR: I see it as an inevitable conflict.

TH: But not as something by which you judge the townspeople—or Lucille, for that matter.

MR: Exactly.[22]

Robinson says that Sylvie and Ruth are not suited to be a family; the reader, together with the townspeople should be anxious—for all they know, Ruth and Sylvie did in fact die at the end of the novel. Robinson strives to give equal voice to both the townspeople and to Sylvie. It is this attempt that is remarkably admirable: Robinson does not shy away from a complicated and dangerous conflict.

The town in itself is a legitimate organization. In fact, Robinson praises the small town as one of the few places conducive to the cultivation of the individual: "I must say too how beautiful human society seems to me, especially in those attenuated forms so characteristic of the West—isolated towns and single houses. . . . We have colonized a hostile planet, and we must staunch every opening where cold and dark might pour through and destroy the false climates we make, the tiny simulations of forgotten seasons beside the Euphrates, or in Eden" (*Child,* 93).

This is the role of both the town and the house, to protect the inhabitants from the hostile planet, to create a small space that reminds us in a small way of paradise. The isolated town is perhaps more palatable for Robinson because it is still a frontier, quite close to and always interacting with the wilderness. For Robinson, the quintessential communities of the West are the small towns, perhaps because they are more transient than established, older, larger towns and cities. The West is more permeable to and at times threatened by nature. As Ruth writes of Fingerbone: "There was not a soul there but knew how shallow-rooted the whole town was. It flooded yearly, and had burned once" (177). Due to transience, the western town is potentially more democratic because the systems of power and privilege that that can calcify and stagnate more established political communities have not been erected. Indeed, Robinson portrays the sheriff of the town, not as a monarchical ruler, but as a representative of the good of a town that is continuously threatened. Ruth writes that he should be pardoned even for coming to her house to check on Sylvie and notes his tolerance of transients, which is why they haunt Fingerbone (178–79). The isolated town is also superior to a larger town or city in the sense that it is more difficult to be anonymous in Fingerbone. The townspeople initially try to help Sylvie and Ruth, visiting them and bringing them casseroles. Although their attempt is comic, it is well-intentioned.[23] The town has a reasonable interest in cultivating the good of its members; the women of the town are not to be judged for worrying when Sylvie and Ruth stay out all night on a little boat on the lake (186).

While the town can serve as a place in which the individual is cultivated and developed, it can also, conversely, seek to wield social control. It is this attempt at social control, particularly through categorizing Sylvie as disabled and dangerous, that concerns Robinson. Foucault is similarly concerned with the social control derived from the historical construction of mental illness: "The [modern] man of madness communicates with society only by the intermediary of an equally abstract reason which is order, physical and moral constraint, the anonymous pressure of the group, the requirements of conformity."[24] By separating reason from madness, reason was historically exalted and madness was controlled and excluded—it was considered something shameful that had to be hidden, it was bound by moral supervision, it was institutionalized, it was repressed.[25] Foucault longs to, through a recognition of the history of human theorizing regarding madness, to get back to undivided Reason and Unreason. Robinson, likewise, identifies two human urges—the appreciation of loneliness and the urge to shore up one's civilization against the threats of nature. While it is not imperative for Robinson that these two things exist in one person, undivided, it is important for her that society value both of these human urges. Problems arise when civilization and housekeeping trump and attempt to assimilate and colonize the loner, the mystic, the prophet. Thus it is not the town that is inherently problematic; rather, it is the town that seeks to squelch any difference it encounters. Perhaps the most striking expression of social control that Robinson critiques is Fingerbone's attempt to separate the family of Sylvie and Ruth. The "isolated town" of Fingerbone threatens the "single house"; one form of community attempts to be the only form. It is this move that pushes Sylvie and Ruth to leave, perceiving themselves to be no longer welcome there: "The sorrow is that every soul is put out of house" (179).[26]

The Family

Like her portrayal of Sylvie and the townspeople, Robinson's portrayal of the institution of the family is polyphonic. Robinson recognizes that some families are full of problems and struggles; nonetheless she highlights the irreplaceable strength of family connections. Before they flee, when Sylvie recognizes that the women of Fingerbone see her as an unsuitable caregiver to Ruth, she appeals to them: "Families should stay together. Otherwise things get out of control." And again, "Families should stay together. . . . They should. There is no other help" (186). Ruth agrees: "It is a terrible thing to break up a family," although this is of course what happens (190). Through her depiction of the conflict between the family and the town, Robinson argues that one form of association should struggle to support and keep alive other forms of association. The town stepping into the family is portrayed as a tragedy. While the townspeople's concern for Sylvie and Ruth was legitimate, Robinson points the reader to openness and democratic deliberation in which each party's voice is heard and respected over intervention. The relationship among different types of association is particularly relevant to disability. At times in American history people with disabilities, as well as the children of people with disabilities, have been un-homed and separated from both their family and the community. In the past, this has happened through institutionalization, while in the present, group homes are often only tangentially connected to the community. Sometimes the children of people with disabilities have been placed with other families.

Not only is Sylvie and Ruth's family broken up, but so are other families that Sylvie knows. Sylvie tells the story of a woman she once knew:

> I knew a woman once who was so lonely she married an old man with a limp and had four children in five years, and none of it helped at all. . . . She was probably crazy. I thought at the time, "She doesn't have children any more than I do." . . . Well, if she did, I feel sorry for them. . . . If the woman on the bus was as lonely as she said she was, she'd have her children with her. Unless she didn't have any children, or the court had taken them. That's what happened to the other little girl I was talking about. (66–68)

Ruth narrates her response to Sylvie's story: "Such a separation [being taken from Sylvie], I imagined, could indeed lead to loneliness intense enough to make one conspicuous in bus stations. It occurred to me that most people in bus stations would be conspicuous if it were not for the numbers of others there who would otherwise be conspicuous in the same way" (68–69). Here, it is ironic that Sylvie identifies someone as "probably crazy" and that, as a result, she'd feel sorry for a child left with her; she ironically affirms the community's interest in ensuring that a mother can care well for her children. Yet Ruth also connects appearing "conspicuous in bus stations," something associated with not only transience but also mental illness, to communities separating mothers from children. Here not only is it the presumption of mental illness and danger that causes the community to separate a family but also the community separating the family that leads to an apparent mental illness or at least to being "conspicuous in bus stations." At the same time that being "conspicuous in bus stations" is rare, Ruth points out that it is also a common situation. Loneliness is part of the human condition, and therefore "most people in bus stations would be conspicuous." This is yet another articulation of Robinson's position on disability: it only makes sense to talk about disability, or what is conspicuous, in the midst of what is conventional. When we recognize that convention itself is simply an attempt to hide conspicuous difference, the exclusion of disability and difference becomes nonsensical.

Another of Sylvie's acquaintances whom she describes as "probably crazy" also shows the importance of family. This woman did not seem to care for her children when they were young. Sylvie reports, "She'd give them string beans for breakfast and she never even cared if their shoes matched" (185). As usual, her story is thick with irony: Sylvie herself offers Ruth and Lucille odd food at odd times and pays little attention to their clothing and grooming. Her story continues: "I knew her when she was old, and she had nine little beds in her house, all made up, and every night she'd go from one to another, tucking the children in, over and over again. She just had four, but after they were all gone she had nine!" (185). This echoes Sylvie's earlier attention to invisible children, trying to lure them out with crackers or marshmallows (148). When her children were gone, she realized how important they were to her. Here, Sylvie's friend who is "probably crazy" bears witness to the universal truth that "families should stay together" (186).

Finally, a seemingly random newspaper clipping that Sylvie shares with Ruth also speaks to the importance of family and its intersection with disability. Sylvie finds a newspaper clipping of "a woman in Oklahoma who lost an arm in an aircraft factory, but who still manages to support six children by giving piano lessons" (105). Here a woman becomes disabled but continues to contribute to her household economy and to the education of her community. She is able to keep her family together and to support her children. Sylvie is particularly attentive to this story; her attentiveness to this article seems whimsical but is also telling. It speaks to Sylvie's eagerness to keep her own family together in spite of the townspeople's suspicions of her; it speaks of her own potential to contribute to her family and to her community.

Echoes of Sylvie: The Dog Called "Crip" and "Connie Bronson"

Not only does Robinson portray Sylvie and the townspeople polyphonically, but whenever disabled characters appear in *Housekeeping*, or in the short story that anticipates it, "Connie Bronson," Robinson also articulates them as fully valid voices that mirror Sylvie in important ways. Ruth tells about a dog that she and Lucille encounter, joining Robinson in giving voice to those whose voice is often suppressed. This dog parallels Sylvie's social exclusion and foreshadows Ruth's later disappearance with Sylvie:

> But we went there, leaving the house at dawn, joined on the road by a fat old bitch with a naked black belly and circles of white around her

> eyes. She was called Crip, because as a puppy she had favored one leg, and now that she was an elderly dog she favored three. She tottered after us briskly, a companionable gleam in her better eye. I describe her at such length because a mile or so from town she disappeared into the woods as if following a scent and never appeared again. She was a dog of no special consequence, and she passed from the world unlamented. Yet something of the somberness with which Lucille and I remembered this outing had to do with our last glimpse of her fat haunches and her palsied, upright tail as she clambered up the rocks and into the dusty dark of the woods. (111)

Ruth simultaneously makes and does not make something of the appearance and disappearance of this dog. The dog was called "Crip"—the others who named her focused on the weaknesses of her body, although Ruth describes her as tottering briskly and, more importantly, companionably. She joins Ruth and Lucille and then leaves them to wander off alone. Her loneliness, the fact that she is marked by others as disabled, and the fact that she passes "from the world unlamented" all are a hint of Ruth and Sylvie's later choice. While Sylvie is perceived by the townspeople as disabled and dangerous due to her antisocial ways and odd approach to housekeeping, the dog is perceived by its namers, presumably the people of the town, to be disabled due to its bodily difference. And the dog's story ends with its loneliness, which may have preceded or followed the townspeople's characterization—"she clambered up the rocks and into the dusty dark of the woods." The brief description of this dog not only ties Sylvie's experience of loneliness and social exclusion more closely to disability but also shows the importance to both Robinson and Ruth of the inclusion and recognition of different perspectives. Although a dog cannot speak, Ruth's description means that it does not remain a dog "of no special consequence" that "passed from the world unlamented."

Another of Robinson's characters that resembles certain aspects of Sylvie is Connie Bronson, the title character of Robinson's only published short story, a work that she has said seemed to anticipate *Housekeeping*.[27] Like *Housekeeping*, "Connie Bronson" offers a polyphonic consideration of difference, possibly disability, in the eponymous character. If Sylvie is portrayed as potentially dangerous, even more so is Connie. Connie both dangerously disregards societal norms and may exhibit insights into reality that those societal norms have missed.

Impairment and disability, as well as social exclusion, are present throughout the story: one of the first things the reader learns about Bronson is that she had brain fever and missed a year of school as a result. The boys at school hate her and tease her, calling her "Bones," despite her mother's attempt to make friends for her by throwing her many parties. Even the pony her mother buys her is "old and sickly" and bites her hand, breaking her finger, which never heals properly, and for which the boys at school make even more fun of her. She certainly has a mean and troubled streak: Connie traps and roasts over fires all the living things she catches near the river—frogs and butterflies, fish and tadpoles—and pinches her only friend, the story's narrator, from time to time. At least in part due to physical illness and impairment, Connie is excluded by the children at school; moreover, while, like Sylvie, she is fascinated by and drawn to nature, she also torments it.[28]

Even more than Sylvie, Connie is portrayed as dangerous, both to the animals she kills and to her friend, the narrator. Connie and her friend spend a lot of time one summer, the last summer of their friendship, by a river near their house from which they had been repeatedly told to stay away. Not only is this the place of her collecting and burning animals and bugs, but Connie threatens her friend with physical harm, pulling her by the wrist toward the river. Connie's mother intervenes in time to save the narrator, and what Connie would have done to her is ultimately unknown. In a similar fashion to *Housekeeping*, "Connie Bronson" explores apparently dangerous, rough and complex, and possibly mentally troubled difference; the narrator is simultaneously intrigued and repulsed by it.[29]

It is more difficult in "Connie Bronson" than in *Housekeeping* to see the insights that the main character offers, but they are present in nascent form. Robinson writes of Connie: "Connie, however, cared about none of this [her social exclusion], meeting hatred with hatred as intense, yet of another order, preoccupied and entirely self-possessed. She apparently accepted the world as hostile and decided to conform herself to it without defensiveness or apology—even with a sort of detachment."

While Robinson expresses this in neutral language here, we have seen self-possession and detachment as positive attributes in *Housekeeping*. Connie's connection to nature and the river, although the place for her destructive practices, can also be seen as having a positive aspect; she chooses not to be formed by society but rather to connect to the broader natural reality. Finally, even Connie killing living things and threatening to pull her friend into the river expresses something developed as a positive characteristic in Sylvie: Connie overcomes her fear, including her fear of the river and of death; in this sense, she exists in porous relation to the spiritual world.[30]

To the disability movement, which has within it both forces of independence and of community, Robinson offers an imaginative, dialogical portrayal of "a life lived otherwise," a picture of a potentially fruitful dynamic that could provide insight for contemporary problems. The disability movement reflects the tensions of individualism and community, of dependence and independence. This is seen in the independent living movement, which emerged in America in the 1960s and focuses on equality, attempting to maximize opportunities for disabled peoples' independence. On the other end of the spectrum, Eva Kittay has observed that we are all some mother's child, a perspective on disability that emphasizes the ubiquity of dependence.[31]

Through providing a voice for Sylvie and Ruth, as well as for the townspeople, Robinson models for the reader the mutual respect and engagement she longs to see in political society, and that she believes will benefit both individuals and society as a whole. She simultaneously critiques political and social exclusion, particularly the kind that occurs through categorizing people as disabled. Robinson does not give a clear answer to the question of whether or not Sylvie is mentally ill. This ambiguous treatment of Sylvie is what makes the townspeople's voices at least partially legitimate. But even if Sylvie is different from the townspeople in ways that may threaten them or are possibly dangerous, her difference still offers a constructive critique by pointing to certain human truths that these more conventional types attempt to avoid. This nuanced discussion of disability permeates every aspect of the novel, from its treatment of the family and its relationship to the town to its description of a physically disabled dog. Robinson's novel is profoundly democratic, giving voice to characters that political society has often made voiceless. To Robinson's attentive ear, Sylvie, the wanderer, the transient, becomes a prophet, a mystic, a member of the community whose perspective is invaluable.

Notes

I am grateful to the editors of this volume, Shannon Mariotti and Joe Lane, for their helpful feedback on this essay; I would also like to thank Lewis McCrary and Kathryn Krall for their insightful comments on drafts of the essay.

1. Marilynne Robinson, *Housekeeping* (New York: Farrar, Straus and Giroux, 1980), 46. Hereafter cited parenthetically.

2. It is unclear here whether Sylvie is denying the truth that the boat belongs to the man or whether she is seeing the truth that things belong to everyone, at least in some way.

3. Christine Caver does consider Sylvie to have the characteristics of a trauma survivor. However, the only evidence that she offers is the correspondence between Sylvie's actions and the common results of trauma. In addition, Caver's diagnosis of trauma in Sylvie tends to do what Robinson warns us against: explain away Sylvie's chosen lifestyle as a result of circumstances beyond her control. For instance, Caver reduces Sylvie's loneliness to a psychological response to trauma, which is at odds with Robinson's own explanation: "One common result of trauma is social isolation; in the absence of others who mirror different aspects of the self, a survivor's identity as survivor may overshadow all other facets of personality. Survivors often withdraw from relationships, believing that others cannot understand—a perception too often confirmed by the disappearance of friends and even family who do not know what to say or who half-believe that misfortune is contagious" (Caver, "Nothing Left to Lose: *Housekeeping*'s Strange Freedoms." *American Literature* 68, no. 1 [1996]: 122).

The most attention to disability in *Housekeeping* comes from an unlikely source—Roger Ebert's excellent review of Bill Forsyth's film version of *Housekeeping.* While Robinson neither wrote the screenplay for the film nor directed the film, Forsyth does pick up on Sylvie's eccentricities and instability. Ebert writes: "In a land where the people are narrow and suspicious, where do they draw the line between madness and sweetness? Between those who are unable to conform to society's norm and those who simply choose not to, because their dreamy private world is more alluring? That is one of the many questions asked, and not exactly answered, in Bill Forsyth's 'Housekeeping,' which is one of the strangest and best films of the year. . . . The role requires her [Christine Lahti, playing Sylvie] to find a delicate line; she must not seem too mad or willful, or the whole charm of the story will be lost. And although there are times when she seems to be indifferent to her nieces, she never seems not to love them. . . . It is important that the action takes place in a small, isolated community, in a place cut off from the world where whimsies can flourish and private notions can survive. At the end of the film, I was quietly astonished. I had seen a film that could perhaps be described as being about a madwoman, but I had seen a character who seemed closer to a mystic, or a saint" (Ebert, "*Housekeeping*," RogerEbert.com, www.rogerebert.com/reviews/housekeeping-1988). Much of Ebert's review, unlike other reflections on *Housekeeping*, reflects on Forsyth's treatment of Sylvie and the line between madness and whimsy. Of course, as Ebert intuits, Forsyth follows Robinson in not adjudicating between madness and whimsy; rather, Ebert astutely notices that Sylvie is presented simultaneously and inseparably as madwoman and mystic.

4. Maggie Galehouse, "Their Own Private Idaho: Transience in Marilynne Robinson's *Housekeeping*," *Contemporary Literature* 41, no. 1 (2000): 125–26. This emphasis on transience contrasts with some interpretations of *Housekeeping*, perhaps most notably that of Maria Moss, who argues that *Housekeeping* is about a search for sanctuary and that the problem of the book is that Ruth is denied it (Moss, "The Search for Sanctuary: Marilynne Robinson's *Housekeeping* and E. Annie Proulx's *The Shipping News*," *American Studies* 49, no.1 [2004]: 6).

5. This is starkly illustrated in the novel when Lucille leaves Sylvie and Ruth's home to move in with Miss Royce, the home economics teacher (140). Before she does, she begins devoting herself to socially acceptable, "womanly" activities, such as sewing (125).

6. Caver, "Nothing Left to Lose," 112.

7. William Burke, "Border Crossings in Marilynne Robinson's *Housekeeping*," *Modern Fiction Studies* 37, no. 4 (1991): 718.

8. Ibid., 724.

9. Roberta Rubenstein, *Boundaries of the Self: Gender, Culture, Fiction* (Chicago: University of Illinois Press, 1987), 219.

10. Robinson most explicitly refers to disability in her nonfiction, especially in the essay "When I Was a Child," in *When I Was a Child I Read Books* (New York: Farrar, Straus and Giroux, 2012). Hereafter cited parenthetically.

11. Americans with Disabilities Act of 1990, as Amended, www.ada.gov/pubs/adastatute08mark.htm.

12. "Towards a Common Language for Functioning, Disability and Health: The International Classification of Functioning, Disability and Health," www.who.int/classifications/icf/training/icfbeginnersguide.pdf, 9–10.

13. Marilynne Robinson, "Facing Reality," in *The Death of Adam: Essays on Modern Thought* (New York: Picador, 1998), 80. Hereafter cited parenthetically.

14. Marilynne Robinson, *Mother Country: Britain, the Welfare State, and Nuclear Pollution* (New York: Farrar, Straus and Giroux, 1989).

15. Ibid., 90.

16. Mikhail Bakhtin, *Problems of Dostoevsky's Poetics*, ed. and trans. Caryl Emerson (Minneapolis: University of Minnesota Press, 1984), 6, emphasis in the original.

17. Ibid., 7.

18. Marilynne Robinson, "Writers and the Nostalgic Fallacy," *New York Times*, October 13, 1985, http://graphics8.nytimes.com/images/blogs/readingroom/robinson.pdf.

19. Joan Kirkby, "Is There Life after Art? The Metaphysics of Marilynne Robinson's *Housekeeping*," *Tulsa Studies in Women's Literature* 5, no. 1 (1986): 95–96.

20. Ibid., 96.

21. Thomas Schaub, "Interview with Marilynne Robinson," *Contemporary Literature* 35, no. 2 (1994): 243.

22. Marilynne Robinson and Tace Hendrick, "On Influence and Appropriation," *Iowa Review* 22, no. 1 (1992): 3–4.

23. Roger Ebert notices the importance of the isolated town in his review of the film version of *Housekeeping:* "It is important that the action takes place in a small, isolated community, in a place cut off from the world where whimsies can flourish and private notions can survive" (Ebert, "*Housekeeping*").

24. Michel Foucault, *Madness and Civilization: A History of Insanity in the Age of Reason,* trans. Richard Howard (New York: Random House, 1965).

25. Michel Foucault, *Mental Illness and Psychology,* trans. Alan Sheridan (Berkeley: University of California Press, 1954), 69, 71, 74, 80.

26. Robinson is attentive to the tendency toward social control that may arise in a democracy, a problem similar to what Tocqueville predicts when he writes about the possibility of soft despotism—whereas ancient tyranny expressed itself as the despotism of one or a few over the many, tyranny in the democratic age may express itself, both politically and socially, as the tyranny of the majority or the intolerance of a community toward difference. Robinson identifies the problem as not enough democracy; Tocqueville predicts that it is a natural tendency of pure, unmoderated democracy. Tocqueville's solution is a relinking of individuals with each other and with the public good through local associations—particularly local government, religion, and the family. He maintains that it is through associations that democracy's excesses and tendency toward social control will be moderated. Although Robinson suggests her solution to the problems of the pressure of social conformity in the contemporary world in terms of individualism, emphasizing Robinson's affirmation of the community of single houses and isolated towns paints her in a more Tocquevillian light (Alexis de Tocqueville, *Democracy in America,* trans. George Lawrence; ed. J. P. Mayer [New York: HarperCollins, 2006]).

27. About "Connie Bronson," Robinson says: "I wrote that story in college. I had a sort of fondness for it because it seemed to me to anticipate *Housekeeping,* though I had written it more than a decade earlier" ("Marilynne Robinson, The Art of Fiction No. 198," interview by Sarah Fay, *Paris Review,* www.theparisreview.org/interviews/5863/the-art-of-fiction-no-198-marilynne-robinson).

28. Marilynne Robinson, "Connie Bronson," *Paris Review*, www.theparisreview.org/fiction/2766/connie-bronson-marilynne-robinson.

29. Ibid.

30. Ibid.

31. Eva Kittay, *Love's Labor: Essays on Women, Equality and Dependency* (New York: Routledge, 1998).

PART II

Faith and Skepticism

Religion, Secularism, and Humanism

CHAPTER 6

The Ministerial Exception

Matthew Scherer

Marilynne Robinson's fiction quietly answers one of the great questions posed with particular urgency to our generation: What place is there for faith, and for the faithful, in American public life? Her answer is strictly personal and enmeshed with highly individualized practices of reading and writing, but it addresses the fate of American religion and its connection to the fate of American democracy. The answer it poses to this question is particularly tuned to the tense relations between religion and politics in the United States, and it suggests ways of negotiating this terrain without pretending to resolve the difficulty once and for all. What is at stake in Robinson's fiction is the possibility of reinventing and continuing a faith tradition—the Congregationalist tradition aligned with the theology of John Calvin—under the centrifugal forces of modernity, under the pressure of skepticism, and under the force of materialism. In short, she analyzes the life of faith in a secular age. To answer this question about the place of the faithful in modernity, Robinson suggests that faith traditions must not only adapt and grow in order to survive and flourish but must also maintain deep and vital connections between faith and life in this world, between religion and politics. Both of those imperatives appear as antidotes to the potentially corrosive effects of secularism and suggest the modification of dominant understandings of the proper means and ends of secularism itself.

This essay reads Marilynne Robinson's fiction—focusing on *Gilead* in particular—as an exercise in speaking for religion, both in defense of religion as a viable framework within which to craft a conscientious and fully modern life and also in defense of religion as an indispensable component of collective, public, and political life. *Gilead* constitutes an extended reflection on the history of American religion and its intimate connections with the larger, more general movements of American history. It meditates at the same time on the continuation of religious tradition into the future, suggesting that faith must maintain its connections both with the historical and the ongoing concerns of American politics. This reflection, moreover, is undertaken from the perspective of a privileged representation of religion, a pastor. *Gilead* not only discloses the parameters of modern spiritual life from an internal perspective, but it also seeks to speak on behalf of religion with the intense particularity not only of a specific tradition, but of a uniquely situated individual human voice. This gesture challenges the deep assumption that modern secularism requires the separation of religion and politics and suggests how and why religion and politics continue to be entwined in modern life, insofar as it suggests both that a pastor's life and words must be engaged with the world, and that his or her words must carry beyond the walls of any given church.

Oceans of ink have been spilled of late on the contours of the secular condition of Europe, America, and the world at large, at the outset of the twenty-first century.[1] Indeed, the very notion of "the secular" is currently the subject of vigorous scholarly debate.[2] Scholars have also considered how Robinson fits into these debates, specifically whether she is a postmodern writer, whether she is a liberal or post-Protestant, and whether she belongs in the Calvinist tradition.[3] Rather than seeking to situate her in those latter debates, I will try here to bring out the uniqueness of her claims on behalf of religion in America today. For Robinson, secularity is marked by a relatively uncontroversial threefold condition in which science produces the preeminent and dominant forms of knowledge, in which traditions of learning, ethical formation, and social organization are in disarray if not crisis, and in which religions persist, albeit uncertainly, in that modern life world. She associates secularism, in turn, both with aggressive, polemical positions that tout the advances of science and seek to restrict the role of religion in public life, as well as with the concrete institutional formations (exemplified by the organization of industry, courts, and universities, for example) that institute and defend the separation of public life from spiritual tradition and practice. Secularization, finally, while it is attended by a declining adherence to mainline churches—and the Congregational and Presbyterian parishes are diminishing in *Gilead*—seems to be marked more by a reconfiguration and relocation of spiritual needs than by a decline in religion simply put.[4] These concerns are clearly legible in her nonfiction writing from

The Death of Adam to *When I Was a Child I Read Books*, and they function as a consistent frame of reference for Robinson's published work.

In the fictional world of her most recent novels, Robinson grounds her reflections on secularity within the distinctly American histories of Protestant Christianity, racialized slavery, and segregation. Part of Robinson's intervention is to show how spiritual traditions are lived in relation to, and evolve along with, major political problems and developments; in *Gilead*, the key problems are slavery and its aftermath (though poverty and the depopulation of rural communities are also present in its pages). One implication of this intervention is that the continuation of spiritual traditions depends in large part on their continued engagement with the profound problems of American political life, and the inheritance of America's complex histories. While it may seem obvious that religions are and should be tied to public life on some level, many powerful intellectual and institutional currents aligned with secularism work to both obscure and attenuate those ties. To further draw the political implications from Robinson's fiction, it will help to step down from this initial level of abstraction—*What is the place of religion in modern America?*—and to begin looking more closely at the precise configuration of secularism in modern American politics that her work challenges and supplements.

Somewhat paradoxically, contemporary political contests over the shape of American secularism are being played out in the language of "religious freedom." Although it is often assumed that the distinctly American form of secularism dictated by the United States Constitution protects religious freedom by positing the strict and absolute separation of religion and politics, Robinson's fiction suggests on the contrary that religion is necessarily entangled with the everyday experiences of public and political life. Furthermore, her work suggests that this entanglement must be maintained if religious traditions are to be continued. An important recent U.S. Supreme Court decision, *Hosanna-Tabor Evangelical Lutheran Church and School v. EEOC* (2012), exemplifies the conventional understanding of secularism that *Gilead* challenges, and I will turn briefly to that decision to illustrate two of the concerns that are at stake in *Gilead*. First, this decision articulates the fundamental logic of American secularism as the separation of church and state that Robinson's work might help to supplement and refine. Second, the Court's decision connects these large-scale questions about secularism with the fine grain of Robinson's fiction insofar as both

Hosanna-Tabor and *Gilead* seek to articulate the place of ministers within their respective faith traditions and in relation to American politics. Insofar as the Court is charged in *Hosanna-Tabor* with weighing the significance of ministers within contemporary churches, and for articulating the proper constitutional relation between ministers, churches, and government, the connections between this text and *Gilead* in particular are direct and significant. I will briefly review the facts of the case before drawing those points out further.

The pertinent facts in *Hosanna-Tabor* are as follows: a teacher at a K–8 school run by a Lutheran church was fired from her job after taking a medical leave in apparent violation of the Americans with Disabilities Act (ADA). When the teacher sued the school, her case was summarily dismissed in a district court on the basis of a doctrine of "ministerial exception" that precludes government from interfering with a church's appointment and removal of its ministers. The Supreme Court upheld this ruling on constitutional grounds, arguing that religious freedom requires that government respect the autonomy of churches. Although on its face, *Hosanna-Tabor* is a run-of-the-mill labor dispute—in which an employee claims discrimination, retaliation, and wrongful termination—it becomes a site at which the Court wrestles with the meaning of modern religion, and the place of religion in America's constitutionally mandated mode of secular governance that is required to define, regulate, and protect it. As in Robinson's *Gilead,* these questions crystallize around the understanding of a minister's exemplary role within faith traditions.

The key to the Court's decision in *Hosanna-Tabor* is its definition of churches as autonomous communities, and its framing of the appointment and dismissal of ministers as essential to the continued maintenance and integrity of those communities. During oral arguments, the justices returned time and again to the problem of defining the ministry—they asked repeatedly, "What is a minister?"—and the Court's decision sets the answer to this question beyond the competence of courts. Absent a clear and reliable test, the justices determined that "churches" are the competent bodies to determine who and what a minister is, because to question their determination would be to violate their autonomy and draw the Court into consideration of theological doctrines. The Court invokes James Madison as a key authority, and its reasoning is consistent with the argument of his *Memorial and Remonstrance against Religious Assessments* that religion "is precedent, both in order of time and in degree of obligation, to the claims of Civil Society" and that religion is therefore "wholly exempt from the cognizance of civil society."[5] To put that argument more directly, the Court follows Madison in saying that churches come before states, that they are older and more important, and that governments therefore must respect the autonomy of churches.[6] The Court presents a clear and parsimonious argument that is representative of the ideal separation of church and state at the heart of the modern secular ideal, but it also runs contrary to historical experience, and, as Robinson will suggest, this approach may ultimately be corrosive of spiritual life and detrimental to the requirements of a democratic society.

Although the argument of Madison's *Memorial and Remonstrance* suggests that religion predates government, taking a long historical perspective, it would be more accurate to view religious and political institutions and discourses as developing through history in relation with one another. The institution in question in *Hosanna-Tabor,* the Lutheran Church Missouri Synod, for example, was founded well after the United States. Geneva predated and grounded Calvin and Calvinism. Religious traditions are born and reformed within political contexts that play a role in shaping them, and that they often reshape in turn. Courts cannot merely distinguish the activity of government from a preexisting, and already autonomous, sphere of religion. In the modern world, courts in particular are called upon to determine what actions are religious, to determine over and again what is religious and what is political in ways that confound strict ideas of separation.[7] Modern religions, in turn, exert pressure on governments to shape and reshape the perceptions, values, and judgments that inform collective life. In *Hosanna-Tabor,* the Court defines the ministry within the law by deciding that a minister is whomever a church holds out to be a minister, and it also defines churches as institutions that are to be set apart and rendered autonomous from social and political pressure. My point is not to argue that either definition is wrong necessarily; it is instead to focus attention on the fact that both definitions of religious institutions are imposed through contestable decisions that carry real consequences for politics insofar as they bear on the rights of citizens, and for religion insofar as they bear on the relative power of religious hierarchies. Church and state are not in any natural or essential sense separate, and although we often draw lines between them, we do so in contested and uneven fashion, case by case.[8]

Hosanna-Tabor reveals a central bind of modern secularism by showing how the Court is required to speak in defense of religion and on religion's behalf but also prohibited from occupying any religious perspective and from speaking in the language of any religious tradition. The Court must enter into relations with religious traditions insofar as it must define the boundaries of religion through the law, but the Court is also prevented from hearing and engaging with the particular claims of these traditions. Although this approach to governing the intersection of religious tradition and political power is intended to protect the freedom and integrity of religion, it patronizes the very traditions it seeks to protect; in rendering them silent, it risks caricaturing, distorting, and undermining these traditions. Those dangers, furthermore, go to the heart of the question of living one's faith in our modern secular age. In my view, Robinson helps to provide grounds for departing from the Court on this fundamental point. In the view of the Court, ministers must be sheltered within the autonomous community of the church because faith itself can and should be sheltered from interference. But Robinson helps us to see why ministers, precisely, must be exposed to profound and continuous engagement with the world in order to fulfill the central terms of their calling, and why faith, too, by extension must be exposed to the world if it is to live at all.

Gilead and the Open Structure of Address

Having posed the contours of the problem, we can now turn to the ways in which *Gilead* departs from the conventional wisdom of secularism embodied in *Hosanna-Tabor* that religion is "other-worldly," that religion is a "private" affair of "conscience" or a matter of "belief" and that churches are "autonomous" institutions. In following the lives of three generations of ministers, *Gilead* traces the transformation and evolution of religion through the evolution of a Congregational church and in connection with the great events and dilemmas of public life throughout nineteenth- and twentieth-century American history. It is attuned to the ways in which spiritual life, and spiritual traditions, are grounded in our collective shared world. This recognition presents the first modification of the Court's assumption that religion is something that autonomous communities pursue in isolation from the other concerns of public life. It suggests instead that religions must be thought of as living traditions that evolve precisely through their constant and profound engagement with the world. Compared with that large-scale perspective, another part of *Gilead*'s contribution is to focus on the ways in which religion infuses life at the levels of language and conscious thought, and also in still more intimate embodied forms through perception, emotion, affect, and sense. That recognition presents another modification of the Court's assumptions about the privacy of religion and the nature of faith. For insofar as religion is lived through the body in its unavoidable interconnection with the bodies that surround it (natural, human, spiritual bodies), individuals carry religion, and irreligion as well, with them throughout their lives and not only within churches. To draw these points out in more detail, I will briefly introduce the novel and then analyze it at three levels: first through its structure of address, then through its appeal to the senses, and finally through its presentation of religion's engagement with the world in and through narrative and tradition. These different levels show the different methods *Gilead* employs to challenge the Court's assumption that religion and politics must be kept separate for the health of democracy.

Gilead is structured as a long letter composed in the small town of Gilead, Iowa, in 1956 by a seventy-four-year-old Congregationalist minister, John Ames, to his seven-year-old son, Robert Boughton Ames, whom he calls Robby. Ames's first child died shortly after birth along with her mother when Ames was a young man, and Robby is his second child. Ames is now old, and after a long life alone as a widower, he experiences his second wife, Lila, and their child as an unexpected delight, joy, blessing, and grace. The first third of the text unfolds as Ames's serene and joyous meditation on the unexpected and incomparable grace bestowed upon him by his second family. From the outset Ames's joy is tinted by melancholy, for he is not only old, but he knows his heart to be failing. Ames anticipates his own death sometime soon, and must imagine his son's fatherless life. Having descended from a long line of ministers and inherited his vocation as a birthright, Ames suffers from the thought that he will not be able to transmit this tradition to his son.

The second two-thirds of *Gilead* present a problem that threatens Ames's tenuous blessings, and a resolution to this problem that deepens, confirms, and transfigures Ames's blessings through a moment of redemption. The problem arrives in the form of John Ames Boughton, known as Jack. Jack is the son of Ames's best friend, Robert Boughton, and he was named for Ames at a time when it seemed certain that Ames, already long a widower, would never have a son of his own. In a sense, Jack is Ames's as well as Boughton's son, and he has called Ames "Papa" since his youth. As Ames's letter slowly discloses, and as the narrative of *Home* extends and confirms, Jack is charming, intelligent, and well-read but also shy, elusive, inscrutable, and a rogue. He has spent time in prison. He is an alcoholic with neither career nor steady employment. He has taken advantage of vulnerable women, and he has abandoned at least one child. Jack lacks faith in God, and despite his efforts to believe, he is an atheist. One is given to suspect this fact is intimately related to the rest.

Ames's address to the son he loves, who appears to him as by grace, Robby, is interrupted, in ways that are resisted and imperfectly acknowledged, by the arrival of Jack, a son who in many respects cannot be loved, cannot be accepted, and who threatens to unmake the late and tenuous blessings of Ames's world. Jack is, on one level, the right age to be Robby's father and Lila's husband, and thus a potential rival. On another level, Jack embodies the faithlessness and fatherlessness that Ames fears for his child Robby. The latter two-thirds of *Gilead* unfolds the relationship between Ames and Jack, the place of each in the other's life, and ultimately the kind of redemption each can and cannot offer the other.

The relatively simple story told in *Gilead* is complicated by the novel's structure of address. Its epistolary structure imposes a certain form on the novel by controlling perspective and determining the pace of exposition, but more importantly for our concerns here it bears upon one of the novel's key themes, the continued public circulation of religion. To the extent that one can generalize in this way, Christianity is an evangelical religion in the sense that it is grounded upon the pronouncement and promulgation of the "gospel" and "good news" to the world.[9] In a more particular sense, American Christianity today, and particularly in the Calvinist tradition that is Robinson's concern, faces fundamental questions about the transmission of its tradition: How will religion be passed from one generation to another? More precisely, how will scripture and worship be communicated? Who will be the pastors of these texts and traditions, and what will they reveal today under the novel conditions of modernity? Answering those questions goes to the heart of the ministry, and Ames worries over them as he considers how he inherited his faith from his father and grandfather, and how he will not be able to pass it along directly to his own child. However, these are not merely Ames's questions. Robinson's novel works to draw its readers into their orbit, that is to say, to slip these questions from Ames's world to that of the reader.

While Ames's letter is addressed to Robby, *Gilead* is also addressed to its readers, some of whom will be of Robby's generation, some of whom will be of the generation of Robby's children, many of whom, like Robby, will not themselves be ministers. I would expect that most of *Gilead*'s readers take its open structure of address for granted, and that they are not surprised by the fact that its words are both directed to Robby and also open for the reader, for anyone and everyone. What is significant here is the connection between this formal structure and the thematic content of the novel. The point is not merely that texts circulate openly, or merely that Robinson has written a novel about faith from the perspective of a minister. The point is that Robinson's novel suggests that it is of the essence of the ministry (in the tradition she imagines), and of the essence of faith itself, to be expressed in language that is in principle addressed to all people, and that knows no boundaries. Even letters addressed to particular individuals—even private letters addressed from father to son—*Gilead* seems to emphasize, cannot only circulate more broadly by chance but are structurally open to a potentially infinite audience. If Ames's letter is to mean anything for his son, Robby, it will be meaningful for a wider, anonymous audience on the very same account, for the criteria of meaning and interest are necessarily public. What bears emphasis here is the radical departure this represents from the Court's secular ideal of a minister as an individual whose communication and care is primarily concerned with his or her autonomously bounded community. In Robinson's conception, faith and the ministry of faith, like language itself, cannot be properly conceived within a narrowly bounded community but must of their nature extend and circulate beyond any boundaries posited between people.

The thematic importance of *Gilead*'s structure of address is perhaps most apparent in the novel's opening, which I quote here in full to draw out its effect:

> I told you last night that I might be gone sometime, and you said, Where, and I said, To be with the Good Lord, and you said, Why, and I said, Because I'm old, and you said, I don't think you're old. And you put your hand in my hand and you said, You aren't very old, as if that settled it. I told you you might have a very different life from mine, and

> from the life you've had with me, and that would be a wonderful thing, there are many ways to live a good life. And you said, Mama already told me that. And then you said, Don't laugh! because you thought I was laughing at you. You reached up and put your fingers on my lips and gave me a look I never in my life saw on any other face besides your mother's. It's a kind of furious pride, very passionate and stern. I'm always a little surprised to find my eyebrows unsinged after I've suffered one of those looks. I will miss them.[10]

The novel's reader, of course, is given no bearings here at the outset, and this apparently direct form of address deposes, confuses, and frustrates the reader. We read, "I told you last night," and yet know we are not the one being addressed: who is speaking?, who is addressed?, and when was last night? It stages, surely, a scene of intimacy between two people, and this intimacy is reinforced by the sparse punctuation that leaves quotation and narration undistinguished, and produces a single stream of words in shared but partial and fractured experience. One finds here a report on two things that "I told you" last night, and based on their tone and content one might infer that they are spoken by an authoritative adult. The first thing "I told you" is that I am going away soon, and the second is that your life will be very different when I am gone. Punctuating and responding to those statements, one finds reports of a rapid play of tender, intimate, and emotional responses characteristic of the comportment of children: asking why, contradicting, touching, claiming to know already, taking offense at seeming to be mocked. The reports of words spoken are interwoven with "your hand in my hand" and "your fingers on my lips," with bodies and parts slipping their boundaries, intertwining, and perhaps not incidentally enacting a gesture—fingers to lips—associated with prophetic address. The scene is sealed by a look proper to one face, "your mother's" appearing on another face, your own. We can read this in retrospect as a conversation between Ames and Robby, reported in a letter from one to the other once its context is established. However, it is written in a way that loosens those connections and allows this text to break from its context and circulate much more broadly. On first read, before a proper context for it can be established, it confronts the reader with a distinctive feature of language in its propensity to slip context and circulate promiscuously.

The structure of *Gilead*'s address is open in a variety of ways. For example, it opens a question about who is communicating, Robinson or Ames. If it is Ames, it leaves one to ponder the simultaneous presence of an Ames living and writing, and an Ames who is now long-dead. And similarly, if Robby is addressed, one must consider the coincidence of Robby as a child known to Ames, and Robby as a grown man reading these letters. One might take Robinson to be implying these questions insofar as a distinctive feature of her fiction is its tendency to cut events, images, words, and language loose from their historical locations, subjects, and relations. On the one hand, this suggests that the texts of our lives may never have been as closely tied to their contexts as common sense supposes, and that we might uproot ourselves from contexts, defying what seemed possible, necessary, and right. Abstractly stated, that possibility is inherent to the spiritual freedom Calvin imagined so clearly, it is the very idea of faith as that which allows one to transcend worldly interests.[11] On the other hand, this also suggests that the texts of our lives are subject to continual disturbance by the unwilled irruption of various contexts that surround them. Jack, and all the memories and troubles associated with him, erupt this way in the text of Ames's life. Slavery and abolition, with the violence, turmoil, and trauma associated with them, interrupt his text this way as well. Ames's text is continuously interrupted and punctuated by memories of his father and grandfather, of John Brown and killings in Kansas, of poverty, of war, of this multifaceted landscape of American historical experience.

Ames reflects upon the relation between language, knowledge, and experience as follows, "My point here is that you never do know the actual nature even of your own experience," and then he radicalizes this point even further, "Or perhaps it has no fixed and certain nature" at all (95). Language in general, and as we shall come to, religious doctrines in particular, pass through our lives. They wash over us as images do and are shared to an extent with others. They also remain partially opaque to each of us as well. They are susceptible to interpretation and given trust, patience, and common effort may become the subject of agreement, understanding, and peace. If Ames theorizes this point, the novel's structure of address stages the condition of ignorance, delusion, and misinterpretation as a function of the circulation of language itself. One might register this relation to language as a key part of Robinson's inheritance of Calvin's theology, insofar as our being out of joint with respect to language reflects humanity's fallen condition and imperfect knowledge of the world.[12]

Ames's gloss on his lifelong practice of writing as prayer reinforces this interpretation: "For me writing has always felt like praying, even when I wasn't writing prayers. . . . You feel that you are with someone. I feel I am with you now, whatever that can mean, considering that you're only a little fellow now and when you're a man you might find these letters of no interest. Or they might never reach you, for any of a number of reasons . . . I pray for you. And there's an intimacy in it. That's the truth" (19).

Ames acknowledges just how tenuous communication is rendered by language, even communication between fathers and sons, applying Calvin's "first rule of right prayer, that we abandon all thought of our own glory, that we cast off all notion of our own worth, that we put away all our self-assurance, in our abjection and our humility giving glory to the Lord," to each act of meaningful speech.[13] Despite the human insufficiency with respect to language, Ames finds "truth" and "intimacy" in the use of language as prayer, that is, when it is addressed not directly to another person but is instead addressed to, and mediated by, God. One conforms then to Calvin's second rule of prayer, "truly to sense our own insufficiency, and earnestly ponder that we need the things we seek from God for ourselves and for our benefit," insofar as one requires communication but manages it only by grace, not by one's own sufficient mastery of language.[14] This further intensifies the point that language circulates independently of our intention and control. Ames gives us a glimpse of a minister who experiences faith rather as a disposition that one adopts with respect to language, particularly with respect to its challenges, limitations, and insufficiencies, and who knows faith only in relation to God, to whom he must attempt to adhere and speak authentically.

One might hold different views both about the nature of our relation to language and about the ways in which we can live that relation. Robinson herself, for example, largely agrees with Ames about our condition, noting in an essay that it "is not by any means fanciful to lay a great many of the unspeakable difficulties to which we [human beings] have always been liable to language."[15] But rather than turning to prayer as Ames does, when speaking in her own voice Robinson suggests that we might instead "develop language that will acknowledge that it does fray, and where it does, and that those things we do not understand are not mere gaps to be closed by extensions of existing ways of thinking," such that we allow mystery to persist at the rough edges between human, language, and world rather than pretending the gaps between can be neatly closed.[16] There are, of course, many compelling ways of sketching the human predicament in language, and probably just as many ways of responding to it. What matters is the idea of faith that Robinson sketches through it, and the sense in which it bears very little resemblance to the idea of faith, minister, and church sketched in *Hosanna-Tabor* and assumed by the idea of modern secularism more generally. Where the Court seeks to make churches autonomous, self-enclosed communities in order to isolate and protect faith, *Gilead* shows us a minister whose faith requires him to acknowledge that he is constantly undone, decentered, and deposed by and within language itself. This is a minister who knows that the words he uses have come from afar and that they will circulate beyond any intended boundaries.

Ames presents his letter as a prayer, meaning in part that it is a faithful address that seeks intimacy and truth while acknowledging that the speaker is inadequate to the task and that the communication's human recipient is unlikely to receive the communication intended. What this prayerful address intends to communicate includes what it means to be a minister of the church, and what it means to follow a vocation, to have faith, to live a life with faith. Ames's letter is at once then a communication to Robby about faith, and an enactment of language as the faithful address to God. At the same time, one might imagine Robinson's novel as at once a communication to its readers about faith, and an enactment of language as the faithful address to God. One might then ask what "truths" and "intimacies" reside in this communication in Ames's terms, or what "mysteries" are preserved and acknowledged in this use of language in Robinson's terms? Christopher Leise, commenting on *Gilead*, usefully frames the mystery and truth to be communicated as "an experience of the divine in the immediate and the immanent: an experience that stops short of knowing through reason and is content with simply living the experience of the miraculous in the everyday."[17] The structure of Robinson's and Ames's address, that is to say, accentuates the exceptionality (or miraculousness) of experience, but it insists on this as an everyday and ubiquitous exceptionality. The Supreme Court's intuition that ministers and religions must in some sense be special if they are to be anything at all seems right, but its decision to set ministers and religious communities apart from the world does not necessarily follow from that intuition. I would like to turn now to considering in greater depth Ames's and Robinson's conception of the miraculousness of the everyday, and the goodness of creation apprehended by the senses.

The Sense of Our World

That Robinson and Ames find truth, faith, and God in the evidence of the senses poses another profound challenge to the secular injunction to separate religion from public and political worlds, and to settle it within its own autonomous boundaries. Insofar as religion is reducible to creed, doctrine, belief, conscience, or even the practices of a community, one might follow the Court in imagining that these can be set aside, insulated, and protected from life, from public pressure, from political power. However, Ames and Robinson show how religion lives in the sensible, sensory, ordinary world. Leise notes that Robinson might find a basis for this theological conception within some of Jonathan Edwards's lesser-known works, such as "Beauty of the World" and *Images or Shadows of Divine Things,* as well as within the text of Calvin's *Institutes.* "Since the perfection of blessedness consists in the knowledge of God (cf. John 17:3), he has been pleased," Calvin writes, "to manifest his perfections in the whole structure of the universe, and daily place himself in our view, that we cannot open our eyes without being compelled to behold him."[18] Even more directly, Calvin enjoins, "We ought not to rack our brains about God; but rather we should contemplate him in his works."[19] To the extent that one's truth, faith, and God are located within the world and accessed through the senses, the separation of religion from the rest of life that grounds a conception of secularism like the Court's becomes impossible. If, as Calvin puts it, the blessed "cannot open" their "eyes without being compelled to behold" God, it cannot be a sufficient protection of their religion to defend the institutional autonomy of their churches. Conceiving faith as such seems to render conceptions of secularism and religious freedom as separation and autonomy radically insufficient and off track. With that challenge in mind, I want to consider the play of faith and the senses in more detail.

Ames's faith is most powerfully expressed and experienced through his sensuous engagement with our shared world. Channeled through Ames's voice, the aesthetic brilliance of Robinson's prose brings the doctrinal constraints of reformed orthodoxy to life in and within the full range of human possibilities. More precisely, Ames's thinking operates within a set of theological constraints: grace, redemption, revelation, scripture, doctrine, church, congregation, sacrament, sermon, minister, faith, and tradition. And these overlap an experiential set of human possibilities: love, sex, procreation, joy, depression, despair, play, marriage, fidelity, reading, listening, speaking, talking, listening, touching, tasting, seeing, hearing, remembering, dreaming, fearing, hoping, jealousy, friendship, appreciation. As these series are mediated by a set of literary operations—metaphor, dialogue, citation, narrative—Robinson shows, again and again, how doctrine is illuminated within the above-considered structure of human address, how it comes to life within sensory experience, and how the events of human life, properly arranged in narrative, disclose its meaning. Rather than providing an interpretive framework that can be placed over, or separated off from life, doctrine itself only lives within human possibilities.

Part of Ames's and Robinson's work in *Gilead* lies in bringing Calvin's doctrines back to life in the sense of reviving them and showing how doctrine and faith can be revived only when they are deeply grounded within ordinary, lived, sensory, human experience. Her interpretation of Calvin seems, then, to be true to key currents in his thought, while at the same time producing an unfamiliar portrait of him. These points can be pressed further by considering the problems of faith and perdition, first as they are presented in Calvin's *Institutes*, and then as they are reimagined in *Gilead*. The *Institutes* opens with a discussion of the fundamental interrelation of one's knowledge of God, and one's knowledge of oneself.[20] In the first edition, Calvin begins thus: "Nearly the whole of sacred doctrine consists in these two parts: knowledge of God and oneself."[21] He argues that there is no knowledge of oneself that is not grounded in contemplation of "the face of God," which shines through God's creation.[22] One's own "ignorance, vanity, want, weakness, in short, depravity and corruption" can be comprehended only in contrast with the fullness of God's creation. On the other hand, one turns to contemplate the face of God only out of dissatisfaction with one's own condition. For "we cannot aspire to Him in earnest until we have begun to be displeased with ourselves."[23] Calvin is at pains to show how this human predicament is resolved and communion with God achieved, for "cut off and separated from Him by sin, man will find in himself only unhappiness, weakness, wickedness, death, in short, hell itself."[24] A traditional interpretation of Calvin might emphasize "God," "the Son," "the Holy Spirit," and "the Church" as the four avenues to faith. Robinson emphasizes, by way of contrast, that part of God which shines forth throughout creation and which illuminates our sense of this world.

What is perhaps most surprising in Robinson's reimagining of Calvin is her emphasis on the joyous apprehension of the goodness of God's creation. This stands in stark contrast with the tone of fear that dominates the theology of both Edwards and Calvin in most interpretations. That fear plays a key role for these theologians seems beyond argument, as casual inspection of a text such as Edwards's famous "Sinners in the Hands of an Angry God" suggests.[25] And Calvin states quite directly that "pure and genuine religion" is "namely, confidence in God coupled with serious fear."[26] Displacing fear and installing joy as the central affective register of a properly Calvinist piety is a tall order, but in many respects, this seems to be one of the primary effects of *Gilead*. The joy that a reader finds in Ames's company may be the most surprising element of *Gilead*—to put it glibly, it is not what one likely expects from an elderly Calvinist minister—and Robinson gives the text over, to a great degree, to the joy that Ames finds in the beauty of nature and this world.

In his meditations Ames often lands on something that satisfies him, and that his readers might potentially find satisfying, but his meditations often fall short as well. They are by turns soaring and beautiful as well as flat and uninspired. "This morning I have been trying to think about heaven, but without much success," he writes; "I don't know why I should expect to have any idea of heaven. I could never have imagined this world if I hadn't spent eight decades walking around in it" (66). Ames's successful expressions most often come when his thoughts are connected, metaphorically, to sensory experience. His writing most often fails when it is absent of those connections, and he often marks such failures by saying, "that's the pulpit speaking," which I take to mean that that is the voice of doctrine detached from sense, and from life. Ames has accumulated a relatively large library, and a massive collection of his own sermons, both of which have formed his mind, and both of which weigh upon him. In his letter, however, the arguments and the doctrines contained in these texts recede to a large extent to the background. Robinson shows us this learned man in his engagement with the world, when he is outdoors, when he is eating in his kitchen, when he is with his family and friends, when he is recalling his and his family's past. It is here that he is most alive, and insightful, and persuasive, and this may be seen as a discovery made by both writers—Ames and Robinson—that their thoughts are most powerful when they are grounded in the world, rooted in sense. What this suggests is a view in which religion—including faith, grace, piety, knowledge of God—lives within the open, shared world of the sensory experience. If religion is spoken for by Ames in the mode of prayer, the contents of that prayer start and finish with the direct evidence of the senses.

Consider as an example of this the following consecutive paragraphs:

> I'd never have believed I'd see a wife of mine doting on a child of mine. It still amazes me every time I think of it. I'm writing this in part to tell you that if you ever wonder what you've done in your life, and everyone does wonder sooner or later, you have been God's grace to me, a miracle, something more than a miracle. You may not remember me very well at all, and it may seem to you to be no great thing to have been the good child of an old man in a shabby little town you will no doubt leave behind. If only I had the words to tell you.

Robinson shows us here one of Ames's failures of expression, and she shows us Ames noticing his failure to adequately express the idea, emotion, affect he means to convey. You are "a grace . . . a miracle . . . more than a miracle . . . if only I had the words," Ames writes, stammering, reaching for the words and admitting that he does not have the right ones. What the reader comes to see with him is that the plain words of doctrine—"grace," "miracle"—ineffectively convey, cannot quite reach to, the life Ames wishes to express. That life can be expressed, can be reached, however, and apprehended through the senses: sensory experience which when projected metaphorically enlivens the words of doctrine. Ames continues:

> There's a shimmer on a child's hair, in the sunlight. There are rainbow colors in it, tiny, soft beams of just the same colors you can see in the dew sometimes. They're in the petals of flowers, and they're on a child's skin. Your hair is straight and dark, and your skin is very fair. I suppose you're not prettier than most children. You're just a nice-looking boy, a bit slight, well scrubbed and well mannered. All that is fine, but it's your existence I love you for, mainly. Existence seems to me now the most remarkable thing that could ever be imagined. I'm about to put on imperishability. In an instant, in the twinkling of an eye. (52–53)

The miracle, the grace, of his son's existence is expressed, is communicated, is apprehended in "a shimmer," "in the sunlight," "rainbow colors," "tiny, soft beams," "in the petals of flowers," in the "straight and dark" hair of the child. It is apprehended through the senses; it is expressed in sensory metaphor.

Doctrines run into one another in the above-cited passage as Ames shifts from the miracle of his own son's existence, through birth, to the transfiguration of his own existence, through death. His labors will be renewed in the following paragraph: having enlivened the miracle, he will have to supply another metaphor again based in sensory experience, to enliven the doctrine of transfiguration, of an afterlife, and of one's passage to it, "in the twinkling of an eye," for it, too, falls relatively flat on first introduction. It is in the observation of nature—Robinson would have us learn from Calvin—that we find the first knowledge of God, and it is in Scripture and doctrine rightly understood that such knowledge might find relative security and stability. To continually renew this knowledge and to enliven doctrine through expression within human possibilities, within sensory experience, within sensory metaphor is Ames's and Robinson's work.

The opening third of *Gilead,* then, oscillates between failed and successful expression—there are myriad instances of Ames's hesitation and disappointment at his ability to convey what he wishes to convey—but I cite here just one more moment where Robinson lets Ames reach effectively into the sensory world to find expression: "You are standing up on the seat of your swing and sailing higher than you really ought to, with that bold, planted stance of a sailor on a billowy sea. The ropes are long and you are light and the ropes bow like cobwebs, laggardly, indolent. Your shirt is red—it is your favorite shirt—and you fly into the sunlight and pause there brilliantly for a second and then fall back into the shadows again" (112).

This is an expression of the joyous encounter, what Ames goes on to call "those first experiments with fundamental things, gravity and light," and one might assume the splendor of creation, of life, in its pure, glorious, and here blessed transience, "you fly into the sunlight and pause there brilliantly for a second and then fall back into the shadows," and in its constant re-creation, "sailing higher than you really ought to," "again," and again. What Ames communicates most clearly throughout his letter, arguably, is a profound love of this world. This is perhaps surprising insofar as we have said that the purpose of his letter is to communicate to his son, and to us, what it means to him to be a minister. The conclusion thus far, however, is that to be a minister one must love the world. Once more Robinson gives her readers strong grounds on which to question the Court's understanding of both religious communities and their ministers insofar as the latter seeks to insulate and set these apart while the former accentuates their necessary engagement with each other. In the next, and final, analysis of *Gilead*, we will consider the ways in which such a love for the world necessarily draws one not only into the field of shared sensory experience but also into the field of interpersonal relations, and political conflict.

Time, Place, and History

Robinson uses the resources of language itself in *Gilead* to show how faith circulates through the emotions, perceptions, and thoughts of individuals, and between individuals as well. In doing this, Robinson makes significant contributions to our capacity to understand how paradigms that consign religion to the domain of private belief and conscience distort and obscure important facets of lived religion. By extension, this vision of faith as entwined with necessarily public address and enmeshed within shared perceptions of the world presses hard against conceptions of secularism that try to separate religion out from collective life. The last point that I would like to consider in *Gilead* returns us from the fine grain of language and the senses to the broad sweep of American history encompassed within the novel's narrative, and to the place of religion within American democracy suggested by this narrative. Throughout *Gilead*, Robinson traces back the history of Ames's father, his father's father, and so on—ministers to time immemorial—and traces forward the dialectical movement of these generations of ministers from righteous abolitionism, through a "disappointing" pacifism, to a context where Ames is the uneasy inheritor of both histories. The story of the generations' struggles with each other and with changing churches and societies constitutes one of the text's two main plots. The other key story in *Gilead* is that of the struggle between Ames and Jack. Both stories converge, such that the resolution of the struggle between Ames and Jack also functions as a resolution to the struggles between generations of ministers, and such that these generations of struggle are shown to have enabled the fragile and hopeful outcome between Ames and Jack. This narrative resolution, in turn, thematizes the mutual dependence of history and spiritual redemption. Tracing these two connected stories out in somewhat greater detail, then, can open a final perspective on Robinson's argument about the necessary connections among individual faith, faith communities, and politics in the American experience.

Ames's letter traces a number of histories that pass through and intersect in the town of Gilead, touching on the story of his own family as well as the larger history of the United States and connecting these histories to Ames's relationship with Jack. These narratives in turn track the history of slavery and racial injustice in America, showing how spiritual formations and lives are shaped and misshaped by larger political currents. "In the old days towns like ours were a conspiracy," Ames remarks; "Lots of people were only there to be antislavery by any means that came to hand," and that would account for the presence of the Ames family first in Kansas and then later in Iowa (158). Ames's grandfather—a fellow traveler of John Brown's who moved to Kansas from Maine in the 1830s—spent his life at war with the institution of slavery. Ames's father would in turn become a pacifist and spend his life in committed opposition to his own father. Much of the contention between father and grandfather turned on their divergent understandings of their faith and ministry—Ames's grandfather patterned his life on a vision of Christ in chains that demanded the abolition of slavery, through violence if necessary, while Ames's father could find no warrant in his faith for violence at all and found in the scriptures instead the absolute requirements of love and peace.

Ames recalls the moment "when a chasm truly opened" between his father and grandfather, during an exchange in which Ames's father had said: "I remember when you walked to the pulpit in that shot-up, bloody shirt with that pistol in your belt. And I had a thought as powerful and clear as any revelation. And it was, This has *nothing* to do with Jesus. Nothing. Nothing" (84–85). In reply, Ames's grandfather left Gilead, his parting words conveyed in a note that read, in part: "No good has come, no evil is ended. That is your peace" (85). While Ames tells us that he has kept his grandfather's note in his own Bible, his task is much more complicated than that of choosing between father and grandfather, for neither orientation would seem viable or appropriate for Ames in his own time and location. Ames can neither disavow his legacy nor simply embrace it. Reflecting on his childhood attempts to make sense of his grandfather, Ames says that he "was predisposed to believe that my grandfather had done something pretty horrible and my father was concealing the evidence and I was in on the secret, too—implicated without knowing what I was implicated in. I believe I was implicated, and am, and would have been if I had never seen that pistol" (81–82). He adds from his mature perspective, "Well, that's the human condition, I suppose," and further that "the things that happened in Kansas lay behind it all, as I knew at the time" (81–82). This hard-won perspective on history—that it is "pretty horrible," that we are "implicated" in this horror, and that there is no escaping it—informs Ames's faith, his character, and his relationship with Jack. Each of these pastors models his faith and his ministry both in conversation with his forebears and in intimate dialogue with the events of his time. Jack's return to Gilead is set within this larger history, and this longer conversation, about which he can only be partially aware, but in which he comes to figure centrally.

When Jack arrives in Gilead, Ames experiences his presence as threatening in a variety of ways. Ames fears Jack, and he is inclined to hold Jack at a distance, to turn Jack away, and to defend himself and his family against Jack. Ames resists those inclinations out of loyalty to Jack's father, who is also Ames's best friend, out of a sense of his duty to help Jack insofar as he can and out of a more general, principled openness to life, to the world, and to others. This principle is a correlate of Ames's perspective on history, and he states it explicitly as a refusal of defensiveness in terms that fit equally well within spiritual and democratic traditions.[27] "Defensiveness," Ames reasons, "precludes the best eventualities along with the worst. At the most basic level, it expresses a lack of faith. . . . And often enough, when we think we are protecting ourselves, we are struggling against our rescuer. I know this, I have seen the truth of it with my own eyes, though I have not myself always managed to live by it" (154). Ames achieves something like his own redemption by overcoming his fear and aversion toward Jack, by resisting the impulse to act defensively. Ames is ultimately able to bestow his blessing upon Jack, he is able to discover and affirm that Jack is a good man, and he responds to this moment by imagining himself saying together with Jack's father, "This is why we have lived this life!" (242, 243). What redeems Jack's life, in Ames's view, and what makes Ames's own redemption possible, are their commitments to places and people, and this requires their participation within—rather than flight from—the larger historical struggles that constitute American political life. The contrast with the Court's position in *Hosanna-Tabor*, once more, could not be starker; where the logic of secularism that drives the Court's decision would insulate religious communities from interference, Robinson suggests that many of the key experiences, values, and aims of religious communities are to be attained precisely through engagement with the world beyond the immediate boundaries of any given spiritual practice or close community. More subtly viewed, it may suggest that a living community is enacted and sustained by its boundaries, which function not so much as fixed limits but rather as sites of connection and passage between the community and the milieu in which it is situated.

Jack's youth had been marked by flight, and the present moment of Ames's narrative, the mid-1950s, is marked by the departure of people from Gilead as well—both forms of flight symbolize a more general spiritual temptation and danger. Those who have left Gilead in search of a wider world of experience include Ames's brother, who told a young Ames: "John, you might as well know now what you're sure to learn sometime. This is a backwater—you must be aware of that already. Leaving here is like waking from a trance" (26). They also include Ames's father, who abandoned both Gilead and the pulpit for a more comfortable retirement on the Gulf Coast. After leaving, Ames's father would tell him "that looking back on Gilead from any distance made it seem a relic, an archaism," narrow, cramped, and irrelevant (235). Ames's grandfather would flee Gilead as well to wander Kansas, unreconciled to his family and his society.

Even those who have not literally abandoned Gilead, it is suggested, have changed and in doing so have abandoned some of their principles. In a Fourth of July address, near the turn of the century, Ames's grandfather had already indicted the people of Gilead for this abandonment: "The President, General Grant, once called Iowa the shining star of radicalism," he recalled, "But what is left here in Iowa? What is left in Gilead? Dust. Dust and ashes" (176). In living memory of the Civil War those words already had little effect, leading Ames to reflect on "how the times change" such that even in his grandfather's lifetime, "the same words that" had carried "a good many people into the howling wilderness in one generation are irksome or meaningless in the next" (176). Jack, too, would recall Iowa's epithet, "the shining star of radicalism," with skepticism about Iowa's continuing capacity for radicalism (220, 231).

Ames was deeply offended by his father's suggestion that he should leave Gilead behind to make another life, for Ames had deliberately chosen to invest his loyalty and to make his life in that town rather than fleeing "the history we had there" (235). It is around the problem of accepting or refusing one's own history that *Gilead*'s two central stories converge, drawing Jack's story into the trajectory set by generations of ministers. In Ames's view, the most "horrible" part of Jack's history was his youthful abandonment of his first child, and what redeems Jack in Ames's eyes is the revelation that he has since married, become a father, and struggled nobly to hold his family together. His struggle is made unusually difficult because his wife, Della, is "a colored woman" (217). Jack fears that his marriage would shock his father, Della's family does not approve it, and Saint Louis, where they had tried to live, legally prohibits it. While Ames admits "surprise" at the match, he does his best to affect nonchalance for Jack's sake, and more importantly he displays a genuine acceptance of their relationship (217). What is significant here is not Jack and Della's interracial marriage as such but rather the history of political struggle this marriage rests upon and continues.

If Gilead was born in a conspiracy against slavery, one of the questions Ames must ask is how to inherit and further project what is noble in that history—questions such as these must shape his faith and ministry no less than they did his father's and grandfather's, though such questions are always more difficult to perceive and resolve in one's own present context. If Ames's father and grandfather could only touch "horror" and "disappointment" in grappling with American slavery and its legacies—the one engaged to a war that did not bring justice, the other engaged to a peace that denied it still—it is only through acceptance of their histories as his own that Ames can be available to hear Jack's story and be able to find redemption in it. The argument here, as I take it, is that even the most spiritual dimensions of the human predicament—the question of redemption in Robinson's perspective—are tied intimately and inextricably to our shared world through one's relations to time, place, and history. It is because he has chosen to remain faithful to his history that Ames is in Gilead to hear Jack's confession. It is also because he honors this history—embracing noble deeds, horror, and his implication in both—that he is able to accept that confession in all its significance.

In drawing her portrait of John Ames, Robinson gives us a picture of a modern life in which religious discourses circulate freely through the lives of individuals and their communities. She gives us a picture in which the shared sensorial world serves as a common point of entry to spiritual life. This is a vision in which spirituality cannot be figured as private and detached from history but instead can be lived fully only when it is engaged with collective problems, histories, and human relationships. There is a long tradition of arguing that democracy requires faith—either generically, as with Robert Bellah's civil religion, or specifically, as with Tocqueville's Protestant Christian mores.[28] Robinson, however, suggests for us a less common insight, namely that spirituality—modern Christian faith in the reformed or Calvinist tradition, at least—requires a deep engagement in the collective problems, injuries, and commitments of public life.

Robinson presents a distinctive argument about the meaning of religion today that identifies and addresses some of the unintended consequences of secularism exemplified by the Supreme Court's decision in *Hosanna-Tabor.* Even attempts to promote religious freedom, insofar as they project freedom as autonomy, as isolation from the cares, commitments, and claims of society, I take Robinson to suggest, present risks to a spiritual life that requires deep and continuous connection with our shared world for their sustenance and survival. From this vantage, it is not for the purposes of enriching political debate that religion would be drawn into public life. It would be, rather, for the restoration, vibrancy, extension, and depth of spiritual life that it be continuously and openly related to ongoing public affairs. *Gilead* suggests that spiritual traditions must not be walled off and sealed within the boundaries of autonomous communities, for to do so would be to succumb to what Ames calls "defensiveness." Robinson's fiction makes strong claims that faith traditions must, to the contrary, be "drawn back into this world" if they are to continue at all, that they must be engaged in the history of this shared world, lest they find themselves abandoned. It is only in allowing itself to be challenged, perhaps even remade, Robinson suggests, that faith can contribute to the collective responsibility of renewing and re-creating the world. The Reverend John Ames is an exceptional figure, and it is part of the genius of *Gilead*—quite across the grain of secularist common sense exemplified in the logic of the Supreme Court's decision in *Hosanna-Tabor*—to show how a minister can be an exceptional figure and be made all the more exceptional through deep engagement with and in the shared trials and problems of collective, public, and political life.

Notes

1. The pathbreaking work on secularism that is most influential in political theory includes John Rawls, *Political Liberalism* (New York: Columbia University Press 1993); José Casanova, *Public Religions in the Modern World* (Chicago: Uni-

versity of Chicago Press, 1994); Talal Asad, *Genealogies of Religion: Discipline and Reasons of Power in Christianity and Islam* (Baltimore: Johns Hopkins University Press, 1993); Talal Asad, *Formations of the Secular: Christianity, Islam, Modernity* (Stanford: Stanford University Press, 2003); William E. Connolly, *Why I Am Not a Secularist* (Minneapolis: University of Minnesota Press, 2000); Charles Taylor, *A Secular Age* (Cambridge: Belknap Press of Harvard University Press, 2007); and Jürgen Habermas, *Between Naturalism and Religion: Philosophical Essays* (Cambridge: Polity, 2008).

2. Recent collections of essays by leading scholars include Rajeev Bhargava, ed., *Secularism and Its Critics* (New York: Oxford University Press, 1998); Michael Warner, Jonathan Van Antwerpen, and Craig Calhoun, eds., *Varieties of Secularism in a Secular Age* (Cambridge: Harvard University Press, 2010); and Anders Berg-Sorensen, *Contesting Secularism: Comparative Perspectives* (Burlington, VT: Ashgate, 2013). Recent monographs include Hussein Agrama, *Questioning Secularism: Islam, Sovereignty, and the Rule of Law in Modern Egypt* (Chicago: University of Chicago Press, 2012); Julie Cooper, *Secular Powers: Humility in Modern Political Thought* (Chicago: University of Chicago Press, 2013); and Elizabeth Pritchard, *Religion in Public: Locke's Political Theology* (Stanford: Stanford University Press, 2014).

3. See, for example, Christie L. Maloyed, "The Death of Jeremiah? Marilynne Robinson and Covenant Theology" in this volume; David A. Hollinger, "Communalist and Dispersionist Approaches to American Jewish History in an Increasingly Post-Jewish Era," *American Jewish History* 95, no. 1 (March 2009): 1–32; Todd Shy, "Religion and Marilynne Robinson," *Salmagundi* (2007): 251–64; and Christopher Leise, "'That Little Incandescence': Reading the Fragmentary and John Calvin in Marilynne Robinson's *Gilead*," *Studies in the Novel* 41, no. 3 (Fall 2009): 348–67.

4. In "Language Is Smarter Than We Are," *New York Times Book Review*, January 11, 1987, for example, Robinson discusses the preservation of "mystery" within our uses of language, scientific language included.

5. James Madison, "Memorial and Remonstrance against Religious Assessments," in *The Papers of James Madison*, vol. 8 (Chicago: University of Chicago Press, 1973): 295–306.

6. While, on the one hand, the Court is careful to frame the ministerial exception as an *exception* to the rule, and thus to constrain the autonomy of churches to a relatively narrow range of considerations, it grants churches, on the other hand, wide latitude in determining which of its employment relations will fall into this exceptional category and, more importantly, establishes the logical tie between religious freedom and institutional autonomy. What is most important is not that churches function autonomously—they are, in fact, not autonomous—but rather

that courts, citizens, and religious individuals increasingly understand, accept, and experience religion in isolation from other dimensions of social life.

7. Winnifred Sullivan's two studies, *The Impossibility of Religious Freedom* (Princeton: Princeton University Press, 2005), and *Prison Religion: Faith-Based Reform and the Constitution* (Princeton: Princeton University Press, 2009), are instructive on these points, particularly on the impossibility of avoiding a definition of religion in the law and thus a limitation of practices cognizable as exercises of religion, as well as an establishment of certain institutions but not others as religious.

8. I make this argument in greater detail in my book *Beyond Church and State: Democracy, Secularism, and Conversion* (Cambridge: Cambridge University Press, 2013).

9. I mean to note here the uncontroversial points that "evangelical" transliterates the same Greek word, "euangelion," which is translated in English as both "good news" and "Gospel," and that Christianity is typically understood to involve transmitting the contents of the Gospel. For a more controversial and yet quite powerful argument that the impersonal structure of modern public address is grounded in evangelical discourse, see Michael Warner, *The Evangelical Public Sphere in Eighteenth-Century America* (Philadelphia: University of Pennsylvania Press, forthcoming).

10. Marilynne Robinson, *Gilead* (New York: Farrar, Straus and Giroux, 2004), 3. Hereafter cited parenthetically.

11. John Calvin, "Christian Freedom, Ecclesiastical Power, and Political Administration," chap. 6 of his *Institutes of the Christian Religion: 1536 Edition*, trans. Ford Lewis Battles (Grand Rapids: Eerdmans, 1975), 176–227.

12. As discussed below, the opening chapter of Calvin's *Institutes* thematizes the insufficiency of human knowledge, and discusses the human relation to the law in terms that can be taken to analogize the human relation to language.

13. Calvin, *Institutes (1536)*, 68.

14. Ibid., 69.

15. Marilynne Robinson, "Language is Smarter Than We Are," *New York Times Book Review*, January 11, 1987, 8.

16. Ibid.

17. Leise, "'That Little Incandescence,'" 349.

18. Ibid., 359, citing Calvin's *Institutes*, vol. 1, chap. 5.

19. Ibid., 348, citing Calvin's *Institutes* vol. 1, chap. 5.

20. The *Institutes* grows over time, as does this discussion, but it is present in some form from the first edition to the last.

21. Calvin, *Institutes (1536)*, 15.

22. Calvin, *Institutes of the Christian Religion*, vol. 1 [1559 ed.], trans. Henry Beveridge (Grand Rapids: Eerdmans, 1983), 38.

23. Ibid., 38.

24. Calvin, *Institutes (1536)*, 16.

25. Jonathan Edwards, "Sinners in the Hands of an Angry God," in *A Jonathan Edwards Reader*, ed. John E. Smith, Harry S. Stout, and Kenneth P. Minkema (New Haven: Yale University Press 1995), 89–104.

26. Calvin, *Institutes (1536)*, 42.

27. Recent work on the connections between faith and democratic practice includes Patrick Deneen, *Democratic Faith* (Princeton: Princeton University Press, 2005); Cornel West, *Democracy Matters: Winning the Fight against Imperialism* (New York: Penguin, 2005); Stanley Hauerwas and Romand Coles, *Christianity, Democracy, and the Radical Ordinary: Conversations between a Radical Democrat and a Christian* (Eugene, OR: Cascade, 2008); George Shulman, *American Prophecy: Race and Redemption in American Political Culture* (Minneapolis: University of Minnesota Press, 2008); and Jeffery Stout, *Blessed Are the Organized: Grassroots Democracy in America* (Princeton: Princeton University Press, 2010).

28. Robert Bellah, "Civil Religion in America," *Dædalus* 96 (Winter 1967): 1–21; Alexis de Tocqueville, *Democracy in America* (New Yorker: Harper Perennial, 2006).

CHAPTER 7

The Death of Jeremiah?

Marilynne Robinson and Covenant Theology

Christie L. Maloyed

American Puritanism has been marked by the rhetorical tradition of the jeremiad. Often delivered as fiery sermons, jeremiads were used as a rebuke against moral decline and as a call for repentance and reformation. Early American Puritans believed that God had charged them with a special spiritual and moral mission and that if they failed to uphold their end of the bargain, God would punish them. Although there are few defenders of this fiery and apocalyptic vision of Puritanism today, the Pulitzer Prize–winning novelist and essayist Marilynne Robinson has worked to reclaim parts of this tradition. Despite her professed dedication to reviving the religious and political thought of John Calvin and Jonathan Edwards, though, the fundamental Puritan idea of an elect community charged with a special purpose is noticeably absent in her work. In her collection of essays on theology, *The Death of Adam,* she clearly laments the cynicism and lack of reverence that characterize the modern era, but she never suggests that current Americans are, or even that they were, in a state of covenant with God. In her literary works, especially her 2004 novel *Gilead,* she explicitly champions Calvinism but depicts the failures of the jeremiad tradition of preaching. Moreover, the community of Gilead, Iowa, is not held up as a city on a hill governed by a special moral purpose, nor, for that matter, is the country more broadly. In her work, Robinson is more concerned with a reverence for human exceptionalism than for American exceptionalism.

Robinson's effort to rescue Puritanism moves the tradition toward a more inclusive theology and political ideology. This essay traces the diminished role of covenant theology and the jeremiad in Robinson's works as she attempts to offer her readers a less fervent version of Calvinism. In her reworking of the jeremiad, Robinson strikes some of the same notes as the Puritans, but not the full chord. Her effort to make Puritanism more tolerant and focused on the universal human experience is, at times, at odds with the tradition of Puritan political thought. Moreover, her emphasis on the liberal elements of Calvinist thought provides an incomplete picture of the Puritan tradition within American history. Robinson's efforts to correct the negative image of Puritanism go so far as to downplay or ignore any injustices associated with the Puritans. In doing so, her work rightly corrects some common misunderstandings of their theology, but it also revises and sanitizes some of the less liberal aspects of their history and rhetoric. The end result is a view of Puritanism that is more compatible with twenty-first-century mores but one that obscures some of the fundamental teachings and problems associated with that tradition.

Marilynne Robinson: A Modern-Day Puritan

Today not only do Puritans have a reputation as sour and dour, but it is also difficult to find defenders of their theology among popular authors and public intellectuals. This is not to say that Calvinism is dead; far from it, in fact. Congregationalist and Presbyterian churches remain active in the United States along with numerous Calvinist colleges and seminaries. In 2006, *Christianity Today* even published a special issue focused on the rise of reformed theology among young Christians.[1] Despite this, the revival of Puritanism is far from mainstream, even among the conservative Christian movement. But Marilynne Robinson has always fancied herself something of a contrarian.

Robinson's interest in Calvinism is apparent in both her essays and her literary works. Her first extended effort to provide a written defense of Puritan ideas came in her collection of essays *The Death of Adam: Essays on Modern Thought.* In this volume, Robinson's overarching task is to explain how modern thought has been dominated by a scientific view that excludes any religious perspective, and how that exclusion has affected our perception of social and human values. This subject may seem like a horse that has been beaten to death, but Robinson offers a measured and contrarian perspective that breathes new life into this old debate. The title refers to the success of Darwinism in eradicating the teachings of the Book of Genesis, specifically its account of the creation of the earth and humanity. In doing so, Robinson argues, Darwinism discounts the long-standing view of humans as exceptional creatures endowed with the unique capacity for self-reflection and the responsibility to act as stewards of God's creation. With this revolution in modern thought, Darwinism paved the way for values to be defined in economic, not religious or moral, terms.[2]

Robinson's preferred alternative to the scientism of the twentieth century is a return to a tempered and revised Calvinism. She takes up the themes of Calvin throughout *The Death of Adam*, with two essays specifically focused on John Calvin. Paradoxically, Robinson hides their central theme by giving both pieces the title "Marguerite de Navarre" (174–226). In these essays Robinson explains that, given the intellectual and historical baggage with which Calvin's legacy has been saddled, she did not feel comfortable titling the pieces with his name; rather, she chooses the name of his French patroness. In fact, Robinson goes so far as to reject the English spelling of his name and instead uses the original French spelling, *Jean Cauvin*. She attempts to situate Calvin's theology within the greater Christian tradition and the theological debates of his day, especially on contentious matters such as the fall of man, predestination, and the doctrine of total depravity. Little-known aspects of Calvin's theology are also emphasized such as his dedication to liberal education, his lack of attention to the role of Eve in the Fall and also to Satan, and his support for resisting rulers who require subjects to disobey God.

Robinson is also at pains to rescue the reputation of Calvin's theological heirs, the American Puritans, in her essay "Puritans and Prigs," in which she rejects pernicious stereotypes and also paints a corrective picture of Puritan theology. Conventional wisdom portrays Puritans as joyless, fire-breathing evangelizers warning listeners of the eternal consequences of sin. However, Robinson contends this image is far from justified:

> I can say they [the Puritans] are by no means characterized by, for example, fear or hatred of the body, anxiety about sex, or denigration of women. This cannot be said of Christian tradition in general, yet for some reason Puritanism is uniquely regarded as synonymous with these preoccupations. Puritans are thought to have taken a lurid pleasure in the notion of hell, and certainly hell seems to have been much in their thoughts, though not more than it was in the thoughts of

> Dante, for example. We speak as though John Calvin invented the Fall of Man, when that was an article of faith universal in Christian culture. (*Adam*, 151)

In place of these images, Robinson emphasizes the "highly elaborated moral, religious, intellectual, and political tradition" established by Calvin that gave rise to "great universities and cultural institutions and an enlightened political order" in America (150). Robinson draws attention to some of the cultural and political legacies that can be tied to Puritan practices, especially in New England, that have been regrettably ignored. These include an emphasis on youth education and literacy; democratic elements of governance both in civil and church institutions; and early support for abolitionism that spread to the Midwest.[3]

What accounts for the disconnect between the modern image of Calvin and the Puritans and their actual teachings? For Robinson, the problem is twofold. First, the displacement of religious thinking and values by scientific thinking in the eighteenth and nineteenth centuries led to a general dismissal of any and all religious ways of thinking. The second problem is that reformed theology was largely informed by biblical scripture, particularly the Old Testament, which is now often taken to represent exclusionary, hierarchical, and patriarchal systems of power. In fact, Robinson declares that by the early twentieth century, Puritanism "appears . . . to have died" (*Adam*, 150).

Robinson is careful to note that she does not see the Puritan reliance on the Old Testament as a problem itself, only that the public today sees it as problematic. In fact, she contends that along with many other canonical works, most readers encounter the Old Testament only through cherry-picked quotes used to demonstrate how the scriptures represent a backward worldview; however, the full text is actually rarely read, let alone studied. As she explains in her most recent collection of essays, *When I Was a Child I Read Books,* rather than as a collection of works dedicated to a legalistic culture hell-bent on punishing miscreants, Robinson views the Old Testament as a work that champions the poor and commands compassion:

> Modern assumptions about the Old Testament, now an unread classic, make it seem an improbable source for economic and social idealism. In fact, it is more insistent than Marx ever was in championing the

> poor and the oppressed. Its influence is thought to have made New Englanders severe, yet Jonathan Edwards (1703–1758), who is taken to personify their severity, preached an absolute obligation to assist the needy—before their need became urgent, before they were compelled to seek help, despite any question of their own worthiness or of the responsibility of relatives or others to assist them.[4]

Not only does she argue that the Old Testament has been unread and misread, but she goes further to argue that Calvinism is "uniquely the *fons et origio* of Christian liberalism in the modern period . . . and that liberalism has had its origins largely in the Old Testament." While she notes that this claim goes "very much against the grain of historical consensus," her effort to restore the intellectual legacy of the Puritans' reading of the Old Testament fits with other recent scholarly efforts to acknowledge the political and religious contributions of reformed theology, especially within the American context.[5] But while covenant theology and the jeremiad formed a basis for Puritan discourse in the American colonial period, Robinson ignores, discounts, or revises these aspects of the tradition.

This is not to say that Robinson needs to follow Calvin and the Puritans in every particular, just as a person need not agree entirely with Aristotle to be an Aristotelian. In fact, Robinson is clear that even the Puritans departed from Calvin on issues such as revivalism, requirements for church membership and communion, and their interest in Satan. Robinson's project regarding Calvinism appears twofold. First, she attempts to recover ignored elements of Calvin's thought from historical misinterpretation. Second, Robinson uses Calvinism as an intellectual resource to buttress a reworked version of covenant theology for the modern world. Robinson's reading of Calvinism is meant to restore the reputation of the tradition and use that tradition to support a modern, liberal Christianity, though there is debate about just how far Robinson pushes this theology.

Scholarly treatments of Robinson's religious views have thus far been limited, but they offer competing interpretations regarding her use of Calvin. Among those who argue that Robinson overextends Calvin is Todd Shy, who has argued that many of her concerns would have been alien to Calvin himself: "Robinson's theology reflects modern priorities in its elevation of social justice and ethics to thrones formally occupied by less concrete debates" such as those over the Eucharist.[6] This is not to say that Robinson and

Calvin would have been at irresolvable odds with one another but rather that Calvin is a somewhat unusual and unexpected choice of allies. As Shy queries, "But are there no thinkers who write well and are ambitious about human possibility that are closer to the vision Robinson portrays?"[7] By this view, there are many other thinkers Robinson could have drawn upon to support the idea that the most fundamental teaching of Christianity is to live a humble, simple life that is dedicated to serving those in need.

By contrast, other scholars have found more of an affinity between Robinson and Calvin. For instance, Thomas Davis has argued that Robinson offers a "nimble reading of John Calvin and his legacy . . . daring the reader to contradict her, commanding the reader to actually *read*."[8] Where previous legions have criticized Calvin and the Puritans for being repressive, Robinson argues they were either not that different from other Christians of the era, and on some counts, actually more progressive. Davis does express a concern with Robinson's approach, one that I share. Robinson cites neither primary nor secondary sources for many of her arguments. Several of her historical claims—for instance, that the Puritans were more egalitarian in their treatment of women, that they did not show greater concern with hell than other Christians, and that they did not express hatred of the physical world—are never referenced to specific Calvinist or Puritan writings or to historical scholarship on the subject.

In a similar vein to Davis, Christopher Leise has also emphasized the affinity between Calvin and Robinson, but Leise argues that her works approach religion as a fluid way of thinking. As he puts it, Robinson "is consciously reading the Puritan tradition against itself, which too often has the effect of over-amplifying the minor-key notes in Puritanism's historically elegiac understandings of Calvin's writing."[9] From this perspective, Robinson isn't revising Puritanism; she is simply pulling out elements that were already latent, but certainly not prominent, within the tradition.

Robinson's approach to Calvinism is to emphasize some elements of his theology over others. Given that Calvin's *Institutes* alone spans more than one thousand pages, not to mention his individual commentaries on the books of the Bible, there are many legitimate choices to make about which aspects are most central to his overall theology. In this regard, Leise is persuasive when he argues that Robinson's project is aimed at offering a "better model" of Calvinistic thinking.[10] While Davis and Leise are correct to argue that Robinson offers a necessary and corrective view of Calvin and the Puritans, her interpretation also ignores and excludes some of the more contentious aspects of the tradition.

One example is Robinson's argument that Puritan teachings on charitable actions have been overshadowed by claims that they were obsessed with teachings on damnation. She is correct that the Puritans preached in favor of generosity and liberality, but they also preached jeremiads that threatened hellfire and brimstone as consequences of breaching the covenant with God. The Puritans were not the only Christians to express an interest in hell, as Robinson rightly notes, but it is also important to acknowledge that hell was of special importance to their theology. The image of hell was used as a rhetorical tool to try to inspire collective repentance during periods of covenant renewal. Robinson's own favorite Puritan, Jonathan Edwards, is best known for his fiery jeremiads that used the imagery of hell to inspire listeners to awaken and repent. He explicitly argued, for instance, that the eternal damnation of sinners to hell is the greatest evidence of God's glory and confirmation of his infinite justice.[11] Edwards's religious musings went beyond reflections on hell, but it would be wrong to ignore the role hell played in his theology.

Likewise, Robinson attempts to correct the popular view of the holier-than-thou Puritan sure of his own position as part of the elect. While this may be accurate, Robinson does not discuss the Puritans' argument that they were an exceptional and chosen people. Although she writes on American history and politics as particularly worthy of study, she does not write about them in the sense of religious exceptionalism, as chosen and protected under a special covenant with God. However, this is how the Puritans understood themselves.[12] Ignoring this aspect of their theology makes the Puritans appear far more inclusive than they actually were. Quite famously, Anne Hutchinson and Roger Williams were run out of Puritan Massachusetts for challenging the ideas of those who were considered to be part of the elect.[13]

In a similar vein, Robinson seeks to make Puritanism an inclusive theological movement by claiming that, along with the Congregationalist and Presbyterians, the Quakers were also Puritans (*Adam,* 151–52). She ignores, however, that Quakers were publicly beaten, whipped, exiled, and in at least in four cases, executed by the Puritans of New England for their failure to adhere to Puritan theology, leading the Quakers to accuse the Puritans of hypocrisy concerning religious liberty.[14] Robinson does not discuss these instances in Puritan history, and she seems satisfied to say that the Puritans were no more inclined toward persecution than other Christians of the day. Rather than ignore these acts of persecution, they need to be contextualized and, where appropriate, repudiated.

Even beyond her revised version of Puritan history, Robinson's defense of Christianity generally seems resistant to self-criticism. For example, *Gilead* presents a Christian town where "lots of people were there to be anti-slavery by any means that came to hand."[15] But as Christopher Douglas has rightly observed, *Gilead*'s critique of slavery "is marked by an evasion of the historical lesson that Christianity provided a vocabulary not just for the abolitionists (like Douglass and John Brown) but also for slavery's supporters (like Furman)."[16] By ignoring inconvenient strains within the tradition, the history of Christianity is purified.

Likewise, there is much we can infer from what Robinson doesn't consider in her essays. She depicts religion as a driving moral force in American history, to the extent that one is left to consider the implication that secular movements lack moral grounding. When she tackles scientism, she takes Darwin, Nietzsche, and Freud as the banner men of the tradition. Lenin and Stalin stand in for virtually all twentieth-century socialism. As William Deresiewicz has noted, her choices about which American histories to tell have missed much: "The great tide of immigration is missing from Robinson's narrative, and so are two presidents named Roosevelt. Progressivism is missing. Liberalism is missing. Trustbusting, Social Security and the Voting Rights Act are missing."[17] Though tackling each of these simplifications or omissions is beyond the scope of this paper, it points to an overall trend in Robinson's approach to history. When it comes to Christian history, she sanitizes the unsavory bits. When secular history is involved, she tends to either build straw men out of complicated and contested dialogues (for example, evolution) or to ignore secular contributions to progressive movements.

In ignoring these aspects of Puritanism, Robinson offers an incomplete picture, one that revises rather than corrects our understanding of their history and theology. By gaining a better understanding of the Puritans' reliance on covenant theology and the jeremiad, it becomes easier to see why they were so interested in hell, why they believed God would punish sin in the temporal world, and why they were willing to persecute those who they believed were sinful. To understand how Robinson has modified the Calvinist tradition, the following section explores her approach to the jeremiad in her novel *Gilead*.

Gilead and the Jeremiad

The central character of *Gilead* is the aging Reverend John Ames, whose life has been spent as a Congregational minister in the rural town of Gilead, Iowa. The novel is a meditative epistle written as an attempt to impart a lifetime's worth of reflection and insight for his young son to read when he is grown, after his father has died. The letter acts as a memoir of Ames's life, a third-generation minister following in the footsteps of his grandfather and father, both named John Ames.

Though all the Ames men shared the same profession, their theologies differ in remarkable ways. Ames's grandfather is a portrait of Puritan severity. A committed abolitionist, he fought alongside John Brown, lost one eye in battle, and continued to preach with even greater fervency. As Leise has correctly assessed in his analysis of *Gilead*, "in typically Puritan style, the eldest Ames is defined almost as much by what he rejects as by what he believes."[18] Though he closely followed the Puritan commands regarding generosity, including giving essential family belongings away to neighbors, he is portrayed as a principled but misguided figure. Though a source of comfort to others in the community, he is a negligent father to his own family. Grandfather Ames's commitment to the war was so alienating to his own son that the second John Ames became a lifelong pacifist.

To the end of his life, Grandfather Ames remains committed to the central element of American puritanical rhetoric, the jeremiad. Jeremiads trace their history back to the Old Testament's Book of Jeremiah, wherein the prophet Jeremiah is tasked by God with delivering His message to the wayward nation of Israel. In short, Jeremiah reminded the people that they had made a covenant with God whereby He would protect them so long as they worshiped Him exclusively. However, as Jeremiah described with vivid imagery, Israel had become a "harlot with many lovers" and had polluted the land with their "whoredoms and wickedness."[19] Jeremiah informed Israel that God had called upon them to repent of their apostasy and reform their sinful ways. Eventually God promised a new covenant under which he would lead Israel anew and would forgive all their iniquities.

Although virtually every culture and era has a rhetorical tradition that juxtaposes moral decline against some "golden era," the Old Testament jeremiad is distinct in that it is tied directly to Israel's covenant with God. The jeremiad is used to call the chosen people to repent and return to the terms of a specific covenant. In fact, jeremiads became a familiar formulation for sermons and followed a distinct pattern. As Andrew Murphy explains, the Puritan jeremiads always contained three discrete parts. First, they "identify problems that show a decline vis-à-vis the past"; then they "identify turning points" to explain when the decline began; and finally, they "call for reform, repentance, or renewal."[20]

On its surface, the jeremiad can appear to be a rather gloomy form of rhetoric. By emphasizing how much better things were in the past and how recent problems, including internal conflict, war, sickness, failing crops, etc., are the direct result of the sins of the community, the overwhelming message appears to be one of decline. Nevertheless, the take-home message, according to Murphy, is actually one of forgiveness and opportunity: "The jeremiad was always intended as a call to action, an exhortation to reform the community back into the image of its founders and godly ancestors, and *never* as an invitation to pessimism and resignation."[21] In this way, the jeremiad serves as a blueprint for corrective action. The audience must first be reminded of what went wrong before they can hope to repent and reform, but reformation is always the end goal.[22]

In *Gilead*, the jeremiad is associated with Grandfather Ames, who frequently reminds his congregants how the church used to be more active, passionate, and generous and calls on his listeners to repent and reform. When invited to speak at a Fourth of July celebration, the elderly Ames delivers a sermon that admonishes his audience to keep up the cause of liberty and recommit to the principles of radicalism. Though a short sermon, it boils down the jeremiad to its barest essentials:

> Children—When I was a young man the Lord came to me and put His hand just here on my right shoulder. I can feel it still. And He spoke to me, very clearly. The words went right through me. He said, Free the captive. Preach good news to the poor. Proclaim liberty throughout the land. That is all Scripture, of course, and the words were already very familiar to me at the time. But it is clear enough why He would feel they needed special emphasis. No one lives by them, unless the Lord

> takes him in hand. Certainly I did not, until the day He stood beside me and spoke those words to me.
>
> I would call that experience a vision. We had visions in those days, a number of us did. Your young men will have visions and your old men will dream dreams. And now all those young men are old, if they're alive at all, and their visions are no more than dreams, and the old days are forgotten. We fly forgotten as a dream, as it says in the old hymn, and our dreams are forgotten long before we are.
>
> The President, General Grant, once called Iowa the shining star of radicalism. But what is left here in Iowa? What is left here in Gilead? Dust. Dust and ashes. Scripture says the people perish, and they certainly do. It is remarkable. For all this His anger is not turned away, but His Hand is stretched out still.
>
> The Lord bless you and keep you, etc. (175–76)

In his sermon, Grandfather Ames follows the standard form of the jeremiad. He begins by identifying problems to show a decline from the past. In a previous generation, God charged Grandfather Ames, and by implication Christians more generally, to "Free the captive. Preach good news to the poor. Proclaim liberty throughout the land." This they did, but now that "shining star of radicalism" is but "dust and ashes." The turning point is also identified as the time when the new generation stopped listening to God's message, hence there are no more visions, and "the old days are forgotten." Lastly, the sermon ends on a note of redemption, not despair, emphasizing that God's "hand is stretched out still" despite His anger with His people. Taken together, this sermon provides a concise picture of the jeremiad form of preaching.

Despite the zeal that fuels this jeremiad, Grandfather Ames's optimism is deeply tested, and he expresses "doubt that it did much good." The audience for the celebration reinforces his conclusion. Among the few in the crowd who even bothered to pay attention to his sermon, "there was a little laughter of the kind you hear when the outlandishness of a thing is being generally agreed on" (176). Robinson uses this example of Grandfather Ames to show that the Puritan jeremiad is a dying form of rhetoric, much like the aging grandfather himself, that no longer holds the power to sway a modern audience. This is not to say that Robinson herself is condemning the form or content of Grandfather Ames's sermon, only that she is supporting her own claim that Puritanism dwindled and eventually expired in the early twentieth century (*Adam,* 150).

By contrast, the narrator John Ames struggles to come to terms with this fiery Puritan legacy. Much like his grandfather before him, Ames is pushed toward the jeremiad tradition of preaching when confronted with the effects of war. Whereas his grandfather was compelled to war by the righteousness of the cause of abolition, the youngest Ames is driven to preach against the needless deaths of the Great War. In his frustration, Ames composes a sermon to rebuke his congregation, and Americans more generally, for their involvement in the war. The resulting sermon follows the jeremiad tradition closely:

> I said . . . these deaths were rescuing foolish young men from the consequences of their own ignorance and courage, that the Lord was gathering them in before they could go off and commit murder against their brothers. And I said that their deaths were a sign and a warning to the rest of us that the desire for war would bring the consequences of war, because there is no ocean big enough to protect us from the Lord's judgment when we decide to hammer our plowshares into swords and our pruning hooks into spears, in contempt of the will and the grace of God. (42)

In this sermon, Ames invokes the tradition of the jeremiad when he claims that God is punishing his people, specifically with the Spanish flu, for the sin of unnecessarily entering the war. His goal is to get his congregants to repent of the sin of supporting the war. But as a sharp point of contrast with his grandfather, Ames chooses to burn the sermon before he delivers it. Knowing that only the mothers and wives of soldiers would be his audience in the pews, and that they already likely agreed that the war was unnecessary, he concluded, "I seemed ridiculous to myself for imagining I could thunder from the pulpit in those circumstances," for "Mirabelle Mercer [one of the congregants] was not Pontius Pilate, and she was not Woodrow Wilson, either" (42–43). The decision to not deliver the sermon shows a turning point from the jeremiad.

Ames's rejection of the jeremiad, in Leise's view, is an intentional departure from the caricature of Puritan theology: "Instead of dangling his parishioners over the figurative flames of hell, in the way that Jonathan

Edwards does in 'Sinners in the Hands of an Angry God,' he [Ames] drops his own jeremiad into a common household fire in the kitchen stove."[23] The contrast between Edwards and Ames is apt, especially since Edwards is typically taken to be one of the most fierce and hell-bent among reformed theologians. Leise laments, and rightly so, that "it is a shame that most Americans, if they know anything about Jonathan Edwards, know only 'Sinners.'"[24] Among his other works, Edwards composed complex and eloquent pieces of theology reflecting on the nature of virtue and the majesty of beauty, and these are the works of Edwards that most influenced Robinson.

Ames notes in speaking of his uncle, who was named after Jonathan Edwards, that Edwards "was much revered in my grandfather's generation" (86). By the time Ames is composing his letter to his son, World War II had concluded, scientific inquiry now dominates religious thinking, and Puritanism is dead. The hellfire brand of the jeremiad has passed away. The causal arrows here are muddled. Did Puritanism die because the fiery style of preaching was abandoned? This seems to be a conclusion to which Grandfather Ames would surely be amenable. Perhaps the damage wrought by the Civil War and its aftermath irrevocably shook the faith of the residents of Gilead? Or was the change in modern thinking so transformative as to render Puritanism obsolete? John Ames seems willing to blame the invention of modern radio and television for "sowing a good deal of confusion where theology is concerned" (208).[25] His suggestion to correct this problem is the same one offered by Robinson in her essays; he reads to his congregants from the *Institutes,* letting Calvin speak for himself (208). Regardless of the cause, there is a sense of lament at the passing of what Grandfather Ames stood for. As John Ames writes to his son, "I believe the old reverend's errors were mainly the consequence of a sort of strenuousness in ethical matters that was to be admired finally" (90). He concludes his letter to his son on a nostalgic tone that evokes a longing for the strenuous ethics of his grandfather to be reinvigorated: "What have I to leave you but the ruins of old courage, and the lore of old gallantry and hope? Well, as I have said, it is all an ember now, and the good Lord will surely someday breathe it into flame again" (246). This echoes the same sentiment found at the end of Grandfather Ames's sermon suggesting that the hand of God is outstretched still and offers hope that Puritan teachings and rhetoric may one day be revived.

The theology offered by John Ames is one that is more Calvinistic than specifically Puritan, in that he does not rely on the jeremiad or ideas that America is a nation under a special covenant. Ames celebrates the exceptional nature of humanity, the necessity of social justice, and takes the beauty of the natural world as evidence of the divine. His is not a fierce rhetoric that emphasizes hell and God's wrath, and in this, he parts company from his grandfather, Jonathan Edwards, and the Puritan legacy. To better understand how Robinson herself revises Puritanism, it is necessary to look to her essays and her understanding of covenant theology.

The Puritan Link between Covenant Theology and the Jeremiad

The most complete perspective Robinson offers on Puritan history and how Americans have moved away from that tradition is her essay "Puritans and Prigs." In this piece, she is at pains to contrast the devout and humble nature of Puritan thinking with the selfishness and priggishness that characterizes modern thought. She claims that one of the central differences between the two cultures is that the Puritans believed their personal actions were noted and judged by God. As she expresses the difference: "When crops failed in Northampton, Massachusetts, in 1743, Jonathan Edwards of course told his congregation that they had their own wickedness to blame for it. They had failed to do justice (his word) to the poor. He said, 'Christian people are to give to others not only so as to lift him above extremity but liberally to furnish him'" (*Adam*, 151). This type of reasoning is foreign to most modern minds.

The logic that underpins the Puritans' way of thinking is based in covenant theology. Edwards used the rhetoric of the jeremiad to explain why calamities happened: when the people break the covenant, God punishes their disobedience. If they repent and act justly toward one another, the covenant will be reaffirmed. Robinson is also clear that covenant theology anticipates that breaches will occur, but these were opportunities for repentance and reformation: "When things went wrong in Calvinist America, the minister or mayor or governor or president, including of course Lincoln, would declare a Day of Fasting and Humiliation, during which businesses and offices closed and the population went to their various churches to figure out what they were doing wrong and how to repent of it" (*Adam*, 155). In this way, God's punishment can be seen as an opportunity to change; it is a cause not for despair but for hope.

The covenant was the centerpiece of reformed political thought and drew from the Old Testament tradition to support the idea that God made covenants with groups of people. According to reformed theology, God created covenants to ensure that his Kingdom of New Jerusalem would be realized. God rewarded his people if they upheld their end of the covenant. If they failed, however, he would punish them collectively. For instance, in his sermon "Impending Judgments Averted Only by Reformation," Edwards interprets an October 1727 earthquake as a warning sign of more calamitous punishments to come if the people do not repent of their sins. Edwards stresses that even the righteous will be punished for tolerating the sins of their neighbors.[26]

Covenant theology held a central position in reformed thinking from its inception, but it took on special meaning with the migration to the New England colonies.[27] Drawing from the work of Calvin, American Puritans touted America as the "New Israel." For instance, in a 1663 election-day sermon in Boston, John Higginson preached that the practice of true religion "was the cause of God and Israel then, the same is the cause of God and his people now."[28] Urian Oakes even used the term "New England Israel" in his 1673 Boston election-day sermon calling the people to repent of their "sundry unchristian and crooked ways" and renew the covenant.[29]

The covenant was central to American expressions of Puritanism as it informed their understanding of their spiritual mission. As Perry Miller has famously described in his book *Errand into the Wilderness* (1956), the New England Puritans believed that their mission was sacred and directed by God, and they hoped their work would culminate in the purification of the Anglican Church.[30] As Sacvan Bercovitch has noted, they identified themselves as "a 'peculiar people,' a company of Christians not only called but chosen, and chosen not only for heaven but as instruments of a sacred historical design. Their church-state was to be at once a model to the world of Reformed Christianity and a prefiguration of New Jerusalem to come."[31] The emphasis on the covenant began even before the Puritans had landed on American soil. In his speech given on the *Arbella* while still waiting to land ashore in New England, John Winthrop reminded his listeners that they were "entered into covenant with Him for this work"; if they failed to live up to their responsibilities, he warned, "the Lord will surely break out in wrath against us, and be revenged of such a people, and make us know the price of the breach of such a covenant."[32] Given that the American Puritans viewed themselves as founding a "New Israel," it is of little surprise that when they were concerned that their own relationship with God was being compromised, they adopted the jeremiad tradition to remind listeners of the consequences of breaking the covenant.

What made the American Puritans' use of the jeremiad distinctive was that it was a tool to remind the community of their chosen status. This jeremiad represents the first rhetorical expression of the idea of American exceptionalism. As Murphy explains, "What makes the American jeremiad American is its connection to a larger, sacred story tied intimately to the particularities of the nation's origins and development."[33] Because of their view of themselves as the New Israel, John Winthrop and later Puritans chose the image of the American experiment as a "city upon a hill" to set an example of righteous living to the rest of the world. With great expectations comes great responsibility—and also the possibility of great retribution. As a result, the Puritans' faith in the covenant was not the equivalent of blind or arrogant patriotism. There was a real sense of fear that if they did not fulfill the covenant—living righteous lives by rejecting worldliness, luxury, and selfishness—they would be subjected to God's punishment.[34]

The theme of America as a chosen nation loomed particularly large in the preaching of Edwards. For instance, in his sermon "Sin and Wickedness," he claimed, "Many have been the special and distinguishing favors that the nation from the first Reformation, and indeed from the first promulgation of the gospel in it, has been blessed with," but he was also quick to warn that the nation had become "exceedingly corrupted and degenerated."[35] In the typical form of the jeremiad, Edwards contrasts the current state of affairs with a more sanctified past. He recounts the current sins found in America—impiety, Deism, profaneness, licentiousness, debauchery, and political corruption, among others—and he foretells of divine punishments on the nation to follow, namely, he predicts a cataclysmic earthquake. He concludes by calling the people to pray for mercy and repent continually, not only on fast days. The imagery is vivid and violent including having the wicked "overthrown and swallowed up in that earthquake" and warning that "God's fire will pass over the earth" in retribution.[36] The overall tone of the sermon is that America as a nation was given special status and hence special rewards, but by turning toward wickedness, its people are inviting divine wrath and possibly the apocalypse.

This way of thinking may unsettle a modern audience not accustomed to conceiving of natural disasters as proof of God's existence, let alone proof that God is judging his chosen people for their communal moral failings.[37] To be clear, Robinson never actually claims that she believes this either. She remains silent on whether or not the Puritans were a chosen people who had entered into a special covenant with God to establish a New Israel. However, she is clear that the Puritans saw themselves in a special relationship with God whereby they were rewarded and punished for their actions. The point of Robinson's "Puritans and Prigs," and in many ways the larger mission of *The Death of Adam,* is to show how far we have removed ourselves from this mind-set. Of our own time, she declares: "No one bothers us now with the notion that our own failures in this line might be called sinful, though we fall far short of the standard that in Edwards's view invited divine wrath. Nor does anyone suggest that punishment might follow such failures, though the case could easily be made that our whole community is punished for them every day. In one respect at least we have rid ourselves entirely of Puritanism" (*Adam,* 151). Her point is that Americans no longer believe they are held to collective standards of morality or that a failure to uphold moral obligations will be met with collective strife.

If Puritanism is dead, especially the logic of covenant theology that implies that sins are punished collectively, what, if anything, has taken its place? For Robinson, modern society has moved toward a more individual sense of identity and morality and rejected communal definitions of these values. In her view, the rejection of spiritual understanding in favor of scientism has led to a near obsession with individualism. She characterizes this change in terms of a disease: "I suggest that, for us, the sense of sickness has replaced the sense of sin, to which it was always near allied, and that while we are acutely aware of the difficulties surrounding notions of good and evil, we ignore, though they are manifest, the equally great difficulties surrounding notions of sickness and health, especially as these judgments are applied to behavior" (*Adam,* 83). The Puritan prescription for feelings of alienation and despair would have been to repent and turn toward a life of generosity, humility, and simplicity. Modern science offers its treatment in the form of prescription medications.

We have become so far removed from the Puritan way of thinking that the idea has been entirely abandoned that responsibility to each other is a divine command that will be met with divine wrath if ignored. Rather, responsibility is conceived in terms of our obligations to ourselves. Hence,

Robinson would argue the covenant is no longer a part of modern thought. Even though Robinson declares her "heart is with the Puritans," her own response to the modern world does not follow the Puritan form of the jeremiad (*Adam,* 165). The following section explores how the jeremiad and covenant theology are adapted, revised, and in some cases rejected as Robinson draws inspiration from the Puritans in developing her own version of Calvinism.

Robinson's Revisionist Calvinism

Robinson is wistful when she writes about the Puritan past, but she expresses a hesitancy to play the role of prophet and perhaps the role of historian as well. Not all her readers share my view of her work, however. For instance, in his review of *The Death of Adam* and *Gilead,* Pastor Lawrence Wood declared that he admired "the brave unfashionableness of her essays, they are jeremiads."[38] But too often the term "jeremiad" is used to refer to any denunciation of contemporary society that valorizes some past generation. Using precise historical and academic distinctions can help make sense of how this genre of speech emerged and evolved. In the historical sense, jeremiads as a rhetorical tradition developed by the American Puritans explain the occurrence of specific problems in terms of particular sins committed. The audience is asked to repent of those sins and to renew their specific covenant with God. If there is no covenant, though, the jeremiad is merely, as Perry Miller described it, "an incessant and never successful cry for repentance."[39]

Although *The Death of Adam* is a sustained and eloquent lament about the state of modern thinking, it is inappropriate to call it a jeremiad, at least within the tradition of Puritan rhetoric. Robinson never calls her readers to repent of their sins in order to avoid the wrath of God as early Puritans did. Instead, she stresses that if modern people were to rededicate themselves to Puritan values—such as compassion, forgiveness, caring for the poor, responsible stewardship of environmental resources, etc.—they would avoid alienation and ecological collapse. She expresses a social rather than strictly religious covenant. Robinson's characterization of her own essays is instructive: "They are, all of them, contrarian in method and spirit. They assert, in one way or another, that the prevailing view of things can be assumed to be wrong, and that its opposite, being its image or shadow, can also be assumed to be wrong. They undertake to demonstrate that there are other ways of thinking, for which better arguments can be made" (*Adam,* 1). Given the sustained intensity of her project, it is easy to understand how the contrarian nature of the work could be mistaken as a jeremiad. But Robinson resists this characterization. Though her essays juxtapose historical ways of thinking with our own, she insists that she is not trying to valorize the past and vilify the present: "I do not wish to suggest in these essays that the past was better than the present, simply that whatever in the past happens to have been of significance or value ought to be held in memory, insofar as that is possible, so that it can give us guidance. . . . So when I find fault I am not suggesting decline. The vices of the present appear in many cases to be failed correctives to vices of the past" (*Adam,* 5–6).

Hence, Robinson rejects explicitly one of the key features of the jeremiad, namely establishing that moral decline has occurred in America since the time of the Puritans.

On the one hand, she is convincing when she claims that she is not trying to declare that we are in a state of perpetual decline. In fact, she finds modern-day heroes in the abolitionists, in the German Lutheran resisters of the Nazis, and in the lives of numerous other citizens of western America. However, Robinson sometimes strikes a tone that appears downright apocalyptic, in the classic sense of the term, meaning that she anticipates a complete societal collapse. For instance, she claims in an off-handed manner: "One need not have an especially excitable or a particularly gloomy nature to be persuaded that we may be approaching the end of the day" (245). Despite the recent preponderance of dystopian films and literature, it is not clear that the view that the end is nigh is widely shared.

Though she forecasts the end of days, this does not mean that Robinson is issuing a jeremiad. Apocalyptic rhetoric is used to warn an audience that the end is near; whether or not that end can be avoided is a different matter altogether. By contrast, the jeremiad attempts to explain problems or punishments that are already under way in light of past transgressions and calls the listener to repent and resubmit to the covenant. Despite her claim that she was not writing about the decline of the nation, Robinson contrasts the Puritan past and the secular present in a way that challenges her own assertion. She offers the following assessment of the current American mind-set:

> The assumption of present responsibility for the present state of things was a ritual feature of life in this culture for two and a half centuries,

> and is entirely forgotten by us now. Though I cannot take time to make the argument for it here, it is my belief that a civilization can trivialize itself to death, that we have set our foot in that path, and that our relation to the issue of responsibility is one measure of our progress. No matter, it is a self-limiting misfortune—by the time the end comes, the loss to the world will be very small. (155)

For an author who claims to avoid narratives of decline, she is quite clear that she believes we have lost the sense of collective responsibility. Is she undermining her own claim that she wants to turn to the past to rehabilitate old values, not to vilify the present? One way to interpret this passage is to treat it is a mere aberration—a temporary and fleeting moment of exasperation with a self-interested, priggish culture. Given that this passage is found in her most extended analysis of the history of Puritanism, another possibility is that she is expressing a sincere belief that society has changed so dramatically that we will never again be capable of thinking in terms of the personal responsibility demanded by covenantal thinking, and for this she is mournful. If we take her at her word that society is at risk of trivializing itself to death and that it will be no great loss when it ends, it at least suggests that she has deep reservations about the probability of repentance and reform.

While it's possible that Robinson is following in the tradition of the prophet Jeremiah's *Lamentations*, it seems more likely that her essays are aimed at breathing an ember of old courage into flame. But given that she has rejected the idea of America as a chosen nation in covenant with God, her arguments necessarily differ in character from those of the Puritans. While Robinson and the Puritans share a desire to cultivate the virtue of generosity, benevolence, and even an aesthetic sensibility of awe and wonder toward creation, they differ in their tone when it comes to the jeremiad. The temporal and eternal consequences for sin were clear in previous centuries; if, as Robinson suggests, the idea of sin was abandoned in the twentieth century, then the consequences must be reframed.

Robinson is one of many authors who have adapted the rhetorical tradition of the Puritans to fit with the times. As George Shulman has argued, the genre of the jeremiad has evolved along with America to include a broader tradition of prophetic speech, which he understands not as "scripture with fixed meaning but as living poetry open to infusions of new meaning."[40] Today's prophets may invoke themes of the jeremiad that "narrate conduct as a decline from origins, to address a community about its constitutive commitments and current difficulties, to make its future contingent on a 'decision' about its conduct."[41] They need not be Puritans, however. His list of authors who speak prophetically include figures as diverse as Henry David Thoreau, Martin Luther King Jr., James Baldwin, and Toni Morrison.

While she draws from the Puritan tradition, Robinson's reworking of covenant theology and the jeremiad is aimed specifically at the post-Puritan world. In this way, she may have prophetic resonance with a modern audience. In place of a religious covenant, Robinson offers a social covenant. Rather than holding her readers over the proverbial fires of hell, Robinson suggests that the consequences for "sin" are social alienation and climatic decimation. In terms of cultural consequences, Robinson notes that society has become characterized by "profound anxiety," that sickness has replaced the idea of sin, and that in their twin dedications to claims of disempowerment and priggishness, modern people have made "a fetish of concern, of criticism, of indignation" (*Adam*, 86, 83, 78, 168). Likewise, as our values have been ever more defined in economic terms, our physical world has also suffered. In *Mother Country*, Robinson declares that the environmental costs of pollution—specifically the commercial production of plutonium—are dire, warning contributing countries that their actions are "not compatible with their own survival, ultimately. And in the long term, the health of the planet is severely compromised, at very best." The solution is no less radical, requiring that "if the world is to be preserved, our thinking must change altogether."[42] But to what?

Robinson wants to replace the idea of American exceptionalism with the idea of human exceptionalism, meaning that we are all valuable creatures deserving of dignity and compassion. She is out to prove that Calvin and the Puritans shared this view and that it was an animating feature of their thought, perhaps the primary one. Recognizing this dedication to benevolence in the history of reformed theology is an important corrective, but in order to understand the Puritan mind-set fully, it is necessary to not lose sight of the means they used to encourage listeners to be virtuous. It would be an oversimplification to say that the Puritans took a "lurid pleasure in the notion of hell" (*Adam*, 151). However, it is accurate and important to note that the Puritan jeremiad supposed that one must behave benevolently in order to avoid calamities on earth as well as eternal damnation.

Robinson's reworking of the jeremiad makes this rhetorical tradition more acceptable for a modern audience. Most people today are happy that we no longer explain tornadoes and earthquakes as evidence of God's wrath and would take this to be an improvement over Puritan reasoning. But if Robinson abandons the idea of a special covenantal status and also the idea of divine punishment, what exactly is it that she shares with Calvin and the Puritans? An emphasis on treating people with kindness, forgiving even those who don't want to be forgiven, treating the land with great care, and providing for the poor. That is an admirable list of virtues, but it is one that many people of various faith traditions, or no faith, could agree upon. Robinson's covenant theology isn't expressly secular, nor is it necessarily religious. To return to Todd Shy's analysis, there are many places to which Robinson could turn in the history of ideas to find support for her dedication to social welfare and justice without invoking Calvin. Not that she is wrong to call upon him for intellectual support, but other than her own personal connection with the Calvinist tradition, it doesn't seem that an acceptance of Calvin's teachings or those of his Puritan followers is required to share her convictions.

Covenant theology as understood by both Calvin and the Puritans emphasized that God had chosen his people and that they were consequently charged with great moral responsibilities. In carrying out their mission to establish a New Israel in America, the Puritans, at times, took actions that today would seem severe and intolerant. At the same time, their theology emphasized the need for individuals to reject wealth and luxury and instead to be humble, industrious, and generous. Robinson argues that our modern view of Calvin and the Puritans has focused far too long on the former view and has all but ignored the latter. Her writings attempt to correct this misperception by offering a version of Calvinism that is focused on liberality and social justice. Robinson goes so far in her effort to correct our view of this tradition that she does not engage the more troubling aspects of Calvinist and Puritan history. At the very least, this provides an incomplete view of Calvinism and, at times, one that is revisionist rather than corrective.

Whereas the Puritans viewed their own mission as exceptional, Robinson wishes to emphasize human exceptionalism more broadly. Though she does not acknowledge it in her own writings, this leads to a departure from the tradition of Calvinist and Puritan theology and rhetoric. Because of the covenant, Puritans developed a unique brand of preaching that urged listeners to repent of their sins, lest they be collectively judged and punished. The rhetoric was strong and threatened immediate consequences for the community and eternal consequences for individuals who refused to reform.

Robinson is not simply correcting biased views of Puritanism but is actually reworking both covenant theology and the jeremiad. By removing the idea that America is a nation in a special covenant with God and expanding the idea of covenant to include all humanity, she makes the tradition more tolerant and liberal. Because the idea of the covenant has shifted, Robinson also moves away from the rhetoric of hellfire, a rhetoric that she already downplayed as part of reformed theology. Her revised Calvinism replaces the idea of eternal damnation with social estrangement and environmental collapse. The virtues to which society must recommit are liberality, benevolence, courage, and kindness. Robinson's assessment of our current society is stirring, as is her call to readers to commit to a gentler, more courageous way of living together. But using a nostalgic, and at times, purified version of reformed theology and Puritan history to buttress the importance of her vision is unnecessary and unfortunate. In the end, her version of Calvinism may not require Calvin at all.

Notes

1. Collin Hansen, "Young, Restless, Reformed: Calvinism Is Making a Comeback—and Shaking up the Church," *Christianity Today*, September 2006, 32–38. On the Calvinist revival, see also Mark Oppenheimer, "Evangelicals Find Themselves in the Midst of a Calvinist Revival," *New York Times*, January 3, 2014, www.nytimes.com/2014/01/04/us/a-calvinist-revival-for-evangelicals.html.

2. Marilynne Robinson, *The Death of Adam: Essays on Modern Thought* (New York: Picador, 1998), 62. Hereafter cited parenthetically.

3. Robinson has written more directly about Calvin in two other venues. She contributed a paper for the Colloquium of the Calvin Studies Society detailing the history of the polemics used against Calvin, "The Polemic against Calvin: The Origins and Consequences of Historical Reputation," in *Calvin and the Church: Papers Presented at the 13th Colloquium of the Calvin Studies Society—May 24–26, 2001*, ed. David Foxgrover (Grand Rapids, MI: CRC Product Services, 2002), 96–122. She also wrote the preface for a recent volume of Calvin's selected writings, providing an overview of his life and theology (see Marilynne Robinson, pref-

ace to *John Calvin: Steward of God's Covenant*, ed. John F. Thornton and Susan B. Varenne [New York: Vintage, 2006], ix–xxviii). Robinson, *Death of Adam*, 150–51.

4. Marilynne Robinson, *When I Was a Child I Read Books: Essays* (New York: Picador, 2012), 64.

5. Mark Hall, *Roger Sherman and the Creation of the American Republic* (New York: Oxford University Press, 2013); Glenn A. Moots, *Politics Reformed: The Anglo-American Legacy of Covenant Theology* (Columbia: University of Missouri Press, 2010); Michael P. Winship, *Godly Republicanism: Puritans, Pilgrims, and a City on a Hill* (Cambridge: Harvard University Press, 2012).

6. Todd Shy, "Religion and Marilynne Robinson," *Salmagundi* 155/156 (Summer/Fall 2007): 255.

7. Ibid., 256.

8. Thomas J. Davis, "The Death of Adam, The Resurrection of Calvin: Marilynne Robinson's Alternative to an American Ideograph" in *Sober, Strict, and Scriptural: Collective Memories of John Calvin, 1800–2000*, ed. Johan de Niet, Herman Paul, and Bart Wallet (Boston: Brill, 2009), 379.

9. Christopher Leise, "'That Little Incandescence': Reading the Fragmentary and John Calvin in Marilynne Robinson's *Gilead*," *Studies in the Novel* 41, no. 3 (2009): 350.

10. Ibid., 359.

11. Jonathan Edwards, "The Justice of God in the Damnation of Sinners," in *Works of Jonathan Edwards Online*, vol. 19, *Sermons and Discourses 1734–1738*, ed. M. X. Lesser (Jonathan Edwards Center, Yale University, 2008), http://edwards.yale.edu/archive?path=aHR0cDovL2Vkd2FyZHMueWFsZS51ZHUvY2dpLWJpbi9uZXdwaGlsby9nZXRvYmplY3QucGw/Yy4xODoxNS53amVv. On Edwards's use of the jeremiad, see Gerald R. McDermott, *One Holy and Happy Society: The Public Theology of Jonathan Edwards* (University Park: Pennsylvania State University Press, 1992), 11–20; and Harry S. Stout, "The Puritans and Edwards," in *Jonathan Edwards and the American Experience*, ed. Nathan O. Hatch and Stout (New York: Oxford University Press, 1988), 142–57.

12. Though the Puritans understood themselves and America more generally as "chosen," Calvin himself did not express this idea. Perhaps Robinson's "Jean Cauvin" naming convention is chosen in part to emphasize that Calvin was neither an English-speaker nor a father to the nationalistic ideas with which Puritanism would later be associated.

13. Winship, *Godly Republicanism;* Andrew R. Murphy, *Conscience and Community: Revisiting Toleration and Religious Dissent in Early Modern England and America* (University Park: Pennsylvania State University Press, 2001), 27–73.

14. Carla Gardina Pestana, "The Quaker Executions as Myth and History," *Journal of American History* 80 (1993): 441–69; Steven Waldman, *Founding*

Faith: How Our Founding Fathers Forged a Radical New Approach to Religious Liberty (New York: Random House, 2008), 10–13.

15. Robinson, *Gilead* (New York: Farrar, Straus and Giroux, 2004), 158. Hereafter cited parenthetically.

16. Christopher Douglas, "Christian Multiculturalism and Unlearned History in Marilynne Robinson's *Gilead*," *Novel: A Forum on Fiction* 44, no. 3 (2001): 340.

17. William Deresiewicz, "Homing Patterns: Marilynne Robinson's Fiction," *Nation*, September 24, 2008, www.thenation.com/print/article/homing-patterns-marilynne-robinsons-fiction; Douglas, "Christian Multiculturalism," 350–51.

18. Leise, "'That Little Incandescence,'" 356.

19. Jer. 31: 1–2, 31–34 KJV.

20. Murphy, *Prodigal Nation*, 7, 9.

21. Ibid., 32.

22. Just how bleak American jeremiads are is a matter of scholarly debate. Perry Miller found them to be an "uninhibited and unrelenting documentation of a people's descent into corruption" (*Errand into the Wilderness* [New York: Harper and Row, 1956], 15). By contrast, Sacvan Bercovitch has argued that the jeremiad actually strengthened the view that God cared for the American Puritans (see Bercovitch, *The American Jeremiad* [Madison: University of Wisconsin Press, 1978], 8; see also Harry S. Stout, *The New England Soul: Preaching and Religious Culture in Colonial New England* [New York: Oxford University Press, 1986], 62–63). Murphy takes a middle road, finding that Bercovitch "understates the real mood of dark despair" present in many Puritan jeremiads, but even this mood was not one of resignation but of reform (see Murphy, *Prodigal Nation*, 36).

23. Leise, "'That Little Incandescence,'" 358.

24. Ibid.

25. In her essay "Facing Reality," Robinson echoes the idea that the thoughtful study of religion has been undermined by television and even suggests TV may have replaced religion entirely (see *Death of Adam*, 85).

26. Jonathan Edwards, "Impending Judgments Averted Only by Reformation" in *Works of Jonathan Edwards Online*, vol. 14, *Sermons and Discourses 1723–1720*, ed. Kenneth P. Minkema (Jonathan Edwards Center, Yale University, 2008), http://edwards.yale.edu/archive?path=aHR0cDovL2Vkd2FyZHMueWFsZS51ZHUvY2dpLWJpbi9uZXdwaGlsby9nZXRvYmplY3QucGw/Yy4xMzoxMS53amVv; Moots, *Politics Reformed*.

27. Though some have disputed the idea that Calvin could have simultaneously supported the idea of a covenant alongside predestination, others have found that this supposed tension misunderstands Calvin's use of the covenant (see Peter A. Lilback, *The Binding of God: Calvin's Role in the Development of Covenant Theology* [Grand Rapids, MI: Baker, 2001]).

28. John Higginson, "The Cause of God and His People in New-England as It Was Stated and Discussed in a Sermon Preached before the Honourable General Court of the Massachusets [*sic*] Colony, on the 27 Day of May, 1663, Being the Day of Election at Boston" (Cambridge, MA: printed by Samuel Green, 1663), Early English Books Online, http://gateway.proquest.com/openurl?ctx_ver=Z39.88–2003&res_id=xri:eebo&rft_id=xri:eebo:citation:13046131.

29. Urian Oakes, "New-England pleaded with, and pressed to consider the things which concern her peace at least in this her day, a sermon preached at Boston in New-England, May 7, 1673, being the day of election there" (Cambridge, MA: printed by Samuel Green, 1673), Early English Books Online, http://gateway.proquest.com/openurl?ctx_ver=Z39.88–2003&res_id=xri:eebo&rft_id=xri:eebo:citation:13640660.

30. Perry Miller, *Errand into the Wilderness;* see also Nicholas Guyatt, *Providence and the Invention of the United States, 1607–1876* (New York: Cambridge University Press, 2007), 11–52;

31. Bercovitch, *The American Jeremiad,* 7–8.

32. John Winthrop, "A Modell of Christian Charitie," in *The Sacred Rights of Conscience: Selected Readings on Religious Liberty and Church-State Relations in the American Founding,* ed. Daniel L. Dreisbach and Mark David Hall (Indianapolis: Liberty Fund, 2009), 130.

33. Murphy, *Prodigal Nation,* 10.

34. Winthrop, "A Modell of Christian Charitie," 130. Theodore Dwight Bozeman has noted that jeremiads were used throughout the history of the American Puritans, especially as part of the practice of "covenant renewal." However, he notes that although the first generation of Puritans focused on the salvation of individuals within the community, jeremiads preached by the second generation focused on public concerns (see Bozeman, *To Live Ancient Lives: The Primitivist Dimension in Puritanism* [Chapel Hill: University of North Carolina Press, 1988], 298–310; see also T. H. Breen, *The Character of The Good Ruler: A Study of Puritan Political Ideas in New England, 1630–1730* [New Haven: Yale University Press, 1970], 97–110). On American exceptionalism, see George McKenna, *The Puritan Origins of American Patriotism* (New Haven: Yale University Press, 2007).

35. Edwards, "Sin and Wickedness" in *Works of Jonathan Edwards Online,* 14:497–98.

36. Ibid., 14:499.

37. In fact, when Pat Robertson and Jerry Falwell claimed that the 9/11 attacks were a divine punishment from God for America's toleration of sinful behavior, their remarks were met with general furor from the American public. On this point, see Murphy, *Prodigal Nation,* 3–5.

38. Lawrence Wood, "Strife in Gilead," *Christian Century*, February 8, 2005, 40.

39. Miller, Errand into the Wilderness, 9.

40. George M. Shulman, *American Prophecy: Race and Redemption in American Political Culture* (Minneapolis: University of Minneapolis Press, 2008), 3.

41. Ibid., 8.

42. Marilynne Robinson, *Mother Country: Britain, the Welfare State, and Nuclear Pollution* (New York: Farrar, Straus and Giroux, 1989), 26.

CHAPTER 8

Transcendence and Human Purpose

Marilynne Robinson and the Travails of Liberal Calvinism

Ralph C. Hancock

From Marilynne Robinson's essays (especially *The Death of Adam*) we learn that she finds herself in an awkward situation, politically: A liberal Calvinist who does not flinch from pointing up the affinities between secular liberal elitism and "Stalinism," she also distances herself clearly from traditional conservatism.[1] In many ways her political comments simply reflect the frustrations of a "mainstream Protestant" liberal who is as ready to deconstruct secularism (especially in the form of Darwinism) on the left and in the prestigious academy as to lambaste the narrow sympathies of the right. But these frustrations can point us to deeper, perennial problems surrounding Christianity and politics, and to reflect on these problems we find much more substantial material in Robinson's fiction, particularly in her masterpiece of exquisite and understated piety, *Gilead,* and in its mysterious doppelgänger, *Home.*

Reflection on the wisdom as well as the blind spots of the fictional epistolary author of *Gilead,* the Reverend John Ames, will help us explore the problematic relationship between the Calvinist understanding of radical transcendence and meaningful human action, especially political action. The brave democratic liberalism that resonates throughout Robinson's nonfiction is indeed deeply grounded in a Calvinist understanding of radical transcendence. But this understanding, I argue, is more complicit in, or more vulnerable to, the secularism Robinson deplores than she knows. On both Calvinist and progressive democratic grounds, Marilynne Robinson is led to separate ultimate human meaning from any stable and intelligible order, either sociopolitical or cosmic. This separation amounts to a repudiation of teleology and thus yields a broadly materialist understanding of reality. But since human action necessarily implies and presupposes some such order of ends, Robinson's Calvinist and democratic idealism draws heavily from the modern materialism that she professes to abjure.

A few very general remarks on the philosophical and theological problem of purposive action are necessary to prepare this critique of Robinson's Calvinist liberalism. As Aristotle wrote, in the first words of his *Nicomachean Ethics,* not only "every art and every inquiry," but even "every action and choice, seems to aim at some good."[2] Of course, what the proper ends of action are, and whether the various purposes of action can be gathered into a comprehensive final end or greatest good, is as fraught a question as can be (as the *Ethics* amply demonstrates). Still, without pretending to any definitive answer to this ultimate question of practical philosophy, we can affirm that the very possibility of meaningful action presupposes an order of ends that is in some way and to some degree available to human intelligence. To act is to try to bring about some change for the better, and thus action presupposes some idea, or perhaps merely some notion, however implicit, of the human good. Thus, for Aristotle, the understanding of action is inseparable from the question of the good.

Within the perspective of this Aristotelian (and pre-Christian) common sense, moreover, politics is action par excellence. Human beings are by nature political beings, in that their distinctively human ends can be achieved only through cooperation with other human beings; and the political association is the most comprehensive and therefore authoritative association. In this sense, from the natural perspective, the perspective of a certain common sense first articulated in classical Greece, politics is the site where the unavoidable question of human purposes comes most fully to light. Political life brings the question of the human good to the fore in the most vivid and inescapable way.

Christianity, of course, complicates the question of human purpose, to say the least. If Christ's kingdom is not of this world, then human action does not in itself dispose of the final end(s) of human existence. If man's final home is not in the City of Man but in a City of God unattainable by human virtue, then true justice and the common good are beyond humanity's natural reach, even in theory or in principle, and action in the whole and natural sense is impossible. Thus the main purpose of Augustine's *City of God* is to deflate human pride (as most fully articulated by the philosophers) and extol the "power and excellence of humility."[3] Human action is incapable of bringing about any truly adequate or satisfying end, and so all our hope must be directed to the goods of another life, goods that depend decisively on faith in a divine power, supernatural grace.

From this radical restriction of the meaning of action there follows, for Augustine, an equally radical devaluation of politics. Rather than aiming at the fulfillment of human possibilities in virtuous action, politics is now seen as a mere compromise among human wills concerning the necessities of mortal existence.[4] The goods of the soul are deferred to the City of God, leaving the City of Man with responsibility only for some minimal order sufficient to sustain mortal existence. (Of course, this new distinction between religious and political ends only poses the problem of the proper ordering of the two realms and by no means solves it, since these realms can never be wholly separate.)

John Calvin, the founder of the theological tradition that Marilynne Robinson so frequently invokes, radicalizes Augustine's critique of human virtue but thereby paradoxically enhances the meaning of human action, now liberated from the rule of any pretensions to rational and "higher" purpose.[5] Since natural reason can in no way mediate between mortal necessities and some heavenly goods, all hierarchical ordering in terms of "higher" and "lower" human possibilities is excluded. To express this point schematically, geometrically, one can say that the radicalization of divine transcendence undercuts the possibility of all "vertical" transcendence—all ranking of ends in view of an intelligible hierarchy of goods. The result is not, to be sure, the elimination of transcendence but rather what I call the emergence of a resolutely "horizontal" configuration of transcendence. God's otherness from humanity is now affirmed so rigorously that divinity can no longer be conceived as a "higher" order, a City of God that fulfills the noblest possibilities envisioned (if only faintly and imperfectly) in human action. Instead, this horizontal transcendence tends to focus spirituality on the common, material needs and interests of humanity or else express it in a sublime sensibility disconnected from human action. At the limit of this Calvinist radicalization of Christian transcendence, divine power is purged of all prideful, vertical content, all projections of allegedly higher human possibilities (cultivated virtues of the soul, moral and intellectual).

The Calvinist liquidation of prideful, vertical transcendence (the classical virtues, moral and contemplative) leaves open just two possible manifestations of transcendence. First, in the realm of practice, grace-full action is associated exclusively with the power to minister to universal human interests. This horizontal expression of grace contributes to and supports the central role of the idea of equality in modern ethical and political ideals. Second, considered apart from questions of action, the soul is no longer a microcosm of a vertically configured cosmos but only a locus of consciousness of this humanly incomprehensible divine power, the self of modern self-consciousness. This analysis of the two possible expressions, as it were practical and theoretical, of post-Calvinist and anti-Aristotelian transcendence will illuminate both the political spirit of Marilynne Robinson's work (most prominent in her nonfiction), and the author's tendency toward aestheticism, or the privileging of the beautiful or perhaps rather sublime over the good, and thus the apparently apolitical tendencies of her fiction, especially *Gilead*.

Horizontal Grace and the Miracle of Nature in *Gilead*

Marilynne Robinson concludes her mysteriously beautiful epistolary novel, *Gilead*, with the phrase, "I pray that you grow up a brave man in a brave country. I will pray you find a way to be useful."[6] The words are striking and perhaps a little perplexing, since the Reverend John Ames has not been able to present himself as an exemplar of courage or bravery in this diary, especially in comparison with his abolitionist grandfather. Courage is in a way the political virtue par excellence, since its most characteristic expression is found in the soldier's willingness to die for his city or fatherland.[7] And Ames in fact directly ties a "brave man" to his "brave country" and seems to link courage closely with being useful to one's country. Yet *Gilead* is in no obvious way a political and even less a patriotic book; indeed, we are left with no clear indication what Ames might mean by "a brave country": the town of Gilead? The United States of America, circa the reelection of Dwight D. Eisenhower? The City of God, such as it is reflected in a dwindling midwestern community of Congregationalists? Robinson's Reverend Ames has not prepared us to see any of these as a likely arena of his son's brave usefulness.

The political meaning or tenor of *Gilead* is thus far from obvious. (The same can be said of its companion volume, *Home,* set in the same place and time as Reverend Ames's letters to his son, except that the problem of racial justice hovers more heavily over the latter.) This is not to say that political themes are absent in the novel but rather that they might seem to be relegated to the town's and the Ames family's past, and thus to, at best, secondary status. There is perhaps nothing puzzling, much less objectionable, in the fact that a novel would focus on private things (religion, family, love, death) more than on public and political concerns. But a puzzle does seem to arise when we notice that political themes are very prominent, to say the least, in the author's nonfiction, that is, her considerable corpus of essays, and that these essays intersect thematically at numerous points with the novels in question. So a reader of the essays who turns to the novels will be struck by what appears to be the apolitical character of the fiction, especially when compared with the nonfiction. The question naturally arises whether the novels have greater political significance than first appears.

Since *Gilead* is infused with the religious reflections and religious perceptions of a preacher near the end of his life, one might see its mostly apolitical character as owing to Reverend Ames's otherworldly preoccupations. But this hunch is clearly too simple, if not simply wrong, because it presupposes a dualism between this world and the other that Ames is constantly undermining and reconfiguring. Jean Bethke Elshtain has perceptively praised Robinson's "incarnational vision," likening it to her own theme of "the redemption of everyday life," or what Charles Taylor has named "the affirmation of ordinary life."[8] Elshtain contrasts this vision with a modern tendency to abstraction, including the fundamental political abstraction of the "sovereign self" and the ultimate religious abstraction of those who "claim for God a place within our conceptual grasp."[9] Much of the spiritual and social power of the Calvinist tradition, as I have proposed elsewhere,[10] follows precisely from its linking of God's radical transcendence with a sense of the holiness of ordinary life, that is, a life devoted on the whole to the common needs of humanity. But I will argue that the rigorous exclusion of God from any "place within our conceptual grasp" in fact renders transcendence vulnerable to the celebration of a self abstracted from communal norms and purposes.

For the Calvinist Ames, and indeed for the Calvinist Robinson (as can be verified in her nonfiction), God's absolute transcendence of our conceptual grasp, that is, of the categories of discursive reason, undercuts any effort we might be tempted to make to articulate heaven on the basis of the elevation of a supreme good or of certain goods that reason might claim to abstract from our experience in this world. As Ames says in *Gilead:* "The right worship of God is essential because it forms the mind to a right understanding of God. God is set apart—He is One, He is not to be imagined as a thing among things (. . . the sacredness of the Word, the creative utterance . . . is not of a kind with other language)" (138). Ames wants to avoid suggesting "a reality that is simply an enlarged or extrapolated version of this reality" (143). He wishes "to suggest a much more absolute unlikeness" that disqualifies reason's pretensions either to support or to contest an understanding of divinity (143). For Ames, the Creator altogether transcends the plane of the creation on which the contest between "rationalism and irrationalism" takes place. As he states, "The Lord absolutely transcends any understanding I have of Him, which makes loyalty to Him a different thing from loyalty to whatever customs and doctrines and memories I happen to associate with Him" (235).

This is not at all to say that Ames is uninterested in the question of the relation of the goodness of this world to that of the next. In fact, if there is one thing the book is about, it is this question. But the character of this goodness has an absolute and mysterious quality that does not lend itself to conceptual articulation or to what I have called vertical transcendence, that is, the elevation of some features of the world over others in some more or less comprehensive and hierarchical conception.

In the first entry in the journal Ames addresses to his son, he observes that "it seems ridiculous to suppose the dead miss anything" about this mortal existence (3). However, ridiculous as it may seem, Ames spends much of the rest of his diary reflecting on what might be missed, and on what this world's goodness might have to do with the blessings of eternity. "Ah, this life, this world" is a characteristic exclamation. Ames shares his Presbyterian colleague Boughton's speculations about heaven: "Mainly I just think about the splendors of the world and multiply by two. I'd multiply by ten or twelve if I had the energy. But two is much more than sufficient for my purposes" (147). Boughton is right "to enjoy the imagination of heaven as the best pleasure of this world" (166). Indulging in this connection in his own imagination (while acknowledging that "Calvin is right to discourage curious speculations" on such things), Ames confesses that he finds it appealing to think of his much younger wife "finding me a strong young man" on the other side (166). But he immediately reminds himself that "there is neither male nor female" over there, though he does not suppress the thought that "it would be a fine thing" (166).

This touching moment of Ames's indulgence of his male imagination is a kind of exception that points up the generally undifferentiated or horizontal character of Ames's understanding of transcendence. That is, for the most part he understands heaven not as an elevation of privileged features of this world but as an enhancement of the conscious experience of the world in general, the enhancement of worldly experience itself without reference to any vertical differentiation. Observing with the conduct of some "decent rascally young fellows," he confesses, "I really can't tell what's beautiful anymore" (5). He looks at the world with the wonderment of a child, except that, unlike children, he knows by now that he will never "grow into it and understand it"; he is "each morning . . . like Adam waking up in Eden" (66). Among the miracles that Adam has eyes to see is "a thing so miraculous as water" (63).

This intensification of the ordinary experience of the world is presented with mysterious and unforgettable power in the early scene in which young Ames and his father pray at the grave of his grandfather. The boy opens his eyes to behold an exquisite play of light between setting sun and rising moon, "palpable currents of light passing back and forth, or as if there were great taut skeins of light suspended between them," each shimmering disc resting just on the horizon, their communion defining a west-east axis. To interrupt a prayer for this vision would not be an interruption. In a supremely lovely gesture, the boy gets his praying father's attention by kissing his hand. As the flow of time is suspended while the luminous orbs "seemed to float on the horizon," the three generations appear in a sacred light neither quite solar nor lunar, just grave, father, and son—an irreducibly particular past, present, and future—positioned precisely at the heart of Being (14). "And that grave, and my father and I, were exactly between them, which seemed amazing to me at the time, since I hadn't given much thought to the nature of the horizon" (15). This horizontal figure of a radiant transcendence is evoked again on the penultimate page of the novel: "I love the prairie! So often I have seen the dawn come and the light flood over the land and everything turn radiant at once, that the word 'good' so profoundly affirmed in my soul that I am amazed I should be allowed to witness such a thing. Here on the prairie there is nothing to distract attention from the evening and the morning, nothing on the horizon to abbreviate or to delay. Mountains would seem an impertinence from that point of view" (246).

Another reference to moonlight conveys Ames's sense of a shimmering and mysterious transcendence: "The moon looks wonderful in this warm evening light, just as a candle flame looks beautiful in the light of the morning. Light within light" (119). And here Ames points us to the deep link in his sense of transcendence between the light of the horizon and the light of human existence, or human self-awareness: "It seems to me to be a metaphor for the human soul, the singular light within the great general light of existence. . . . like poetry within language" (119). What I have called the undifferentiated or horizontal transcendence of the world is intimately linked with the mystery of self-awareness or individual self-consciousness. The wonder of the sheer existence of things in the world is grounded in or bound up with the wonder of individuated self-awareness: "This is an interesting planet. It deserves all the attention you can give it" (28). Ames develops this observation through a meditation on the use of the word "just," as in "the sun just *shone* and the tree just *glistened*," a usage that calls attention to "a thing existing in excess of itself" (28). This "excess" of the thing points to the miraculous connection between worldly things and human awareness; not knowledge of a hierarchical order but sheer consciousness of existence, being aware of being here, is experienced as a divine gift. Ames's witnessing of a young couple being showered by the shaking of a glistening tree branch after a heavy rain prompts the thought that "water was made primarily for blessing, and only secondarily for growing vegetables or doing the wash" (28). Thus, remembering again the miraculous horizon illuminated by the sun and the moon that he witnessed with his father as a child, Ames recalls "the sweet strength," the rare "joy . . . and assurance" he felt at that moment and is moved to tell his son "what an amazing instrument you are, so to speak, what a power you have to experience beyond anything you might ever actually need" (49). When Ames remarks that "existence seems to me now the most remarkable thing that could ever be imagined" (53), he is talking about the sheer, gratuitous existence of things, and at the same time about the availability of the world of things to human awareness, the "twinkling of an eye . . . that little incandescence you see in people when the charm of a thing strikes them" (53). The splendor "He has hidden from the world . . . the eternal breaking in on the temporal" apart from any hierarchy or teleology, any logic of "cause or consequence," is understood as "a glimpse or parable of an embracing, incomprehensible reality" (238), but the preeminent site of this glimpse, the privileged point of eternity's breaking into temporality, is the human face: God's splendor is "revealed to me in your sweetly ordinary face" (237).[11]

The distinction between nature and grace thus tends to collapse, and Ames's (and we must suppose Robinson's) piety acknowledges its profound affinity with Feuerbach's atheism. It is Feuerbach who saw the natural religious significance of water, which in "its natural character is the image of the spotless nature of the Divine Spirit." Ames insists on sharing his atheist brother Edward's taste for Feuerbach: "Feuerbach is a famous atheist, but he is about as good on the joyful aspects of religion as anybody" (23). According to Ames, his only mistake is that "he thinks religion could just get out of the way and let joy exist pure and undisguised." The Presbyterian minister Boughton clearly holds this mistake against Feuerbach more than does Ames himself; Boughton "takes a dim view of [Feuerbach], because he unsettles the faith of many people." Ames's response, we can gather from Robinson's essays, is very close to her own heart: "I take issue as much with those people as with Feuerbach" (24). That is, there is an important sense in which Robinson has more in common with an atheist who appreciates the wonder (if not the miracle) of sheer openness to existence than with a Christian who implicitly imposes some worldly idea of order upon a transcendent God.

The Ames Legacy: The Exhaustion of Political Courage in *Gilead*

The Reverend John Ames's exquisite celebration of the holiness of ordinary life is certainly the most prominent feature of this book. This respectable Iowa minister, reaching the end of his life in the 1950s, sees the incarnation of eternity, its penetration into time, its distillation and crystallization in the most delicate details of each particular existence, with truly unforgettable clarity and inexhaustible gratitude. And every reader in the least open to this incarnational sensibility must be moved to share in this gratitude. And yet, the more grateful we are to participate in Ames's incarnational sensibility, the more we must be puzzled or even disturbed by the questions that are suggested, upon reflection, by his final evocation: "A brave man in a brave country!" (247). This is what the Reverend wishes for his son: bravery, courage, uprightness, the virtue of standing up for something, and a country experienced as something worth standing up for. But this is the oddest, and on reflection, the most alarming conclusion imaginable to a book of poetic praise for the sheer gratuity of existence, the mysterious surfeit of being in becoming. It is an odd and alarming conclusion to Ames's life, for it cannot but invite us to wonder whether Ames, son of a pacifist and grandson of an abolitionist, has given his son, or us, something to be brave about, something in our soul and our city to stand up for.

To be sure, one might reasonably protest, *contra* Aristotle, and apart from the Reverend Ames's puzzling exclamation, that there is a kind of courage that has nothing to do with politics, that implies no connection between bravery in the soul (or the self) and the affirmation and defense of a particular country, a particular community with its particular conception of a good life. To be clear, in fact, we might distinguish three species of courage, two political and one apolitical.

The first political kind of courage would correspond most fully to Ames's evocation of an inherent linkage between bravery in the soul and bravery in the city. This is an Aristotelian and vertical courage: to stand up for a certain understanding of virtue and of the good life that is praised in one's community and that one aspires to represent in one's own character. This proud and vertical view, when adapted to an otherworldly revealed religion, implies a certain confidence in some continuity between this world and a better world. For example, consider the moment described above when Ames lets down his Calvinist guard enough to begin to envision heavenly bliss as an enhancement of the pleasures and honors of manhood. If Ames were to pursue this non-Calvinist reflection on transcendence further, its political implications might come to light as the affirmation of the goodness of a certain way of life centered on the procreative family and the difference and complementarity of man and woman. Here would be something definite, a particular way of life and the particular qualities of character appropriate to that way of life, qualities a brave man could stand up for, a concrete linkage between a brave character and a brave community. Of course the Calvinist Ames does not indulge this momentary Aristotelian lapse of imagination nearly to this extent.

The second kind of political courage would correspond to the horizontal aspect of Calvinist spirituality described above. This kind of courage does not stand up for any particular qualities of a character or a community, since these are interpreted as prideful and empty from a divine perspective. Rather, this courage manifests the spirit of absolute transcendence in action understood "horizontally," that is, as grounded in concern for universal human needs and interests. A commitment to basic human decency and identification with the common suffering of humanity inform this kind of courageous action, which thus marches under the banner of equality. Clearly the Reverend's abolitionist grandfather represents such courage, but Ames himself neither makes a claim to it for himself, his congregation, his town, or his country nor educates his son to such political action. It is this absence of courage on behalf of racial justice that casts a heavy shadow over the later novel *Home.*

Finally, though, we must acknowledge the possibility of a nonpolitical courage, a courage that is not so much a matter of character and action but rather a more subtle and, one might say, aesthetic personal bearing. In fact, one might say that this courage is even antipolitical, in that it involves a fundamental resistance to political and vertical interpretations of transcendence, that is, to the natural and prideful inclination to attribute purposes to the world that suit one's own character and prejudices. To be open to the "splendor He has hidden from the world" requires a subtle and resolute form of courage, precisely the courage to bracket one's morally, politically, and even religiously conditioned understanding of the noble or beautiful in order to be open to the sheer miracle of existence, a miracle that may be at least as available to the brave and resolute atheist as to the believer.

To the considerable extent that bravery or courage is a theme of Marilynne Robinson's writings as a whole, one can distribute this theme over her works as follows. First, vertical or Aristotelian courage has little place in the articulation of transcendence either of Robinson herself or of the protagonists of her two most recent novels. Such courage depends on prideful, "vertical" affirmations that are excluded as much by Robinson's Calvinism as by her liberalism. Next, insofar as Calvinist courage is understood as an active and political virtue informed by a vision of universal equality, then this is certainly the sensibility that informs Robinson's nonfiction. This virtue is also powerfully present through its tragic absence in the novel *Home:* here the town Gilead's utter oblivion of the demands of racial justice that once constituted it as a community underlie the impossibility of Reverend Ames's namesake Jack Boughton ever finding a *home* there. In *Gilead,* the courage of equal justice is also present mostly by its absence; it belongs to a past that Ames respects but can find no way to honor in practice. This horizontal courage lies at the heart of the midwestern biblical utopianism and progressivism that (as we learn from the essays) William Jennings Bryan represented, and it provides the spiritual backdrop to both the great novels Marilynne Robinson sets in the town of Gilead, Iowa, in the 1950s. But by this time the flame of social reform is barely flickering in what remains of heartland Calvinism. The dying of this flame is more tragic in *Home,* where the tragic character Jack is most central to the story. In *Gilead,* the aesthetic, nonpolitical courage of the dying protagonist seems to provide an alternative to the moral and political exhaustion, even destitution, of the town and its churches that is exhibited in *Home.*

Here we must focus our attention, first on *Gilead,* and then on Robinson's nonfiction.[12] In this epistolary novel, the Reverend Ames (I will call the protagonist of the novel Ames III, the third generation of Calvinist preachers) seems to be immobilized between the mad or inspired but also bloody and criminal political engagement of his grandfather (Ames Sr.) and the pacifism of his father (Ames Jr.)—a pacifism or quietism that finally seems to leave his father defenseless against skepticism. Grandfather Ames understood his vision of Christ as a call with clear and immediate political, and indeed military, implications: abolitionism. He is disgusted by the flaccidity of what has become of Christianity in Gilead, and particularly in his son's church. In a decisive break that leads to Ames Sr.'s departure for Kansas and his ultimate death, he walks out of an apparently pacifist sermon by Ames Jr. ("Consider the Lilies"), only to be similarly disappointed by the apparently no less pacifist preaching ("love your enemies") in the town's black church, which is being driven from the town. The old man's sardonic commentary speaks volumes and hangs like a huge question mark, I suggest, over the whole novel: "Very Christian" (84).

Ames Jr.'s determination is to "forget Kansas"—the militant vision of Christian justice—altogether. He resents his father for leaving a bundle behind, in which sermons and a pistol are wrapped up together. These are buried, exhumed, reburied, and then the gun again exhumed to be smashed and thrown into the river. Ames Jr. eventually seems to become allied with, or to fall into the orbit of, his wayward atheistic intellectual son, Edward. In perhaps the saddest words of the whole novel, we learn that the father of the narrator can no longer preach: Ames Jr. states, "I just can't do it anymore" (234).

Ames III knows full well the superiority, at least in terms of saintliness and its imprint on the world, of holiness in action, of his grandfather to his father. He has saved in his Bible the militant note Ames Sr. left upon his departure to die on the former battlefields of Kansas:

> No good has come, no evil is ended.
> That is your peace.
> Without vision the people perish.
> The Lord bless you and keep you. (85)

After the failure of the Civil War to redeem America and establish true justice, Ames Sr. "had nowhere to spend his courage, no way to feel it in himself" (47). At least he could remember what it felt like. With the additional discrediting of courage in the Great War, Ames III has no direct experience of what it would mean to stand up for some Christian vision on a political or military field. There is a studied ambivalence regarding World War II as well.

The quietism of Ames Jr. and Ames III is not limited to the question of war alone. The will of each father to stamp an identity on his son, to found a line of Ameses and a tribe marked by its distinctive human origins has been shattered or humbled. Ames Jr. has lost his firstborn and most promising son to cosmopolitan atheism. Ames III had a son only very late in life and seems quite passive in many respects concerning his son's education. Though he is writing this journal to explain himself to his son and to praise the beauty and holiness of the goods of ordinary life, he is free of any aristocratic hope that he might chart a course for his son or form him to become like himself. The line of preachers seems destined to end with Ames III.

Nor does the narrator Ames endeavor to shape the course of his town or country. We learn that he has grown up in a town terrorized for decades by the assumed (or imagined) lingering presence of a murderer whom the law was not strong enough to convict. When Ames III's oldest friend and colleague in the ministry, Boughton, indulges in grouchy complaints about how the moral character of society has declined, he is gently dismissive. The narrator Ames can see that television is transforming the way of life he loves, but he has no will to resist it. And, most tellingly, in contrast to his grandfather's militant passion for justice, Ames III casually accepts the town's black population being driven away. Then, what is most shocking, when he learns of his namesake's (Boughton's son Jack's) predicament of having an African American common-law wife and a mixed-race child and finding no community that will accept them, it does not occur to him to use his influence to try to find a balm for them in Gilead.

Ames III has lived a life of service, but mostly of leisured learning, a life that has allowed him to fill an attic with sermons. His appreciation of the ordinary has been refined to an extraordinary degree by a life of Sundays and a theological library presumably acquired from his modest but reliable salary as a minister. But he sees his way of life passing away and sees no point in trying to pass it on to his son; there will be no Ames IV. He can only pray for a brave son in a brave country.

Gilead can thus be read as a portrait of the best of a certain liberal and aesthetic Protestantism and of its telling limitations. Calvin's antihierarchical legacy indeed taught generations to savor the holiness of the ordinary, the common. But once this sensibility was severed from the transformative social and therefore political vision that linked the Puritans to the abolitionists, or once this vision was usurped by a frankly secular progressivism—once the sensibility of horizontal transcendence severed itself from or drifted away from its dogmatic theological anchoring, then there was no one left bravely to take political, philosophical, or theological responsibility for a world or for a regime in which the ordinary could come to light as extraordinary.

Transcendence and the Human Exception in *The Death of Adam* and *Absence of Mind*

Robinson's essays in *The Death of Adam* also conclude with a reference to courage. Here she remarks on the need for a "prevenient courage," analogous to the theological notion of a "prevenient grace," to nourish and support the individual courage. The conditions of courage are social and political: "Courage is rarely expressed except when there is sufficient social consensus to support it." But then, when the author comes to state the content of her liberal political views, her commitment to advancing "the well-being of people," we find all the requisite provisions for the material conditions of their "full enfranchisement," but nothing about the substance of a social consensus, a shared moral framework, that would give people something to stand up for, that would supply a vertical dimension for human action.[13]

Although Robinson bemoans the decline of Sabbath observance under the pressure of commercialism, she expresses no nostalgia for laws that once protected the Sabbath. She sees no role for public institutions in "character formation," a task, she thinks, that "has traditionally been reserved to the family, community, and religion, to the institutions of our diversity" (98, 99).[14] That might require dualism, and an apologetic or defensive stance regarding religion. Robinson, it seems, cannot follow through on her insight into the social conditions for the exercise of courage; to attend more fully to the role of "social consensus" would take the argument in an Aristotelian direction and point to a necessary dependency of horizontal on vertical courage. A society must be able to stand up for and perpetuate itself, its ways, its beliefs, before it can stand up for the cause of universality. To paraphrase the great French philosophical sociologist Raymond Aron: for a society to be just, it must first *be*.

Let us consider the arguments of *The Death of Adam* in order to understand the relation between the author's Calvinism and her liberalism, that is, between her radical understanding of transcendence and her secular political commitments. *The Death of Adam* is a proudly contrarian collection. Unsurprisingly, it is clearer what the author is against than what she is for, but this is not necessarily a debilitating defect, especially if we can manage to make some reasonable positive inferences from her spirited negatives.

The clearest target of Robinson's critique, as she indicates in her introduction, is what I would call scientistic reductionism, or, the persistent tendency of the most ambitious modern thinkers to deny "the expression of human exceptionalism in the arts and sciences that declare the strange exhilarations of our strange life on earth" (2). One kind of reductionism interprets "religion, politics, philosophy, [and] music . . . as means of consolidating the power of a ruling elite, or something of the kind" (3). Another kind of reductionism, the economist's, reads all behavior and institutions as strategies of material self-interest. But the biggest target of Robinson's critique is the subject of her first, longest, and I would say best, essay, "Darwinism." Here she vigorously lays into the neo-Darwinist conceit that the unseemly moral and political implications of Darwinism can now safely be ignored as we accept the irresistible authority of evolutionary science. Robinson follows the vigorous public atheist Daniel Dennett in crediting Friedrich Nietzsche with a profound understanding of the moral implications of Darwinism: "That party of life which takes in hand the greatest of all tasks, the higher breeding of humanity, together with the remorseless destruction of all degenerate and parasitic elements, will again make possible on earth that *superfluity of life* out of which the Dionysian condition must again proceed" (53, quoting Nietzsche, *Ecce Homo*).

What permits us, Robinson asks, to assume that the moral consequences of the "death of Adam" will be more wholesome than those foreseen and even embraced by the likes of Herbert Spencer, Friedrich Nietzsche, and, of course Darwin himself?: "To be free of God the Creator is to be free of the religious ethic implied in the Genesis narrative of Creation. Charity was the shadow of a gesture toward acknowledging the obligations of human beings to one another, thus conceived" (48).[15]

For Marilynne Robinson, the most powerful and noxious force unleashed by the "death of Adam" is the ideology of the "free market," the "classical" "science" of economics she prefers to call "primitive economics": "Primitive, sometimes called classical, economics has long lived symbiotically with Darwinism, which sprang from it" (28). Primitive economics embraces the moral vocabulary of "progress," and though scientific Darwinism now claims to reject it, both fall back on moral language when they dismiss as unnatural and therefore as wrong the humane "desire to mitigate competition and to put aside self-interest" (30). The social prestige of Darwinism as an antireligious ideology has little to do, she argues, with the "notion of natural selection as a chaste, objectively functioning scientific principle," but rather with the anti-Christian ideological force it inherited from Malthus and bequeathed to Nietzsche and, indeed, as she shows, to Freud.

The fundamental theoretical defect of this anti-Christian celebration of cruel "naturalism" is its failure to account for mind and therefore for moral choice: "Mind is not a consideration for [Darwin]. . . . The fact that we alone are capable of describing order in nature is not a significant distinction in his view" (35). It is this failure to attend to what makes human beings special that makes Darwinism in all its forms blind to its own naturalistic mythologizing, whether in its approval of predatory nationalism or its attribution of "selfishness" to genes.

The meaning of this naturalistic suppression of the question of mind is a problem that Robinson returns to at some length in *Absence of Mind:*

> The neo-Darwinism of Hamilton and others shares one consequence with meme theory: both of them represent the mind as a passive con-

> duit of other purposes than those the mind ascribes to itself. It reiterates that essential modernist position, that our minds are not our own. The conviction so generally shared among us, that we think in some ordinary sense of that word, that we reason and learn and choose as individuals in response to our circumstances and capacities, is simply—the one, crucial point of agreement between these otherwise incompatible theories—a persisting illusion serving a force or a process that is essentially unknown and indifferent to us.[16]

The reason, then, why "these innocent scientific ideas veer so predictably toward ugliness and evil," as Robinson wrote in *The Death of Adam,* is that "they systematically disallow the legitimacy of benign, or for that matter merely neutral, motives and behavior" (56).

This is to say that *as a scientific idea,* Robinson regards the theory of evolution as perfectly innocent, and in no way incompatible with Christianity. In fact, she argues, "Judeo-Christian culture has been uniquely hospitable to science." It is indeed hard to imagine a worldview more "congenial to science" than Christianity. "Faith is called faith for a reason," that is, because true religion "does not look for proof of the existence of God, or understand God in a way that makes his existence liable to proof or disproof." Attempts to prove the existence of God that have been made "under the influence of the prestige of Aristotle" should not be taken to mean that Christianity "depended on that kind of affirmation," that is, on an understanding of God which would make Him continuous with the world understood as available to natural reason and thus accessible to rational demonstration. Christianity, according to Robinson, should not allow itself to be implicated in any prideful Aristotelian temptation to articulate vertical transcendence, that is, any rational continuities between this world and some other, higher world (39).

The God of the Bible, Robinson maintains, is hospitable to modern science in general and to evolutionary theory in particular, precisely because, *pace* Nietzsche, "the world of Genesis cosmogony . . . is not in the least degree animistic or demon-haunted or dependent for its functioning on divine intervention." On the contrary, Genesis shows us, "no Watchmaker, as the Darwinists would have us believe, but a God who stands outside his creation. . . . This terse account does as little to invoke the model of a human artisan as it could do. . . . [Everything] has the same origin, and it is all good. *There is no suggestion of hierarchy in the order in which things come in to being*" (39, my emphasis). Moreover, and decisively, "God is not embodied in any part of creation. . . . There are no loci of special holiness, *humanity aside,* and nothing evil or alarming or unclean. The sun and moon are simply 'lights' and the markers of days and seasons. . . . Certainly this cosmogony describes a natural order which is freestanding and complete" (37–38, my emphasis).

God's creation stands as an open field for modern naturalistic science precisely because Creator remains distinct from creation, and therefore the created world is one without intrinsic hierarchy or spiritual differentiation that would present any obstacle to a purely rational explanation of phenomena within the created world. The world of biblical creation is thus a world open to scientific explanation and, as we shall see, to a democratic and progressive understanding of justice.

Note, however, that Robinson sets "humanity aside" from the morally or spiritually undifferentiated phenomena of creation: "Genesis tries to describe human exceptionalism, and Darwinism tries to discount it" (62). What are we to make of the special quality of humanity in relation to the rest of creation? In *Absence of Mind,* Robinson seems to point to two possible ways of articulating the human difference—let us refer to them as the way of the "self" and the way of the "mind," though it is not clear how or whether these two possibilities are supposed to fit together. First, let us consider the account of the human exception in terms of the "self" (which corresponds to the third, apolitical meaning of courage described above):

> Then there is the odd privilege of existence as a coherent self, the ability to speak the word "I" and mean by it a richly individual history of experience, perception, and thought. For the religious, the sense of the soul may have as a final redoubt, *not as argument but as experience,* that haunting I who wakes us in the night wondering where time has gone, the I we waken to, sharply aware that we have been unfaithful to ourselves, that a life lived otherwise would have acknowledged a yearning more our own than any of the daylit motives whose behests we answer to so diligently. Our religious traditions give us as the name of God two deeply mysterious words, one deeply mysterious utterance: I AM. Putting to one side the question of their meaning as the name and character by which the God of Moses would be known, these are

> words any human being can say about herself, and does say, though always with a modifier of some kind. I am hungry, I am comfortable, I am a singer, I am a cook. The abrupt descent into particularity in every statement of this kind, Being itself made an auxiliary to some momentary accident of being, may only startle in the dark of night, when the intuition comes that there is no proportion between the great given of existence and the narrow vessel of circumstance into which it is inevitably forced. (110, my emphasis)

The human self is a mysterious center of awareness that somehow echoes the "I Am" of almighty Jehovah. The self is mysterious because its exceptional quality has no place within a knowable hierarchy of being but instead comes to awareness only by an "abrupt descent into particularity"; the mystery of existence lies in the absolute disproportion between the ultragenerality of "the great-given of existence" and the unqualified particularity of the self's historicity. On this account of human exceptionalism, there is no possible way of ascribing any general quality to this mysterious link between divinity and humanity; no teleology links man to God but only the sheer mystery of the self-awareness of existence (*Absence,* 110).

Robinson only hints at another path for articulating the meaning of the human difference, but this hint, which corresponds to the first, political and "vertical" meaning of courage described above, is worth considering. This is when she writes (in *Absence of Mind*) that "there is that haunting compatibility of our means of knowing with the universe of things to be known" (xiv). The compatibility between the mind and the universe is "haunting," I suggest, because it is in a way more mysterious than the unqualified mystery of the enacting of existence through our self-awareness as radically historical beings. For our awareness of that radical mystery in a way leaves us nothing further to think about, whereas the haunting fact that there is a link (Plato's Socrates says, in *Republic* 508a, a "yoke")[17] between our capacity to know and the (partly) intelligible order of the universe or cosmos would seem to call us to strive to understand this order and the place of humanity in it as best we can.[18] If the universe is in some way the *home* of the human mind and thus of humanity, then it is not so easy to dismiss or compartmentalize human and divine exceptionalism such that they have no implications for the nature of the created order. If the creation and the human mind are made for each other, and if mindful humanity is in the image of God, then it is at best problematic to describe the creation as "free-standing and complete" without reference to the meaning of divinity. In other words, if there is divine meaning in the imperfectly intelligible order of the universe, then Robinson's strategy of conceding rational comprehension of nature to a chaste and nonideological naturalistic science is at risk. It is not so clear, in other words, that Aristotelian Christians were simply wrong to believe that they had an interest *as Christians* in a certain understanding of the natural order and of the place of humanity in it. But this is the vertical understanding of courage and of political action Robinson consistently rejects, on both Calvinist and liberal grounds.

It is instructive to consider Robinson's intriguing half defense of William Jennings Bryan, in *The Death of Adam,* in the light of her attempt to hold together Christian historical self-awareness with a naturalistic understanding of the nature of creation. Bryan's mistake, from Robinson's point of view, is precisely to connect the truth of Christianity with some particular understanding of the natural order as linked with a consensual moral order.

Bryan, Robinson points out, "was a pacifist, an anti-Imperialist and a progressive, and a rapturous Presbyterian" (64).[19] (This description already challenges our contemporary political and religious categories, since a progressive creationist is now almost as hard to conceive as a rapturous Presbyterian.) His midwestern ethic rooted in a "utopian culture of idealism and social reform" freely appealed to the Bible and issued from the Second Great Awakening; its social fruits include "abolitionism, the higher education of women, and the creation of the public school system." This is the liberal Protestantism that Robinson finds so diminished in contemporary politics and society, and for the survival of which she is pleading. Already in Bryan's day, she must acknowledge, "the ethos of reform was dying out . . . the old biblical language of justice and mercy was finally losing its power." And so the world is now out of joint, in Robinson's view, as long as progressives ignore their biblical roots and Bible-believers violate the utopian reformism that she thinks accords with the Bible.

Of course Bryan, a biblical progressive, was by no means as liberal as contemporary progressivism, and so Robinson's apology for Bryan must be qualified in decisive respects. "Bryan won his case," she notes, "insisting on the right of a Christian populace not to subsidize the teaching of an inimical doctrine." On the face of it, the reader might so far be inclined to take Bryan's side in defense of a "Christian populace," whether on the basis of democracy or of Christianity. But such a defense is clearly beyond the pale of contemporary liberal progressivism, and Robinson dismisses it without argument: "The problems of this approach are obvious." The best she can do is to find extenuating circumstances to excuse Bryan's lapse from the obvious soundness of contemporary progressive liberalism: "he was mortally ill and might have done better under other circumstances."

Let us examine more closely the source of Robinson's ambivalence concerning Bryan. On the one hand, we must "remember that his attack on Darwinism came from the *left*, from the side of pacifism and reform," and this much our author endorses without qualification. The limitations of Bryan's wisdom, on the other hand, lie in the fact that as "a biblical literalist"; he "makes no distinction between evolution and Darwinism, the philosophical or ethical system that has claimed to be implied by evolution" (65). We now know better than Bryan, Robinson thinks, that a progressive ethics of human exceptionalism is in no way threatened by a naturalistic explanation of the world, as long as this naturalism is not associated with any moral or political project. That is, Bryan's "argument against Darwinism is essentially political," and he would have done better, according to Robinson, not to contest the naturalistic science that seemed to him to underlie Darwinism as a moral-political project.

The problem of the relation between science and public morality arises again immediately in connection with Bryan's effort to discredit Darrow by citing his recent defense of Leopold and Loeb, who were on trial for the gratuitous murder of a child. Darrow had argued that, since the transmoral Nietzsche was familiar reading in practically all contemporary universities, it was "hardly fair to hang a nineteen-year-old boy for the philosophy that was taught him at the university." Bryan referred to this argument of Darrow's in order to make the case "that schools and universities should not have books in them that might corrupt 'the souls entrusted to them'" (66). Now, of course, Robinson is not going to violate contemporary liberalism by suggesting that the universities ought to beware of the corrupting influence of Nietzsche any more than that of evolutionary naturalism. "This is clearly the wrong conclusion to draw," she avers, again without further argument. And yet she remains ambivalent concerning the *modern* in modern liberalism: "What magic is there," she asks, "about the word 'modern' that makes us assume what we think has no effect on what we do?" (67). What indeed, I would ask—returning the question to Robinson—what makes us think (unlike Bryan, and unlike contemporary creationists, for example) that our understanding of the nature of creation, of the character of the real can simply be separated from our understanding of the human exception, of moral and political purposes? What makes us think that the meaning of divinity can be severed without consequence from the meaning of nature, from the Aristotelian question of distinctive goods and purposes inherent in our natures? How can we be so sure that political courage can do without a vertical dimension, an understanding of the good of nature coordinated with a conception of a good society?

Marilynne Robinson's critique of Darwinist science cuts to its core: "It is certainly one of the oddest features of a school of thought that denies human exceptionalism as its first premise that it finds so much of human behavior contrary to nature—and objectionable on those grounds." But is the moral-political project of modern naturalism a mere accident of Darwinism or a figment of conservative, creationist counter-Darwinism? In fact, Robinson is aware that scientism as a moral-political project is by no means peculiar to Darwinism. "This school of thought—ordinarily referred to as modern thought—tells us nothing more urgently than that we are wrong about ourselves" (68). But Robinson does not seem to consider that it is not only Darwinism, but the modern technological project more generally, a project that promises to compensate the oblivion of the good with material benefits of the mastery of nature, that aims to tell us that we are wrong about ourselves, wrong to think of ourselves and our world purposively, wrong to think of the universe as the home of human purposes. Before Darwin, and before Francis Bacon and René Descartes, it was, after all, John Calvin who, through a rigorous radicalization of the Christian idea of transcendence, told us that we were wrong about ourselves.

Transcendence as Democratic Progress in *The Death of Adam* and *When I Was a Child I Read Books*

Robinson aims to contribute to renewing the collaboration of religion and humanism, which she laments are now too often assumed to be antagonists (*Adam*, 8). Thus she is engaged in a battle on two fronts: on the one hand, she opposes those religionists who are suspicious of humanism (conservatives and fundamentalists), and on the other, those advocates of human progress and human power who are not really humanists because they reduce the human to some subhuman causal ground. Against these she is ready to take up "that old romance of the self," and even ground this romance in the older narrative of the human *soul,* understood as the proper seat of moral obligation as well as of the pleasures of art, music, philosophy, and even philanthropy and revolution. In keeping with the horizontal configuration of transcendence that has deep roots in Calvinism, Robinson associates this religious defense of humanism or humanist defense of religion with democracy, that is, with "the profoundly democratic idea that . . . a biography was the passage of a soul through the vale of its making, or its destruction, and that the business of the world was a parable or test or temptation or distraction and therefore engrossing, and full of the highest order of meaning, but in itself a fairly negligible thing" (*Adam,* 9).

Robinson opposes this democratic idea of religion/humanism to the old and more Aristotelian idea that "leisure . . . was the basis of culture." In fact there is one principle or tendency in contemporary life that is spared from criticism without exception, as far as I can tell, in Robinson's spirited polemics: "democracy." This is an ideal that apparently needs no justification and precious little description; it seems rather to stand as the unquestioned axis of Robinson's moral-political universe,[20] and one that finally seems to exercise more substantive authority than the "Calvinism" concerning which she is so protective, not to say irritable. Certainly there is more of a tendency to judge and to interpret Calvinism by the (implicit, assumed) standards of "democracy" than vice versa. Whatever may have been the contribution of Calvinism to modern liberalism (and I have argued that the contribution is significant), it seems a stretch for her to claim the legacy of Calvinism for the view that "it is in the nature of people to do good to one another" (*Child,* loc. 543).

I take it as obvious that Robinson, who reports that she was led by a deep affinity to migrate from her inherited Presbyterianism and to affiliate with liberal and modern Congregationalists, cannot by any means be considered an integral Calvinist. But this is not to deny a deep connection between her allegiance to Calvinism and her rapturous enthusiasm for modern liberalism and democracy. The link between Robinson's Calvinism and her progressive liberalism is fundamental albeit negative rather than substantial: both Calvinism and modern liberalism negate all claims to hierarchical order in the soul, the city, and the cosmos. This alliance expresses itself most radically in the author's emphasis on the essential mystery of the human condition, the homelessness of the human spirit in the material world, and the rupture between the self's sheer consciousness and any affirmation of a natural hierarchy of ends: "The presence of human consciousness is a radical, qualitative change in the natural order. What are we, after all? Why are we such mysteries to ourselves? Why do we stand apart from nature, even to the extent of posing a mortal threat to its continued life?" (*Child,* loc. 2821).

In keeping with the fundamental mystery of human existence, Robinson thus reduces the idea of soul to sheer "self-awareness," which of course leaves the soul without any stable, intelligible purpose (*Child,* loc. 197). This emphasis on the poverty of our understanding might seem to imply political quietism or, as tended to be the case for Calvin himself, authoritarianism. But for Robinson, as for Rousseau and the revolutionary progressivism he begat, the mystery of the self somehow yields a confidence in History as the matrix of Democracy; the evacuation of order in the cosmos yields the affirmation of some implicit, emergent meaning in history: "To identify sacred mystery with every individual experience, every life, giving the word its largest sense, is to arrive at democracy as an ideal, and to accept the difficult obligation to honor others and oneself with something approaching due reverence. It is a vision that is wholly religious though by no means sectarian, wholly realist in acknowledging the great truth of the centrality of human consciousness, wholly open in that it anticipates and welcomes the disruption of present values in the course of finding truer ones" (*Child,* loc. 96).

"Mystery is openness to possibility" and all possibilities, it seems, are to be welcomed (*Child,* loc. 2785). "Wisdom, which is almost always another name for humility, lies in accepting one's own inevitable share in human fallibility"—and fallibility is but another term for confidence in the progress of democracy (*Child,* loc. 461). Calvin's repudiation of Aristotelian rational teleology thus issues into Jeffersonian rational progressivism: Robinson finds that "Jefferson's words acknowledge an essential mystery in human nature and circumstance" (*Child,* loc. 2328). As she says, "It is not surprising that the leader of a revolution taking place on the edge of a little-known continent, a man clearly intent on helping to create a new order of things, would attempt an anthropology that could not preclude any good course history might take" (*Child,* loc. 2330).

Humility, or "recognition of our radically imperfect understanding," can thus be embraced as "a principle of liberation" (*Child,* loc. 2339). For a moment, Robinson's Calvinist conscience seems to warn her against this very optimistic view of nature and history: "I do not draw any conclusions from the fact of our apparent malleability. Certainly it cannot imply perfectibility" (*Child,* loc. 2047). But, in fact, her unrestrained embrace of Democracy's unbounded progress implies something very much like perfectibility—an ongoing process of transformation toward some indefinite and ever-receding ideal. And since this ideal is inherently indefinite and open-ended, in practice it can only be defined negatively, that is, in terms of what it opposes, what it transforms, what it destroys; "Essentially, decisively, we are at odds with nature" (*Child,* loc. 2628). This is the fundamental kinship between Robinson's progressive Calvinism and the modern scientism she deplores. For Robinson, the mysteries of Christianity and democracy converge in their movement away from all traditional categories and constraints, with their implicit teleological assertions, a movement guided by the "vision of the soul, all souls, realizing itself in the course of transforming everything that has constrained it and them" (*Child,* loc. 94).

> There is a disturbing lack of confidence in democracy in the frightened resistance to the workings of democracy and its continuous evolution beyond the old constraints of traditional society and authoritarian government. It resembles nothing so much as the disturbing lack of faith in Christianity that puts the darkest interpretation on social change, religious diversity, foreign influence, the implications of science, and so much else besides. If Christianity expresses the nature and will of God, and if Christ will be with us even to the end of the age, why all this fear? (*Child,* loc. 198)

What has constrained the mysterious progress of democracy against nature, Robinson thinks, is the crippling (if natural) idea that community depends upon some consensus concerning a substantive common good: "There is a notion with a brutal history that a homogeneous country is more peaceful and stable and, in a very deep sense, more satisfying than one with a complex and mingled population like ours. To an alarming extent, we have internalized this prejudice against ourselves" (*Child,* loc. 434).

Any attempt to affirm and preserve a community's particular understanding of the good, any exercise of vertical courage, is a threat to equality and a closure of possibilities: "In any case, the return to traditional values seems to them to mean, together with a bracing and punitive severity toward the vulnerable among us, the establishment of a kind of religious monoculture we have never had and our institutions have never encouraged" (*Child,* loc. 53).

Against those inclined to stand up for a particular way of life and its associated hierarchy of goods, Robinson affirms the unfettered operation of a purely horizontal transcendence; our ethical imagination must not be limited by any actual habits or loyalties: "They insist that the imagination must stay within the boundaries they establish for it, that sympathy and identification are only allowable within certain limits. I am convinced that the broadest possible exercise of imagination is the thing most conducive to human health, individual and global. . . . Democracy, in its essence and genius, is imaginative love for and identification with a community with which, much of the time and in many ways, one may be in profound disagreement" (*Child,* locs. 449, 472).

In this historicized democratic idealism, this distrust of all substantive consensus except that grounded in an enthusiastic openness to emergent meaning, we see the ultimate complicity between the two styles of anti-Aristotelian courage identified above. The mystery of democratic progress is the meeting ground of egalitarian justice and existential resoluteness. To be sure, Robinson's vision of boundless democratic transformation cannot operate completely without intelligible content, without some understanding of the character of the beings who are assumed to be the subjects and beneficiaries of democratic progress. Even if horizontalizing transcendence is propelled mainly by the negative imperative of leveling prideful hierarchies, some understanding of our common human nature, of universal necessities, inevitably informs one's understanding of democratic progress, just as it informed Calvin's antiteleological reinterpretation of "natural law." The unquestioned norm that effectively drives Robinson's open-ended vision is simple reciprocity in view of "well-being": "Interdependency ought to ensure that we will regard one another as the basis of our own well-being, and will reciprocate, service for service, working out the fine points as circumstance requires. . . . The logic of such mutuality and reciprocity seems irrefutable" (*Child,* locs. 567, 570).

Since all traditional and teleological conceptions of human well-being have been excluded by the mystery of the self and its transformational imperative, the shared or public content of this "well-being" can be nothing at all mysterious or distinctive but only the plain material interests of humanity. Thus Robinson is ready to welcome the secular, utilitarian formula, "the greatest good for the greatest number" (*Child,* loc. 649). Similarly, in the earlier essay titled "Darwinism," Robinson has interpreted human freedom "appropriate to our singular dignity" as action that "serves the collective well-being" (*Adam,* 69).

Like John Stuart Mill, Robinson sees no tension within a public ethic that would combine utilitarian reciprocity with expansive individual autonomy: "Western society at its best expresses the serene sort of courage that allows us to grant one another real safety, real autonomy, the means to think and act as judgment and conscience dictate" (*Child,* loc. 687). Thus she understands the American constitutional principle of religious freedom as "freedom from established religion" and embraces the rhetoric of a "wall of separation between church and state" (*Child,* locs. 1943, 1947).

Thus it is on the ground of a certain Calvinist understanding of the mystery of the self that Marilynne Robinson embraces a political ethic of secularism, including the transformative implications of the radical opposition between human freedom and nature. She seems unaware how much she thus has in common with the modern materialism whose expression in Darwinism she is so keen to combat. Marilynne Robinson cannot see the source of the weakness of liberal Protestantism she laments because she does not seem to see that individualistic and capitalist "Social Darwinism" is not, after all, the deepest and most resilient form of the practical synthesis between the mysterious self and the attribution of purpose to purposeless process.

Human Purpose and the "Nature of the Horizon"

We have seen that the Reverend John Ames's religious sensibility is captured in the dazzling moment of horizontal transcendence on the axis between moon and sun, where the exquisite particularity of the three Ameses' little trinity of boundless finitude appears at the center of existence on the barren Kansas plain, apart from any larger community, a shimmering existence unsheltered by a regime or a cosmos. Whether such a vision of transcendence can be sustained without the help of brave people in a brave country, or without a cosmos in which the noonday sun defines a vertical dimension of high and low reflected in a stable social and moral consensus—this is the question Marilynne Robinson has raised for me. We may still have not given enough "thought to the nature of the horizon."

At the beginning of this essay I began to report Reverend Ames's last words to his son, his hope that the boy would grow up "a brave man in a brave country." But, in fact, the very last words of the novel are these: "I'll pray, and then I'll sleep" (247). For those of us who must also act, there remains, beyond the self's experience of sheer miracle of existence, the question of purpose in the soul and in the city.

Notes

1. While citing favorably a column in which David Brooks criticized what Robinson calls "stick-figure anthropology," she is careful to reassure readers that he is an author "with whom I almost never agree" (*When I Was a Child I Read Books: Essays* (New York: Farrar, Straus and Giroux, 2012), Kindle loc. 2119). See below for Robinson's critique of traditionalism.

2. Aristotle, *Nicomachean Ethics*, trans. Joe Sachs (Newburyport, MA: Focus, 2002), 1.

3. Augustine, *City of God*, trans. David Knowles (Middlesex, UK: Penguin, 1980), 5.

4. Ibid., 877.

5. Here I can only outline my interpretation of Calvin's theology (or, more strictly, his antitheology). For a full elaboration based for the most part on a careful reading of Calvin's *Institutes of the Christian Religion*, see my *Calvin and the Foundations of Modern Politics* (1989; South Bend: IN: Saint Augustine's Press, 2011). This interpretation is further developed in the context of my reflection on vertical and horizontal figures of transcendence in chapter 3 of my *Responsibility of Reason* (Lanham, MD: Rowman and Littlefield, 2013), "The Rule of Reason and Paradoxes of Transcendence."

6. Marilynne Robinson, *Gilead* (New York: Picador, 2004), 247. Hereafter cited parenthetically.

7. Aristotle, *Nicomachean Ethics*, 48.

8. Jean Bethke Elshtain, "The Incarnational Vision of Marilynne Robinson," *Cresset: A Review of Literature, the Arts, and Public Affairs* 73, no. 3 (2010), http://thecresset.org/2010/Lent/Elshtain_L10.html. See Charles Taylor, *Sources of the Self: the Making of the Modern Identity* (Cambridge: Cambridge University Press, 1989), 209.

9. Elshtain, "Incarnational Vision."

10. Hancock, *Calvin and the Foundations of Modern Politics.* See also Hancock, *The Responsibility of Reason,* 100–104.

11. The natural gratuity or miraculous character of water informs the religious ritual of baptism: "for us the water just heightens the touch of the pastor's hand on the sweet bones of the head, sort of like making an electrical connection" (63).

12. Much would need to be said about the problem of courage and purposive action in *Home.* Here I can only suggest that the boundless and dreadful sadness surrounding the lost soul, Jack Boughton, lies precisely in the impossibility of his finding a *home,* that is, a community of shared purpose in which his action might have some stable and intelligible meaning. Jack finds no balm in Gilead, in part because the Congregationalist commitment to justice has largely succumbed to Presbyterian respectability. But Gilead's failure to sustain a connection between Protestant piety and meaningful action seems to have a deep theological root in the Calvinist doctrine of predestination. Jack tends to understand his own homelessness, his failure to act within a meaningful community, according to this doctrine, and Reverend Ames has no alternative to offer; in fact he links the doctrine of predestination with a deterministic view of human nature: "Generally, a person's behavior is consistent with his nature, which is to say that his behavior is consistent. The consistency is what I mean when I speak of his nature" (225). Only Ames's unlearned wife, Lila, is sufficiently free of the burden of the Calvinist doctrine of predestination to offer hope to Jack: "A person can change." But even for Lila the possibility of change does not refer to meaningful and deliberate action within a stable cosmos and community of meaning but rather to the evangelical miracle of transformation: "Everything can change" (227).

13. Marilynne Robinson, *The Death of Adam: Essays on Modern Thought* (New York: Picador, 1998), 255, 258. Hereafter cited parenthetically.

14. I owe this observation to an unpublished manuscript by Peter Augustine Lawler, "Robinson and Tocqueville on American Exceptionalism." Professor Lawler similarly notices and seems to appreciate Robinson's immanent critique of modern liberalism. But, by coming at the subject somewhat sideways, through a comparison with Tocqueville, he invites us to ask just what it is that elicits or preserves the beauty of the ordinary: what makes time holy and prevents the ordinary from sinking into the merely banal, not to say the vulgar, or from being mobilized by the abstraction of History? The Puritans established colonies without lords or economic classes—in this they might indeed be described as antidualist—but not without God or without Sunday, without a distinction between the ordinary and the extraordinary (even if these categories were not assigned to distinct social classes). Tocqueville insists on the necessity of a certain dualism between body and soul, the secular and the sacred, for sustaining what is distinctive in human existence. Robinson thinks the notion of "transcendence" is based upon a mistake (and here,

indeed, she is drawing upon a Calvinist rejection of Aristotelian "dualism"). But is Robinson insufficiently protective of a basic dualism from which ordinary life at its best draws extraordinary meaning? She thinks poetic narrative is our best clue to the meaning of life, but would there be any great stories to tell without people who looked up to some abstractions and were willing to sacrifice the ordinary for some conception of what is extraordinary? Is the beautiful so sovereign over the good and the true?

15. Robinson seems to me to obscure this argument and detract from its power when she immediately identifies the obligation of Christian love with unquestioning support of the left-liberal agenda concerning the welfare state: "It was a burden under which the people never stopped chafing—witness this unfathomably rich country now contriving new means daily to impoverish the poor among us" (48).

16. Marilynne Robinson, *Absence of Mind: The Dispelling of Inwardness from the Modern Myth of the Self* (New Haven: Yale University Press, 2010), 71. Hereafter cited parenthetically.

17. Plato, *Republic*, trans. Allan Bloom (New York: Basic, 1968), 188.

18. See my discussion of the significance of Plato "yoke" for reflexive and political responsibility in *The Responsibility of Reason* (60–63).

19. All the quotations in this and the next paragraph are from this page.

20. Marilynne Robinson, *When I Was a Child I Read Books* (New York: Farrar, Straus and Giroux, 2012), Kindle locs. 46, 119, 123, 472, 1988. Hereafter cited parenthetically.

CHAPTER 9

The Romance of the Self

Marilynne Robinson's Existential Humanism

Anna Hadfield and Roger Berkowitz

In 1933, a document entitled "A Humanist Manifesto" was published in a small but burgeoning American magazine called the *New Humanist*. The manifesto—which was cosigned by more than thirty writers, Unitarian ministers, and academics, including the philosopher John Dewey—announced a "new religion" forged from "the materials of the modern world." Religion had shown itself to be powerless before the demands of the twentieth century; at least in its traditional practice, religion was ill-suited to an age shaped by "vastly increased knowledge and experience." A new worldview was therefore necessary, one that would "formulate its hopes and plans in the light of the scientific spirit and method" and discourage "sentimental and unreal hopes and wishful thinking." This religion would recognize human beings as a part of nature and so reject any supernatural or cosmic accounts of human life and human values. It would look to many like "a complete break with the past," for it would "affirm life rather than deny it." This new religion, the manifesto declared, would be called humanism.[1]

In the years following the publication of the "Humanist Manifesto," the term "humanism" became associated with a rejection of religion and a championing of science and rationality as the conjoined hope of the modern age. Several English and American organizations aligned themselves explicitly with the humanist cause. In 1941, the American Humanist Association was founded, an outgrowth of the previously existing Humanist Fellowship at the University of Chicago. In 1967, the Union of Ethical Societies, a British organization founded in the late nineteenth century, changed its name to the British Humanist Association. And in 1972, the Rationalist Association, another British organization and press, changed the name of its long-standing magazine to *New Humanist.* Today, humanism remains as widespread a term as ever before, perhaps even more so due to the term's appropriation by a group of popular atheist writers, called the New Atheists, whose viewpoints many in the humanist community have embraced.[2]

The core of modern humanism has been the promise of liberation from bondage to religion and tradition. "Man is at last becoming aware," proclaims the 1933 manifesto, "that he alone is responsible for the realization of the world of his dreams, that he has within himself the power for its achievement. He must set intelligence and will to the task."[3] As science teaches us about the universe and about ourselves, we overcome the limitations to human freedom and progress that once were ascribed to divine will, human sinfulness, and fate. A society guided by science and humanism will not only be free from the constraints of religious dogma but will be animated by a universal benevolence, as religious belief is regarded as one of the primary sources of hatred and conflict.

One of the first thinkers to recognize the danger of modern humanism was the poet T. S. Eliot. In the late 1920s, Eliot wrote two essays following the publication of a new book by Irving Babbitt, his friend and former teacher. Babbitt envisioned humanism as a modern alternative to religion, an ethical stance suited for the individual who believed in the importance of acting according to one's own sense of right and wrong rather than in response to any external authority. Though Babbitt's humanism was not yet a polemical atheism, Eliot saw the latent tendencies in Babbitt's metaphysical assumptions.

To fully reject religion, Eliot argued, was to reject the idea that there is anything that makes human beings unique or distinct from nature. "If you remove from the word 'human' all that the belief in the supernatural has given to man," he remarked, "you can view him finally as no more than an extremely clever, adaptable, and mischievous little animal."[4] The new conception of atheist humanism, Eliot asserted, was a departure from what he called "true Humanism," a cultural attitude necessary to society and to religion.

"True Humanism," as Eliot described it, was a "mediating and corrective ingredient" in civilization, a sensibility that operated against fanaticism. It was "concerned less with reason than with common sense" and acted as a complement to religion and philosophy rather than as a substitute for them, always remaining "critical rather than constructive."[5] Indeed, Eliot thought that one of the possible functions of humanism was to reenliven religious belief when it was in danger of falling into mere ritual and habit.[6] But he feared that humanism would become more and more a positive philosophy, destructive rather than critical, dogmatic in its opposition to all religious or transcendent understandings of human life.

If Eliot's true humanism has a contemporary advocate, it is the novelist and essayist Marilynne Robinson. Robinson sees the decline of a humanistic sensibility as a loss of belief in human exceptionalism, the idea that there is something finally mysterious and special about the human person that makes us fundamentally different from other animals. And like T. S. Eliot, Robinson rejects the modern opposition between religion and humanism, asserting that humanism inheres in the recognition of human beings as endowed with thinking and thus nonmaterial souls.

In articulating her vision of humanism, Robinson emphasizes the distinctly aesthetic dimension of humanism, the way in which such a sensibility is grounded in appreciation of the arts of civilization—an appreciation that is gradually being superseded by a sense of the humanities as unscientific, sentimental, and useless. She writes in the introduction to *The Death of Adam: Essays on Modern Thought* that "what used to be meant by 'humanism,' that old romance of the self, the idea that the self is to be refined by exposure to things that are wonderful and difficult and imbued with what was called the human spirit . . . has ended."[7] Robinson imagines a human self that can create and thrive within a humanly created moral and political world. "Humanism," she writes, "clearly rested on the idea that people have souls, and that they have certain obligations to them, and certain pleasures in them, which arise from their refinement or their expression in art or in admirable or striking conduct, or which arise from finding other souls expressed in music or philosophy or philanthropy or revolution" (8–9). Against scientific humanism that elevates truth over the humanly created meaning found in art, religion, and revolution, Robinson insists that religious and ethical truths are part of the human world, one intimately connected to the humanist culture of literacy.

Literacy in Robinson's work is more than simply the capacity to read and to write. It is the facility for joining into the world made by Western civilization:

> Literacy became virtually universal in Western civilization when and where it began to seem essential for people to be able to read the Bible. All the immeasurable practical benefits that came with mass literacy, its spectacular utility, awaited this unworldly stimulus. Clearly mere utility is not sufficient to sustain it at even functional levels, though the penalties of illiteracy are now very severe. Reading, above the level of the simplest information, is an act of great inwardness and subjectivity, and this is why and how it had such a profound meaning while it did—the soul encountered itself in its response to a text, first Genesis or Matthew and then *Paradise Lost* or *Leaves of Grass*. Great respect for the text and great respect for, and pleasure in, the reader's subjectivity flourished together. Now they are disparaged together. (9)

Human beings become human in thinking, writing, and reading within a given natural world and a humanly created cultural world that transcends our material and biological realities. Literacy is at the foundation of Robinson's humanism because the human world is a mythic and aesthetic world even as it is also a biological and material one. The fact that humans transcend their material foundations and live in a meaningful spiritual world is the basic insight that Robinson's humanism works to preserve.

In this essay, we argue that Robinson's writing manifests an alternative humanism to the new humanism of the New Atheists. Robinson's humanism affirms that being human does not have anything to do with any objectively definable "human nature" but rather comes from the *experience* of being human. And this experience of mind and consciousness is utterly irreducible to scientific calculations or social scientific descriptions and theories; it can only be looked at with a kind of wonder, as "a radical, qualitative change in the natural order."[8] She worries we have come to devalue the very testimony that would recognize the "felt experience" of consciousness, of subjectivity and intuition. And in the face of this ever-growing impulse to distrust and debunk human experience, the humanistic sensibility attests to the profound importance of this sense of wonder at human exceptionalism, which is not only especially called for in our secular and reductionist age but has always been fundamental to human existence.

Darwinism

Darwinism has become almost synonymous with the new, or "exclusive," humanism that emerged in the twentieth century. Leading Darwinists like Stephen Jay Gould, Richard Dawkins, and E. O. Wilson are all past recipients of the Humanist of the Year award, given by the American Humanist Association. Indeed, the modern humanist worldview has partly become popularized today through the work of these evolutionary thinkers—particularly Wilson and Dawkins—and they have come to play key roles in the contemporary articulation of scientific humanism. Robinson's humanism is rooted above all in her critique of this type of Darwinist thinking and, in particular, reductionist arguments that invoke evolution in order to make certain pseudoscientific claims about the nature and purpose of human life.

In the United States, the debate over evolution has been cast—not inaccurately—as a battle between secularism and religious fundamentalism. In this polarized climate, Robinson represents one of the few dissenting voices that does not take issue with Darwin on the basis of creationism;[9] nonetheless, her critique of Darwinism illuminates and clarifies the differences between thinking about human life from a human exceptionalist and "religious" frame versus a reductionist and animalist frame. Without contending with evolution scientifically, or giving credence to creationist arguments, we intend to examine how popular scientific accounts of evolution reject the idea that human beings have intrinsic worth by assuming that human beings are fundamentally explainable in biological terms. We argue that, by taking for granted that human beings are no more than the sum of their parts, Darwinism offers a radically devalued conception of what it means to be human. Darwinism—as a theory rather than a science—rejects the very idea of mankind that underlies so much of human civilization and the modern justification of human rights.

First, it is important to see that Darwinism means not simply evolution but the claim that "natural selection is the overwhelmingly significant causal factor in evolution."[10] In her essay "Darwinism," Robinson distinguishes between "evolution, the change that occurs in organisms over time, and Darwinism, the interpretation of this phenomenon which claims to refute religion and to imply a personal and social ethic which is, not coincidentally, antithetical to the assumptions imposed and authorized by Judeo-Christianity" (*Adam,* 30–31). Darwinism, as opposed to evolution, is a materialist worldview in which self-interest is the prevailing rule in human and animal relations, and the universe is both completely intelligible (at least in principle) and ultimately purposeless.

The connection between Darwinism and modern humanism rests on the belief that human beings have no privileged status in the hierarchy of life. Evolution disproves any biological distinction between human beings and animals. But Darwin and Darwinism go further, rejecting the possibility of any nonbiological, transcendent, and meaningful aspect of human thinking. The Darwinian worldview challenges human exceptionalism and empties the world of what Max Weber called "mysterious incalculable forces."[11] The fact that human beings are the product of a long sequence of evolutionary adaptations is understood as proof that there is nothing unique or surprising about humans; the nature of mind, however complex it may be, is held to be fundamentally explainable in terms of biology. Against classical, religious, and humanist affirmations of the mystery of human consciousness and intelligence, humanist Darwinism reduces human beings to simply the highest evolutionary form of mechanistic animal.

The antihumanist implications of his theory were clear even to Darwin himself. In a well-known letter to his friend, the philosopher and political economist William Graham, Darwin summed up the dangers inherent in the evolutionary account of mind: "But then with me the horrid doubt always arises whether the convictions of man's mind, which has been developed from the mind of the lower animals, are of any value or at all trustworthy. Would any trust in the convictions of a monkey's mind, if there are any convictions in such a mind?"[12]

Darwin rightly feared that if our mind is only a complex mechanism—if our deepest convictions are nothing more than elaborate products of a fundamental and all-encompassing struggle for survival—then human beings would lose the sense of intellectual and moral freedom that distinguishes us from other animals. And if morality is nothing more than a means by which our species ensures its own survival, then we reduce the highest human ideals to simple animalistic impulses.

A second way that Darwinism rejects human significance is through Darwin's controversial embrace of a progressive view of natural selection. From the very beginning, Darwin described natural selection as not only bringing about general advancement but also working toward biological perfection. According to most accounts, the crucial piece of the theory of natural selection—that favorable variations are preserved and unfavorable variations destroyed—was inspired by Thomas Malthus's 1798 *Essay on the Principle of Population*. The basic thesis of Malthus's essay was that population increase would always outstrip the growth in food supply, thus causing periodic misery and famine; Malthus counseled that food assistance should thus be withheld from the poorest and weakest.[13]

What Darwin lent to the Malthusian idea was the gloss of scientific natural laws; it was ultimately nature, not man, that dictated the necessity of abandoning the weak: "Man, like every other animal, has no doubt advanced to his present high condition through a struggle for existence consequent on his rapid multiplication," Darwin wrote, "and if he is to advance still higher, it is to be feared that he must remain subject to a severe struggle."[14] While Malthus's ideas were prescriptions for a society too long beholden to the Christian charity ethic, Darwin's competition was already at work in the natural world, as human society owed its very existence to such unrelenting competition.

Robinson is contemptuous of the attempt on the part of contemporary Darwinists to distance Darwin from the progressivism inherent to his thinking. Indeed, even the title of Darwin's seminal work, *On the Origin of Species by Means of Natural Selection, or the Preservation of Favored Races in the Struggle for Life*, indicates the importance of the notion of racial progress to his conception of evolution. The title "clearly implies that whatever is is right, and—even less tenably—that whatever is is the product of raw struggle, and—still less tenably—that there is a teleology behind it all, one which favors and preserves" (*Adam*, 43–44). Darwin conceived of natural selection as governing not only teleologically but also morally; its workings were judgments of value. As a moral theory, natural selection opened the door to thinking of all creatures and all races as having greater or lesser value in accordance with the ruthless struggle for existence.

It is partially out of recognition of these implications that neo-Darwinists reject evolutionary progressivism, particularly given the rise of social Darwinism in the mid-nineteenth century and its progeny, eugenics, in the early twentieth. But just as Darwin's ostensibly scientific claim that human advancement was the product of severe struggle and competition was heavily entangled with the prejudices of his society and class, so, too, does neo-Darwinist thinking continue to vault the bounds of science and make pseudoscientific claims about the nature and purpose of human life.

One example of this pseudoscientific tendency to enfold human beings into nature can be found in the thinking of the prominent Darwinist Stephen Jay Gould, who stresses that natural selection is only a principle of local adaptation, not of general advance or progress.[15] In *The Structure of Evolutionary Theory,* he argues that human beings arose "as a fortuitous and contingent outcome of thousands of linked events, any one of which could have occurred differently and sent history on an alternative pathway that would not have led to consciousness."[16] This improbability leads Gould to conclude that human life is "a relatively minor phenomenon that arises only as a side consequence of a physically constrained starting point."[17] While describing human life as a "relatively minor phenomenon" may make sense strictly in the context of evolutionary development, Gould then goes on to paraphrase Freud's remark that great revolutions in the history of science have one feature in common: "they knock human arrogance off one pedestal after another of our previous examples of our self-importance."[18] Humans are not simply evolutionary products, Gould argues, but minor beings irrationally possessed by an inflated self-worth. Similarly, in *Darwinism and Its Discontents,* Michael Ruse argues that "seeing evolution as a progressive process leading up to humankind is a human-created picture rather than a disinterested reflection of reality."[19] To truly understand evolution, Gould and Ruse suggest, is to finally abandon the consoling fiction that human beings are special and somehow different from nature, a conclusion that has less to do with evolutionary science than a pantheistic antihumanism.

Another example of the pseudoscientific materialist reduction of human life is found in the neo-Darwinist approach to altruism, of particular concern for Robinson. From the perspective of evolutionary biology, the "problem" of altruism has to do with how a trait can survive if it causes the organism to behave in a way that makes it less likely to leave descendants. For Robinson, however, the obsession with altruism is one example of the Darwinist tendency to simplify aspects of human experiences that refuse to fit into a preconceived model of how human beings can and should act.

Richard Dawkins's pivotal text *The Selfish Gene,* which applies the theory of natural selection on the level of genes, attempts to deal with the problem of altruism by arguing against the possibility of altruistic actions altogether. Though Dawkins clarifies in the introduction that the definitions of altruism and selfishness in this context are "*behavioral,* not subjective,"[20] meaning that he is not going to draw conclusions about whether altruistic behavior is actually the result of secret or subconscious selfish motives, this disclaimer that he is only speaking in metaphor allows him to make sweeping and often provocative statements about the supposed "selfishness" of genes while at the same time claiming that he is speaking purely from a scientific point of view. Among such statements are the assertions that "a predominant quality to be expected in a gene is ruthless selfishness"[21] and that "we must expect lies and deceit, and selfish exploitation of communication to arise whenever the interests of the genes of different individuals diverge."[22]

In Dawkins's framework, selfishness becomes a general rule that the actor, who is not only not in control of their actions but unaware of this fact, is powerless to resist. In doing so, it embodies another crucial implication of the Darwinist school of thought: that we do not and cannot know our "real" motives, that the world of genes and traits that dictates how we act is almost entirely unknown to our conscious minds. However, in their insistence that altruism is an illusion, Darwinists fail to account for the human need to justify our actions to ourselves; after all, even if altruism is a delusion, its importance and prevalence as an idea would still testify to the moral dimension of human experience. Indeed, Robinson argues that it is such so-called moral and spiritual delusions that "make up a great part of the margin between ourselves and the other creatures that we call our humanity."[23]

Robinson insists on an indissoluble distinction between human beings and all other species. Whereas Darwinism and other social sciences imagine humans to follow rules (survival of the fittest, struggle, pursuit of self-interest), she insists that real human beings are more complicated. The very idea that mankind can put an end to life on earth is, for Robinson, persuasive reason to conclude that humanity is "exceptional among the animals." Such a human capacity, she writes, "surely complicates the idea that we are biologically driven by the imperatives of genetic survival. Surely it also complicates the idea that competition and aggression serve the ends of genetic survival" (*Adam*, 63). For Robinson, much of contemporary Darwinism is simply bad science, a confusion of scientific evolution with the ideological pseudoscientific claims of materialist humanism.

Parascience

In *Absence of Mind: The Dispelling of Inwardness from the Modern Myth of the Self,* Robinson refers to the reductionist thinking Darwinism exemplifies as parascience (akin to scientism, a word Robinson also employs). Parascientific literature always proceeds from "a genesis of human nature in primordial life to a set of general conclusions about what our nature is and must be, together with the ethical, political, economic and/or philosophic implications to be drawn from these conclusions."[24] It is the idea that our essential selves are contained in our origins, accompanied by an often drastically simplistic idea of these origins. Parascience is attractive to new humanists because its simplifications offer comprehensibility and thus mastery of the humanly built world.

Parascience is dangerous, however, because it throws human agency into question. The idea that our true motivations exist at a great remove from our own lives, set into motion by natural impulses or by impersonal forces generations before we ever came into being, suggests that even as we can understand human motivations, individuals are powerless to influence the direction of change. Robinson traces this position in part to the modernist conviction that "our minds are not our own"—that our thinking, choosing, and learning is only "serving a force or a process that is essentially unknown and indifferent to us."[25] She does not take issue with parascience in the name of an alternative view of human beings as entirely rational agents; indeed, Robinson reiterates that it is the nature of human consciousness to elude final explanation and understanding. Rather, her problem with parascience is that it teaches us to look upon our own intellectual and moral experiences with cynicism, to distrust any sense we may have of the meaningfulness of these experiences.

In focusing on the parascientific view of mind, Robinson reframes the religion/science debate in terms of two radically different approaches to thinking about reality and human consciousness. She rejects the idea that there is any inherent conflict between science and religion: "The great breach that separates the modern Western world from its dominant traditions of religion and metaphysics is the prestige of opinion that throws into question the scale of the reality in which the mind participates. Does it open on ultimate truth, at least potentially or in momentary glimpses, or is it an extravagance of nature, brilliantly complex yet created and radically constrained by its biology and by cultural influence?"[26]

The real opposition is not between science and religion, but between an understanding of reality that preserves mystery and an understanding of reality that implies that mystery can be conquered. In one understanding, the mind is "properly an object of wonder," sufficient unto itself, indicative of the special status of human beings within the framework of the universe.[27] In the other, the mind is a myth that is gradually being debunked, a relic of a time when we could not reverse-engineer the brain.

The idea that science could "disprove" religion or render the questioning it encompasses unnecessary or irrelevant is a fallacy. In her essay "Cosmology," Robinson argues that in parascience description has come to be equated with explanation.[28] Consider, for example, Richard Dawkins's provocation at the beginning of *The Blind Watchmaker* that "our own existence once presented the greatest of all mysteries, but it is a mystery no longer. Darwin and Wallace solved it."[29] The problem that the two scientists solved, according to Dawkins's own account, is how the complex design of living things could have arisen; the "solution"—that is, natural selection—displaces not only other possible scientific explanations for human existence but somehow *all* explanations, effectively ridding us of the need to contemplate or question the "mystery" of human existence any longer. At the core of the parascientific enterprise is the scientific optimism that we have crossed a historical threshold after which all illusions are somehow irrevocably and miraculously dispelled. Robinson worries that if parascience emerges victorious and every belief that is not empirically verifiable is discredited, it will no longer be possible to see the world and human life as unconditionally meaningful. There is the threat of a new "emptiness" that hangs over human experience.[30]

If Robinson's opposition to much of modern thought seems at times startlingly sweeping, it is because she believes that the reductionist picture is one that has become a foundational assumption for a variety of disciplines, particularly the social sciences. In her essay "Freedom of Thought," Robinson describes her experience as an undergraduate: "At a certain point I decided that everything I took from studying and reading anthropology, psychology, economics, cultural history, and so on did not square at all with my sense of things, and that the tendency of much of it was to posit or assume a human simplicity within a simple reality and to marginalize the sense of the sacred, the beautiful, everything in any way lofty."[31]

We consider sacred or call beautiful that which resists the bounds of our understanding but which nonetheless strikes us as profoundly meaningful. The objective viewpoint of the social scientist, however, does not accommodate this internal sense of wonder or awe.

Though Robinson does not propose that we can arrive at a definition for religion, or that religion can be thought of as an "alternative" to scientific reductionism in any instrumental sense of the word, her work does offer a nonreductionist way of thinking about religion. For Robinson, wonder and awe at the infinite richness and meaningfulness of that which cannot be known is the essence of a religious frame. She rejects the idea that we can arrive rationally at an account of our reality, or even that we can make a definitive assertion as to the existence of God. We have no basis in our experience for such a claim, as "we have no way of knowing the true nature of the reality in which we are immersed, of the substance of which we are composed."[32] Religious belief is thus not a matter of affirming particular propositions about the universe. It resides, rather, in the assumption that life, whatever its ultimate meaning, has a profound significance, and that human beings fit into the universe in a miraculous if endlessly mysterious way.

It is because a belief in exceptionalism is integral to what Robinson means by a religious perspective or frame that her humanism is religious. She has remarked in an interview that "the feeling of amazement that I think is appropriate to an alerted sense of what being is leads very naturally to deep comfort with the assumption of God."[33] For Robinson, as for Eliot, there is no strictly secular language that can articulate human exceptionalism. In reference to Thomas Jefferson's declaration that "all men are created equal, that they are endowed by their Creator with certain inalienable rights," she asks: "What would a secular paraphrase of this sentence look like? In what nonreligious terms is human equality self-evident? . . . Jefferson's words acknowledge an essential mystery in human nature and circumstance. He does this by evoking the old faith that God knows us in ways we cannot know ourselves, and that he values us in ways we cannot value ourselves or one another because our intuition of the sacred is so radically limited."[34]

To speak of the "essential mystery" of human beings is to speak in terms that allow for intrinsic worth, that do not crumble under rationalizations of what is valuable or invaluable, advantageous or disadvantageous, in the sense of survival. In our secular age, human exceptionalism is increasingly cast as an anachronistic and hubristic delusion. What Robinson continually affirms is that it is in recognition of the exceptional capacity of human beings for immense destruction as well as good that we must speak of human uniqueness: "we cannot know ourselves."

Fiction

If Robinson aims in her nonfiction to lay bare the pseudoscientific trends that impoverish our experiences and minimize our humanity, her fiction offers a vision for the continued salience of a meaningful humanism. Her first novel, *Housekeeping*, is a portrait of consciousness, an exploration of the inherent slippage between memory, imagination, and perception. Ruth, the narrator, remarks: "I have never distinguished readily between thinking and dreaming. I know my life would be much different if I could ever say, This I have learned from my senses while that I have merely imagined."[35] The ambiguity and final inscrutability of experience never leads Ruth to doubt her own reality; reality is not some final and knowable state that lends itself to confirmation. Indeed, "reality" in the context of the novel translates into something like the interaction between consciousness and the external world; it could never be abstracted or separated from the work of the individual mind within its environment.

Robinson's second novel, *Gilead*, is more explicitly religious, offering an idea of how religious faith—faith in the way that Robinson conceives of it, in the sense of recognizing the ultimate mystery of existence—can awaken and heighten perception, make the world more real and more meaningful. Set in the small town of Gilead, Iowa, the novel is written from the perspective of the Reverend John Ames, an elderly Congregationalist pastor who is nearing the end of his life.

As with Ruth in *Housekeeping*, there is a reciprocal relationship between Reverend Ames's individual consciousness and the world, as consciousness does not strictly create meaning but rather recognizes and articulates what is already in some way given. The framing power of religious practice is that it helps the individual to recognize what is already latent not just in our experience of the world but also in the world itself. When the world just begins to make sense, "it is a remarkable thing to consider," Ames remarks several times in his private reveries. *Gilead*, like *Housekeeping*, is replete with descriptions of moments of quiet remarkability. One such description is Ames's discussion of baptism: "There is a reality in blessing, which I take baptism to be, primarily. It doesn't enhance sacredness, but it acknowledges it, and there is a power in that. I have felt it pass through me, so to speak. The sensation is of really knowing a creature, I mean really feeling its mysterious life and your own mysterious life at the same time."[36]

Baptism is a brief moment of awakening that affords one a glimpse at an underlying reality often missed in daily life. This is, more broadly, one of the responsibilities and values of religion: to alert us to the existence of this underlying reality and help us to see the sacredness of the ordinary.

Ames's narration is imbued throughout the novel with a pure and wholehearted astonishment that recalls the ancient Greek idea of *thaumazein*, or wonder at what is. Reflecting on his meetings with members of his congregation, Ames describes this wonder at "the life that is the real subject of it all": "By 'life' I mean something like 'energy' (as the scientists use the word) or 'vitality,' and also something very different. When people come to speak to me, whatever they say, I am struck by a kind of incandescence in them, the 'I' whose predicate can be 'love' or 'fear' or 'want,' and whose object can be 'someone' or 'nothing' and it won't really matter, because the loveliness is just in that presence, shaped around 'I' like a flame on a wick, emanating itself in grief and guilt and joy and whatever else" (44–45). When Ames qualifies his use of the word "life," he shows that what he means to privilege is really *human* life over a strictly scientific and biological sense of the word. Such life is defined by that almost mythic "I" that is itself meaningful without qualification, a human presence that is singular in its very ability to utter "I," regardless of what follows. That this presence "emanates itself" is a particularly beautiful turn of phrase in that it emphasizes the agency of the human presence, and the metaphor itself—the flame on a wick—implies a subtle but important connection between some sort of internal core of selfhood and an external presence that shines into the world.

The notion that there is some sort of internal core in each person, an essence that flames forth yet remains mysterious even to the individual himself, is embodied in the character of Jack Boughton, the son of Ames's friend. When he was young, Jack fathered a child but refused to take responsibility for it and left town. His return home decades later unsettles Reverend Ames, who finds himself unable to forgive his namesake for this and other offenses. Ames describes how, even before the incident with the girl, Jack seemed unable to be good and had a particular and mysterious sadness about him. "His transgressions were sly and lonely," Ames writes, "and this became truer as he grew up. . . . There was no sense in what he did, unless his purpose was to cause a maximum of embarrassment and risk a minimum of retribution" (182). Though Jack has caused others much pain in his life, there is the sense that this was always somehow despite himself. He is the prodigal son of his family, beloved by them but inexplicably compelled to reject their love or disappoint it.

As he struggles with his feelings about Jack, Ames finds peace in the idea that there is a strange and profound beauty in human fallibility; to acknowledge this beauty is to emulate God's seeing of the world. He recalls an idea of John Calvin's, that each person is an actor on a stage and God is the audience. "That metaphor has always interested me," Ames says, "because it makes us artists of our behavior, and the reaction of God to us might be thought of as aesthetic rather than morally judgmental in the ordinary sense" (124). That God somehow takes pleasure in human fallibility frees us from the need to account for the mystery of our existence, to render it explainable.

Toward the end of the book, as Ames is sitting with Jack on his porch, he reflects: "I wished I could sit at the feet of that eternal soul and learn. He did then seem to me the angel of himself, brooding over the mysteries his mortal life describes, the deep things of man. And of course that is exactly what he is" (197). Jack's transgressions, though they are terrible in the eyes of Ames, are in the same moment worthy of a kind of awe. In showing the way in which our actions often elude final explanation and rationale, they testify to the ultimate mysteriousness of mortal existence. If what constitutes goodness is ultimately a mystery to us, what should be celebrated, acknowledged, even exalted is not goodness, but what Ames calls "the exquisite primary fact of existence" (190).

Intrinsic to Robinson's conception of the singularity of each person is a kind of existential individualism, stemming from the deep interiority within each person. Following the passage about Jack quoted above, Ames observes:

> In every important way we are such secrets from each other, and I do believe that there is a separate language in each of us, also a separate aesthetics and a separate jurisprudence. Every single one of us is a little civilization built on the ruins of any number of preceding civilizations, but with our own variant notions of what is beautiful and what is acceptable—which, I hasten to add, we generally do not satisfy and by which we struggle to live. We take fortuitous resemblances among us to be actual likeness, because those around us have also fallen heir to

> the same customs, trade in the same coin, acknowledge, more or less, the same notions of decency and sanity. But all that really just allows us to coexist with the inviolable, untraversable, and utterly vast spaces between us. (197)

There is an integrity and majesty to this idea of each person as a civilization unto themselves, but it is an integrity that, as in *Housekeeping*, does not resolve into being completely comfortable in the world. There is always an irremediable otherness within worldly encounters and experiences that can only be acknowledged and honored, as Ames comes to do with Jack. Indeed, there is a sense in which solitude is for Robinson the most fundamental human experience, for it is in solitude that one answers to oneself and apprehends one's individual, subjective existence in its relation to the whole of existence, or to being, or to the divine.

Conclusion: The Romance of the Self

Humanism, or what used to be called humanism, acknowledges the intrinsic worth and infinite complexity of human beings; it believes in the meaning of a "self," some being that can neither be understood nor made complete sense of. In the face of the social scientific and Darwinist reduction of human reality to objective measures, Robinson holds fast to her idea of humanism as the romance of the self.

Humanism concerns the mind as opposed to the brain and the self in contrast to the subject. "The mind," Robinson writes in *Absence of Mind*, "whatever else it is, is a constant of everyone's experiences, and, in more and other ways than we know, the creator of the reality that we live within, that we live by and for and despite, and that, often enough, we die from."[37] The mind is that part of ourselves we approach in silence and solitude. It is where we are by ourselves and with ourselves.

But the mind is simultaneously where we dream and think thoughts we share with others. As Emerson writes in "The American Scholar," in lines that Robinson cherishes: "In silence, in steadiness, in severe abstraction, let him hold by himself; add observation to observation, patient of neglect, patient of reproach, and bide his own time,—happy enough if he can satisfy himself alone that this day he has seen something truly. . . . For the instinct is sure, that prompts him to tell his brother what he thinks. He then learns that in going down into the secrets of his own mind he has descended into the secrets of all minds."[38]

Emerson writes these lines in response to a painter who admonished him to believe that what is true and most one's own is true for all of humanity. In these lines is an appeal to a self-reliant truth that, in the Emersonian sense, is transcendent and thus true. The self, Robinson's flame emanating from the wick, is as fecund as it is still, as unique as it is universal.

Emerson's invocation of the self can only cause perturbation today, Robinson writes, in light of the rise of parascience and the modern humanist rejection of the human soul and the mysteries of the self. At a time when "the self is no longer assumed to be a thing to be approached with optimism, or to be trusted to see anything truly,"[39] the venture of art and its quest to explore and probe the infinite and unknowable can rarely appear as anything but untimely. And yet it is just such a fiction that Robinson offers us: to spin from the human mind memories of the transcendent and the eternal.

The imperative of memory is the inescapable claim of history. "If history has any meaning or value," Robinson writes, "as we must assume it does, given our tendency to reach back into the past (or what we assume to have been the past) to account for present problems, then it matters to get it right, insofar as we can" *(Adam,* 11). What history offers is an account of our human path, the contours and guideposts of the world we have created in our writing, acting, and creating. History, as does memory, brings us into the human world. And insofar as we learn history through books, literacy is the first means by which one becomes a self-aware member of the human community. In this way, it is also for Robinson the grounding for democracy, as it is through reading that we come to develop "imaginative love" for people we do not know, and find ways to see and approach others in good faith, whatever deep conflicts we may have with them.[40]

Near the end of *Housekeeping,* Robinson writes: "Memory is the sense of loss, and loss pulls us after it."[41] The memory of loss is a yearning for a reunion with the whole, a unity we have been torn from. Of the first loss, the first event—the "expulsion" from the Garden—she writes, "the force behind the movement of time is a mourning that will not be comforted" (192). The inextinguishable power of mourning is the force that moves time forward from the cut of expulsion to the wholeness of reconciliation.

Amid these reveries on memory, loss, and reconciliation, Ruth wonders what would have happened if her mother had not driven into Fingerbone Lake, where her grandfather also lost his life. Ruth answers her own query: "We would have known nothing of the nature and reach of her sorrow if she had come back. But she left us and broke the family and the sorrow was released and we saw its wings and saw it fly a thousand ways into the hills, and sometimes I think sorrow is a predatory thing because birds scream at dawn with a marvelous terror, and there is, as I have said before, a deathly bitterness in the smell of ponds and ditches."[42]

Sorrow breaks families apart, just as Cain broke the family of Adam and Absalom twice split the family of King David. It is this sorrow and the memorial mourning it unleashes that fires Robinson's stories. To be human, she suggests, is to repay sorrow with words.

What holds our humanity together in the end is simply a web of words, as Ruth writes in *Housekeeping:* "It had never occurred to me that words, too, must be salvaged, though when I thought about it, it seemed obvious. It was absurd to think that things were held in place, are held in place, by a web of words."[43] Humanism, as Robinson imagines it in her work, is a sensibility that preserves this common web and attests to the sense of beauty in the human act. Humanism finds an "aesthetic pleasure in the human presence," even in its darkest moments (*Adam*, 27).

Notes

1. American Humanist Association, "Humanist Manifesto I," last modified 1973, www.americanhumanist.org/Humanism/Humanist_Manifesto_I.

2. See http://newatheists.org. The writers associated with the New Atheists include the recently deceased journalist Christopher Hitchens, the scientist Richard Dawkins, the writer Sam Harris, and the philosopher Daniel Dennett.

3. American Humanist Association, "Humanist Manifesto I."

4. T. S. Eliot, "Second Thoughts on Humanism," in *Collected Essays* (New York: Harcourt, Brace, 1950), 433.

5. Ibid., 436.

6. T. S. Eliot, "The Humanism of Irving Babbitt," in *Collected Essays* (New York: Harcourt, Brace, 1950), 423.

7. Marilynne Robinson, *The Death of Adam: Essays on Modern Thought* (New York: Picador, 2005), 8. Hereafter cited parenthetically.

8. Robinson, *When I Was a Child I Read Books: Essays* (New York: Farrar, Straus and Giroux, 2012), 199.

9. In fact, Robinson describes creationism as "the best thing that could have happened to Darwinism, the caricature of religion that has seemed to justify Darwinist contempt for the whole of religion" (Robinson, *The Death of Adam,* 40).

10. Michael Ruse defines natural selection as "the key Darwinian mechanism for evolutionary change, claiming that a small percentage of organisms in each generation survive and reproduce owing to characteristics which other members of the population do not possess; these adaptive characteristics are passed along to offspring" (Ruse, *Mystery of Mysteries: Is Evolution a Social Construction?* [Cambridge: Harvard University Press, 1999], 282).

11. Max Weber, "Science as a Vocation," in *From Max Weber: Essays in Sociology,* trans. and ed. H. H. Gerth and C. Wright Mills (New York: Oxford University Press, 1946), 7.

12. Charles Darwin, "Darwin, C. R. to Graham, William, 3 July 1881," from *Darwin Correspondence Project.* University of Cambridge, last modified 2014, www.darwinproject.ac.uk/entry-13230.

13. Thomas Malthus, *An Essay on the Principle of Population: Text, Sources and Background, Criticism,* ed. Philip Appleman, Norton Critical Editions (New York: Norton, 1976).

14. Charles Darwin, *The Descent of Man,* in *Darwin: Texts, Commentary,* ed. Philip Appleman, Norton Critical Editions, 3rd ed. (New York: Norton, 2001), 253.

15. Stephen Jay Gould, "The Evolution of Life on Earth," in *The Richness of Life: The Essential Stephen Jay Gould,* ed. Paul McGarr and Steven Rose (New York: Norton, 2006), 209.

16. Ibid., 215.

17. Ibid., 213–14.

18. Ibid., 220.

19. Michael Ruse, *Darwinism and Its Discontents* (Cambridge: Cambridge University Press, 2008), 202.

20. Richard Dawkins, *The Selfish Gene* (New York: Oxford University Press, 1976), 4.

21. Ibid., 2.

22. Ibid., 69–70.

23. Marilynne Robinson, *Absence of Mind: The Dispelling of Inwardness from the Modern Myth of the Self* (New Haven: Yale University Press, 2010), 62.

24. Robinson, *Absence of Mind,* 32–33.

25. Ibid., 71.

26. Ibid., 31.

27. Robinson, *When I Was a Child,* 193.

28. Ibid., 197.

29. Richard Dawkins, *The Blind Watchmaker* (New York: Norton, 1996), xiii.

30. Robinson, *Absence of Mind,* 23.
31. Robinson, *When I Was a Child,* 5.
32. Robinson, *When I Was a Child,* 192.
33. Marilynne Robinson, interview by Bob Abernathy, *Religion and Ethics Newsweekly,* Podcast audio, March 18, 2005, www.pbs.org/wnet/religionandethics/episodes/march-18–2005/interview-marilynne-robinson/4226.
34. Robinson, *When I Was a Child,* 162–63.
35. Marilynne Robinson, *Housekeeping* (New York: Picador, 1980), 215–16.
36. Marilynne Robinson, *Gilead* (New York: Picador, 2004), 23. Hereafter cited parenthetically.
37. Robinson, *Absence of Mind,* 1.
38. Qtd. ibid., xvii.
39. Ibid., xviii.
40. Robinson *When I Was a Child,* 28.
41. Robinson, *Housekeeping,* 194.
42. Ibid., 198.
43. Ibid., 200.

CHAPTER 10

Merism and the Mermaid in a Ship's Cabin

A Conversation with Marilynne Robinson

We conducted this interview on September 19, 2014, in Marilynne Robinson's Iowa City home, an inviting space where one is surrounded by books on all sides and photographs that hold significance for her. The interview was done toward the end of our publication process, with all of the essays completed and the book nearly ready to send to press. We were curious to see how Robinson's most recent novel, *Lila*, would fit in with some of our authors' arguments. But unfortunately, the timing of things did not allow us to include a consideration of this latest book in our collection. *Lila* was scheduled for release in early October 2014, just about the time we were preparing the manuscript for the publisher. But *Lila* did figure into our interview in an especially serendipitous way. Just as we were leaving Robinson's house after finishing the interview, we noticed a very large box outside of her door. We offered to carry it inside for her. Robinson said that the box probably contained her advance copies of the new book, and, if so, she would like to give us each a copy of it. So we eagerly carried the box inside and indeed, it was *Lila*! Robinson graciously gave us each a signed copy, and we had the most absorbing reading material possible for our flights back home.

JL (Joseph Lane): I would like to start with a quote from the overall series editor's introduction. Patrick Deneen writes that a study of American political life "is incomplete if it neglects American literature, one of the great repositories of the nation's political thought and teachings. American literature is distinctive because it is, above all, intended for a democratic citizenry." He goes on: "An astute political interpretation of an American literary tradition requires careful, patient and attentive readers who approach the text with a view to understanding its underlying messages about citizenship and democracy." We wanted to get your reaction to that underlying philosophy of the series. As somebody who writes literature that approaches political questions from oblique angles, and an essay writer who writes directly on political issues in books like *Mother Country,* how do you think literature illuminates our understanding of politics, and how do you approach politics differently as an essayist and as a novelist?

MR: Literature—fiction, or poetry, I guess, like Walt Whitman—makes a conceivable model of relationships. I think that with very rare exceptions, politicians themselves, and I'm not using the word invidiously, tend to have to simplify because they are focused around certain issues and certain solutions. In terms of meditating on the actual nature of problems and questions, I think fiction and poetry are much more accommodating to that sort of thinking.

SM (Shannon Mariotti): Yes, I think there are a lot of questions that you can explore more deeply through fiction than you can through politics, and a lot of the pieces that are in this series, I think, will illuminate that.

JL: When you sit down to write something like *Mother Country* or other essays on political issues, do you feel your thinking is meaningfully different than when you're meditating on those things through something like a novel?

MR: It's different in emphasis. I wouldn't call it qualitatively different, really. I think you have to be engaged with the world to write fiction. And it's a different kind of engagement from politics. It's an interesting thing, even to think what politics is. Because it does tend to be so specifically addressed to a moment, to a problem, to an electorate, as it's understood in a certain period of time. Perhaps I'm overgeneralizing, but I don't think we have political theorists operating now, particularly. Paul Krugman perhaps, but I can't think of anybody else. We went through a very strange period in this country where we let political discourse be dominated by things like Marxism. Which was turned into this strange jungle of theory. By people who didn't read Marx, people who didn't study economics. It sounded cosmic and global and everything, but I think it took our mind away from what mattered, that address to a democratic populace. And the odd effect, I think, of academic Marxism was to create an elitism of political thinking, because it really never touched ground as far as most people's experience was concerned. I would really like to see the reemergence of people who talk about politics with real respect and interest for democratic politics, democratic equality.

SM: So when you talk about political theorists, it sounds to me like you're talking about people who think about politics with an eye toward practice, too, and people who think about politics with an eye toward what it's like to live on the ground. Do you mean that Paul Krugman is an example of that way of thinking?

MR: Yes, that. And then, you know, I read him pretty often, although frankly I agree with him so much I'm frightened to read him [*laughs*]. But he talks about the persisting crisis in Europe. And I think it is actually a reconstruction of European society. The reason they don't solve it is because they don't want to solve it. I mean, it has moved the whole continent radically in another direction from the one that it seemed to be heading in, before this financial crisis. And if you read economics historically, one of the ways to maintain political power is to maintain high levels of unemployment. And that's what you have all over Europe now. And God bless him, dear old Paul Krugman asks, "Why are these people not fixing this?"

SM: You would argue that there's not the political will to fix it.

MR: Exactly, or not anyway among the people that have any power to fix it.

SM: Can you say more about how you understand political theory?

MR: It seems to me that there is a degree of traditionalism in academic political thought that assigns little value to current realities. With all respect to Locke and Burke and Smith and Tocqueville and Marx and Weber and all the rest, the world has changed sufficiently to deserve a profound rethinking. Krugman has an admirable loyalty to this world and this country in this time. So he looks at the data and considers the influences and their implications. The nostalgists and the dystopians are not engaged with reality, by definition. I think Krugman is mistaken in some of his assumptions about what is going on in the world economy, but he is attending to it and thinking very scrupulously about it, and he is capable of making evaluative statements—which are political in the best sense, implying the potential efficacy of public awareness and public policy.

SM: You bring up Marx, and in one of your essays, you write about the experience of really reading Marx. You write often about the experience of really reading the books that we sort of think we know or think we're familiar with and having this new experience of finding things that we didn't think we would find there. And you talk about reading Marx in that same way. So, what did you bring away from that experience of really reading Marx?

MR: Well, he describes England in its industrial period, and he's indignant. I mean, it was profoundly inhumane, without question the most radical polarization of wealth and poverty that could be contrived. He tries to see beyond this in a way by imagining that some ultimate good will emerge from it, but the tenor of his writing—he writes like Luther. Like Luther and Dickens. Because he is ironic, and he has a very strong ethical sense focused around really bitter injustice.

SM: And suffering.

MR: And suffering. And you know, he was read in this country for a long time, not just because he wrote a column for the *New York Daily Tribune,* but also *Capital* was read here for a long time. I think if people read Marx now they would see analogies between what he's described and what we're tending toward. And then if you read the people that consider themselves anti-Marxists, like the British economists that came after him: they were basically proceeding on the same assumption, that if the working class gets unruly, you simply ship the jobs overseas and this sort of thing. And so they are simply calling good what he calls evil. It's the same model.

SM: When I teach Locke in my political theory class and then I teach Marx, sort of the father of capitalism, the father of communism, and they're very similar, they're just calling different things good and bad. I think you're exactly right that reading Marx has to begin in some ways with what we think we know about Marx.

MR: If some great magnet could pass over the continent and erase . . .

SM: Yes! I do this silly exercise with students: I say close your eyes, forget everything you think you know about Marx, and let's just try to read this like we read other things.

MR: Exactly. And you know, people have a sort of superstitious attitude toward books: I can't read that, it'll jump into my mind and change me [*laughter*]. It's just bizarre.

JL: Is that the sort of feeling that you were trying to capture in the discussion between Gloria and Jack about taking Marx out of the library or taking Du Bois out of the library?

MR: Exactly.

JL: That they would get this infection.

MR: It's very sad. I would like to see where that enters in, because it is premodern, this fear of books. And here we are producing hundreds of thousands of books every year, every imaginable kind, but there are certain ones that are just stigmatized. You know it, and it's like the *Malleus Maleficarum*, the book on how to deal with witches.

SM: Are there other books that you find yourself returning to again and again to reread and to discover things anew continually? I mean, you've written about the Bible obviously in the same kind of context, but are there other books you return to?

MR: Well, I keep reading things that I haven't read before. John Wycliffe, for example. How bizarre that he's not more well-known. I'm actually writing an essay that suggests that there was a cultural environment in which Shakespeare spoke that didn't come from the upper class, that came from these dissident traditions like Wycliffe, who was in print and available, although you got burned for having him.

JL: Going back to the Marx again, in writing *Mother Country*, did you see yourself in some ways trying to bring out on behalf of the people of Cumbria and the North Sea Coast the same type of indignation and sort of cry for attention and justice that you thought Marx was using for the working class in Manchester and Birmingham and the industrial cities of Britain a century earlier?

MR: I came across this Sellafield business. And it's outrageous: anybody who knows anything about plutonium or the state of the sea—just baldly, on its face, it's outrageous. I was trying to figure out why it would have happened. Because in this country, it's very characteristic, there's a sort of spectrum of what we consider possible or likely. Too many things fall off the end. I mean, they're manufacturing plutonium. People would say, Well why would they do that? As if the fact that it's crazy means that it wouldn't happen. And this is true of very many things. Europe and Britain are a huge blind spot for us; we never really look at them. You know, I lived in France for a while, and when I came back here I was trying to follow French news and honestly, honestly, there was a strike of pastry chefs! That was basically what the *Times* was concerning itself with. We make Europeans cute. It's just ridiculous. It's embarrassing, really.

SM: On the question of Europe, did you have any thoughts on the Scottish vote for independence? And as far as we know, we still don't know the outcome of it, right? We were checking the news before we came over this morning.

JL: It looks like it will be "No."

MR: Oh, I don't know. Scotland has a much stronger educational culture, much stronger labor unions, God knows. A stronger health system, all these kinds of things. And this is despite the influence of London, right? But even granting all difficulties, I would be interested to see what Scotland would do.

SM: On its own?

MR: Yes.

JL: Do you think that such votes, and the talk of other peripheral areas moving away from their centers, is a reaction to the types of injustices you've talked about in your writings on neoliberalism and austerity and the defects of austerity-driven political economics?

MR: I think that that can be a factor, sadly enough. When people are deprived by their own governments, they tend to turn on minorities. It's very hard—people try to identify with the core. We see it in this country all the time, exactly the people that would be benefited by having the influence of the larger culture just can't accept it at all. And that's happening all over, even in places like Sweden. It's very alarming because it's so irrational and it's so potent.

SM: Yeah. With immigration in the U.S. we're seeing that right now, too.

MR: Yes, exactly.

SM: We had some questions we wanted to talk about with respect to democracy as well. In *When I Was a Child I Read Books,* you invoke an ideal of democracy, and in one of the quotes that I think is really powerful, you say, "To identify sacred mystery with every individual experience, every life, giving the word its largest sense, is to arrive at democracy as an ideal and to accept the difficult obligation to honor others and oneself with something approaching due reverence." I wonder if you could just expand a little bit more on what you think that practice of democracy looks like in action. What it means to live this kind of democratic life on an individual level.

MR: Right. Well, I think that democracy has to be collaborative. Because it's very easy to demonstrate that people do each other profound good by cooperative behavior of every kind. I mean, democracy as an ideal is a pretty harsh light on democracy as we have ever succeeded in practicing it, but that's the nature of an ideal. Not only that, but it's what has made us do things better than we did one hundred years ago. I always tell my classes, I say this so incessantly it's embarrassing, but I seem to be alone saying it: A human brain is the most complex object known to exist in the universe. And what a profoundly democratic gesture on the part of, I would say God. Others would say, what? Evolution? But nevertheless, there's nothing evolutionary about it because it's an absolutely true statement about anybody. And that means we don't know what people are capable of. And the way that we create ability in other people is by supporting their health, by giving them options that they can turn into other options that we would never have anticipated. So, I think openness of that kind would be the most direct way toward achieving democracy. Heightened democracy. We don't know what people are. We don't know what they could do. It really bothers me to hear all this talk about reforming the educational system, which is really narrowing options and making people into little more than efficient workers.

JL: Or capitalists? They might share that in common [*laughter*].

MR: Well, morphologically it's capital accumulation with economic power being the center of power.

SM: It's interesting to me, because it does seem like your thoughts on democracy really remind us of the root of the word, which is to give the *demos kratos,* to give the people power. You're talking about empowering people by respecting their uniqueness, by respecting their experiences.

MR: By teaching *them* to respect them. That's one of the things that really drives me crazy. I think that we're encouraged to have some low ceiling on our expectations. On what basis? That whole thing about our culture being immature or declined—the kinds of categories that we are put into as a culture. This is purely destructive. We say to a black kid, to an Asian kid, to whatever, we say, "You can do anything you want to do." Then we turn around and say, generalizing them, "Since you are Americans, you are probably kind of dim." We engage in such generalizations about this population that is so wildly diverse and diversified. I just can't imagine how people think that's a meaningful way to talk.

JL: So really mindfulness, to use your word, as a democratic virtue is being mindful of the mind.

MR: Absolutely. I mean, there are lots of ways in which other creatures are more elegant than we are. But we do have that.

SM: Do you see any of the characters in your novels really adopting that unique disposition that you are describing? Are there particular characters that you feel embody that spirit of mindfulness, of some reverence for the minds of others, the lives of others, the experiences of others?

MR: I suppose John Ames comes as close anyone does. But it's a very difficult thing to do. I think the achievements of people in that way are very limited.

SM: I think you alluded to this earlier. It's the struggle that matters, because you never fully attain that ideal.

MR: Exactly.

SM: It's the working toward it. It's that striving toward democracy as an ideal that you will never really fully achieve.

MR: Right. And I think, objectively speaking, to the extent that this culture and country is democratic, we have done extraordinarily well. It's because we have these sort of cosmetic visions of Europe and England, particularly, that we can't evaluate what we ourselves have done and decide simply what has worked well, which I think is always an important thing to be aware of.

JL: Tying into that and evaluating what we have done well and particularly citing John Ames as a good example of this, one of our authors in the volume, Emily Nacol, writes about the relationship that you see between old age and democracy. This is, in some ways, the inverse of a common perception of democracy that associates democracy often with the young, with the rebellious, with doing untraditional and unconventional things. I wonder if you could talk some about that connection. In what way is democracy informed by or enriched by age and its aging population? What should we look for there?

SM: In your writing there is a reverence for old things. Ames talks about how he realizes that the things he loves the most he calls old, like "old Boughton." So is this reverence for old things, for old people, for aging, actually tied to the strengthening of democratic communities?

MR: One thing is simply that people who have lived a long time: they have big data [*laughter*]. I sometimes talk to students that say nothing ever changes. I remember the pre–civil rights period. I remember the prefeminist period. Things change. There's a kind of activism that builds on good, earlier activism, and there's a kind that just kind of goes haywire on the assumption that everything, except for their immediate circle or something, is foolish and corrupt. I have felt for a long time that we have models in our history for doing well, for making good reform. It's very unusual to make a reform that actually becomes a part of the cultural fabric. But the question is, how do you go about it? The answer is, find out how earlier generations have gone about it. Characteristically in this country, every generation has enhanced the experience of the next generation. Not true now, I am afraid.

SM: It seems to me that your mind is skeptical. You question things. You challenge assumptions, especially some of the ones that we take to be most commonplace. But in talking with you, you're a skeptic without being cynical. I think you seem optimistic about our potential and about especially what Americans have been capable of in the past and what they would be capable of in the future.

MR: I am. Again, it's history and it's also comparative cultural things that I attend to. People think it's like ancestor worship or something, where you look at the abolitionists, who are not my personal ancestors. But what I'm really saying is, how do these people do this? How did they get purchase on a situation like this? Getting rid of slavery in the States would be like getting rid of the computer industry or something today. It was completely embedded and enormously economically generative. What they did is really amazing. They tend to be stigmatized as violent because of old John Brown, but slavery was so violent that the fact that the stigma would fall on the abolitionists is just extraordinary. I mean, it's persisting racism of a very profound kind.

SM: You have this way of returning to the past and to abolitionists in general as a touchstone. Is there a space today, and if so where would it be, for the Grandfather Ameses of the world? Or have we totally foreclosed the possibility for that kind of radical abolitionism that he lived and embodied?

MR: Well, the world is so different now. The issues are so different. I think that one of the things that the abolitionists had going for them was a very clearly defined problem. Another thing, slavery was an international phenomenon, and the French and the Spanish and the Portuguese and so on continued the slave trade almost to the end of the nineteenth century. So it's not as if the phenomenon of global economics is novel. Nevertheless, people can't wake up to the fact that this kind of globalism has a long history, and it is always a pitting the poor against the poorer still. You set up a factory in Malaysia, the wages go up a little bit, so you abandon the factory in Malaysia and go somewhere where the people are more desperate. The consequence of that is that it makes poverty an economic resource for governments. I mean, I'm sure that's one of the reasons wages never go up here, because of this model of competition.

SM: It's strategic.

MR: Yes. Exactly.

SM: Thinking more about race and the way that fits into your fictions . . . I hope it's okay: we call him Grandfather Ames because . . .

JL: When people write about *Gilead,* it becomes a real issue. Ames, Ames, Ames.

SM: There are so many Ameses, like Ames Senior, Ames Junior. So we call him Grandfather Ames. But he embodies one way of responding to racial injustice, and Jack, the other sort of unlikely hero, mirrors him in a lot of ways but represents a very different way of responding to racial injustice. If we see those as two different models of how to deal with the problem of racial inequality, which do you think is the better approach today? Is it Jack's personal way of living these ideals in his own construction of his family, or is it Grandfather Ames's more radical approach? Or, in your mind, what's the difference between those two approaches to dealing with racial injustice?

MR: Well, I think we have sort of passed the time when you put a pistol in your belt. I guess we haven't. I guess I wish we had.

JL: Right. In most places.

MR: But Jack is somebody who doesn't identify with a particular role in society. So he's much more just simply open.

SM: Right.

MR: He encounters this woman who was very gracious to him and probably kind of reminds him of home, because of her own family. His sorrow, his ineptitude, and so on, make him simply grateful for the kindness that she shows him and the other people in this church that he starts being involved in. I mean, he's sort of ahead of his time simply because he has no place in his time.

JL: I had this strange experience last year, last fall, with my first-year students. *Gilead* was what they were supposed to read over the summer before they came to college. When we got to talking about it, there was part of the class, not everybody, but a significant part that said: "Dr. Lane, you keep bringing up the racial stuff in this book. That's there, but it's not what the book is about." That was very funny to me, because I thought that was *all* of what the book was about. But they didn't see it. They saw it mostly as being about fathers and sons and not necessarily about race. But it at least awoke me to the idea that there is something kind of strange about deciding to tell the story of race and racism in America in a small all-white town in Iowa with white Anglo-Saxon characters. At least on screen that's whom you see, so to speak. Why did you think that was an interesting way to approach the problem of racism in American in a book that wasn't about an African American character?

MR: Well, the experience of life, for black Americans, was very, very strongly formed by people who don't think about them at all. The abolitionist movement was very strong in Iowa. This town was nearly wiped out by the number of men that went into the Union army. The thing that struck me so powerfully when I began to know something about that history is that people here don't know that history. They don't know their history at all, actually, unless it's that their ancestors were from Czechoslovakia or something like that. Who knows why we turned into an all-white state? Historically the two most radical egalitarian states in the union are Maine and Iowa. Both snow-white. Who can explain this? For a long time we had great difficulty bringing minority writers to the Iowa Workshop because it was in Iowa. But the first MFA given in the world was given here to a black woman named Elizabeth Catlett, who was a sculptor and painter and very well regarded. You can see a statue that she made in the student union. She donated it out of gratitude. But in any case, black opera singers would come here because our graduate programs accepted them. Nobody else. So we've always had this history, and we're actually quite proud of it. At the same time there is a conception of what this state is that is so potent. But now, thank God, the dam broke somehow or other, and we're getting a lot of minority kids who do very well. But that's the thing. If minority people feel that something is a closed world, a white world, they are not going to trifle with it. It took us a long time to get past that. I mean, people would say we didn't admit black people. But they didn't apply.

JL: Well, that's fascinating. Thank you. In your essays you talk about the relationship between the American people and the wilderness and the settlement of the West as being really a foundational moment and interaction of people and landscape that shapes who we are, and you lament, at times, that some of the better virtues and attributes that we received from that action are being lost. I wondered whether the townspeople's distrust of Sylvie, in a certain way, reflects the burying of those old values that you thought had a certain importance for American society but are being lost because they can't stand her ruthlessness. They can't stand the idea that she would pick up and go somewhere.

SM: Transience.

JL: She won't stay put.

MR: Well, she takes this little girl out overnight in a leaky boat. She has given every sign of being a strange character. The sheriff comes. He knows he's supposed to do something about it, and he doesn't have the heart to do it. So if that were to happen and you were to read about it in the newspaper, you would say, "Where were the people who should have been protecting this child?" So I feel sometimes as if the things that you write get put into the mold that is preestablished. I'm not on a side. I mean, I don't feel—I'm sympathetic to the town. I'm sympathetic to everybody, you know.

SM: That comes through.

MR: I hope so, but I think it's quite true that people that stay in these towns, nevertheless, feel and understand the desire to just walk off into the mountains, and would be probably less suspicious of Sylvie than an ordinary town would be. I think we misunderstand the frontier because so much of it was really quite idealistic. The Homestead Act, which is, as the British economists always say, the biggest handout by a government in the history of the world. All these kinds of things were huge instances of putting public wealth into public hands in ways that were meant to enhance life. If you read the economics that's contemporary with the Homestead Act, they thought of giving people plots of land as an answer to destitution. Of course, it was much more generous in scale than anything these rather nasty little European economists dreamed about. And it did create a tremendous autonomous wealth among a very large part of the population. This country was mainly agricultural until—I mean in terms of how people were employed—until the end of the 1950s, I suppose. And so the people were basically being given the primary means of subsistence in the economy. It was a huge thing to do. People act now as if it were just pushing and shoving and grabbing and all that sort of thing. So everything turns into an advertisement for the NRA in terms of thinking about our history. But places like Greeley, Colorado, a lot of these were utopian communities.

SM: It's impossible to imagine something like that on that scale happening today. It's extraordinary.

MR: It's just amazing.

JL: Is that why you speak of the biblical scale of the whole thing, calling the Homestead Act "like Deuteronomy"?

MR: Yes, exactly. Yes, because in Deuteronomy: unalienable property. This was distributed through the whole population.

SM: This is one of the problems that you encounter when teaching political theory. So many of the political ideals that we still have, like equal opportunity and so many of these seemingly good liberal values come out of a tradition where they were more realizable in a material sense, giving people land, giving them the means to actually pull themselves up by their boot straps. But today we have those same values, but they are out of step with the material realities of the world today, of the U.S. today, especially.

MR: Yes, this great emphasis of world economy, it implies that we don't have the luxury of actually creating characteristic laws that would have the effect of sheltering modest ownership and things like that. You can read about it in Marx. You can read about it in William Beveridge.

There is a school of economic thought that will not accept the idea of rights of self-determination. I had a Jamaican student talking to me in my office just yesterday. He was talking about how the International Monetary Fund had stepped in. When he was a little kid, he watched them pouring tons and tons of fresh Jamaican milk into the sea because under the terms of the IMF agreements, they had to buy powdered milk from Europe. I mean, destruction of wealth in the most objective sense. What do you have in the way of autonomy if something like that can be imposed?

SM: That's a really vivid example. Relating to this conversation about the reverence for home that you have. You pair that with the sense that there is a kind of homelessness that also has value, and you've mentioned Jack's openness and his sense of acceptance, that his tolerance comes from maybe not having a space in conventional society. In your writing I think that there's this reverence for home and a reverence for the influence of homelessness that Sylvie represents and that Jack represents. One of the people that I study is Thoreau. I see him as representing that same middle ground. He goes to Walden Pond, but there is a profound domesticity to his cabin at Walden Pond even at the same time he goes there to cultivate this outsider status and to get outside of conventions. In contrast, a lot of times in contemporary democratic theory there tends to be a sharper distinction between the kinds of attitudes that we cultivate at home, this comfortable complacency maybe where everything is familiar. That attitude is sometimes seen as dangerous for a democracy, whereas this ethos of homelessness is seen as valuable for democracy because it sharpens your critical capacities and things like that. But it seems to me that like Thoreau, in a lot of ways, you don't see dichotomy between these two things, home and homelessness, but rather combine them in important ways. I wonder if you could just talk with us a little bit about your thoughts on the value of home and homelessness in a democratic community, the ways that they both have value.

MR: Well, I just sort of attach a democratic value to people doing what they want to do. There is a term that's used in biblical criticism, "merism." It refers to concepts that encompass two ends of a continuum in effect, heaven and earth, phrases that imply everything in between. I think it's a bad habit of mind that we have to assume that unlike things are in opposition to each other. The idea of continuum means that neither end is absolutely estranged from the other. That seems to me a much more realistic and rational way of thinking.

SM: Could you elaborate more on the concept of "merism" and how you see it extending beyond the study of theology? Is this an important orienting concept for your worldview in general?

MR: Sometimes I become aware that there are habits of thought that are important for us culturally and which create rigidity in our view of things. The fact that things that we often regard as in opposition to each other can in fact be two extremes of a continuum, implying a rich and complex intermediate reality lying between them, is interesting and fruitful. Merism is a term in biblical criticism for inclusive extremes, heaven and earth being one example, good and evil being another. I use the idea often, to help myself rethink, reconsider.

SM: You have that one passage in *Housekeeping* about Sylvie like a mermaid in a ship's cabin sunk in the very element that it was meant to exclude. That really seems to me to capture just what you are talking about, that it's both/and: home and homelessness. These things are not opposites.

MR: Right, so few things are, I think, real opposites.

JL: How do we foster that sort of understanding that recognizes that the poles aren't really poles at all? Because they are seeing some action in democratic discourse now, and I'm using the term "democratic" with a small *d* and maybe even with a touch of irony, but I mean the discourse around democracy that wants to drive the wedge as deeply in as it can between this group and that group. The in-group, the out-group, the rich, the poor, the whatever. Instead of taking that sort of more all-encompassing view that says there is this continuum, but everyone along that continuum is part of us. Is that something that can be linguistically overcome?

MR: Well, I think if people try. We are having a fairly profound experience of the futility of this oppositional thinking. I think that all sides have indulged in it in a degree that is very irresponsible. To see these people scrambling around trying to rouse up some fringe group and so on, it's beneath the dignity of democracy and it certainly is not friendly to its thriving or continuing.

SM: Yes, especially when you think about how in the context of the

U.S., our two parties have so much in common with each other. I think that the idea of getting rid of this oppositional thinking also helps us understand the ways that gender plays into your writing and your fiction, because this idea that there is not a dichotomy or sharp distinction between public and private, or between home and wilderness, I think you show that the home can be a wilderness in a lot of ways.

It's liberating for women not to have this kind of public man/private woman dichotomy. I mean, the way that Sylvie engages in this kind of delightful but bizarre form of housekeeping; she comes home to care for her nieces in a way that is very gendered. You have women who come home out of obligation to care for their nieces in a similar way to the way that Glory comes home to care for her father. But none of those dynamics play out in the conventional ways that we might expect with this way that we sharply define public and private.

MR: Well, part of what has to be dealt with is that I am writing about the middle 1950s, before crucial changes in the society. Sylvie comes home, but if the only relative they were aware of was a man, we don't have any reason to think he might not have come home also. Protectiveness is not a monopoly of any gender. In the case of Glory, the kind of cover for her situation is that she's taking care of her father. In fact, she finds shelter with her father because her other life fell apart. So in both cases, I don't think that the roles would take on a gender, except in the sense that if they want to fall into a conventional pattern, then they can claim to be taking on gendered roles.

SM: Yes, I think that helps make sense of it because they're women, but that seems beside the point in a lot of ways. Along those same lines of thinking about gender, one of the things that we noticed and have been thinking about is the role that fathering plays in a lot of your fiction. We have a lot of rich examples of what fathering looks like in practice or of failed attempts at fathering. There's obviously Ames and his son, Robby, but then there's Ames and Jack. Ames is a sort of father figure for Jack, and there's Jack's lack of a relationship with his daughter, who died, and then there's his attempts to have a relationship with his own son. So there's a lot of fathering that goes on. It struck me that we don't have the same kind of rich examples of mothering, although maybe the new book changes that. But I wondered if you were aware of or attentive to fathering in a way that you were not as attentive to mothering in the fiction.

MR: Well, the new novel is a counterexample. It's a funny thing: there's a way in which I think writing is not as intentional as sometimes people think it is. I started this series of novels because I had John Ames's voice in my mind. I think that is the impulse for a lot of writing. You ponder a character by creating versions that are variations, in effect.

SM: When you are writing your essays, do you find yourself inspired in the same kind of way? If you started hearing John Ames's voice and that prompted *Gilead,* is there a similar process that prompts you to write nonfiction? It sounded like *Mother Country* was inspired in a similar kind of way by a sense of outrage.

MR: Well, no, I mean I was shocked . . . and surprised. I have a PhD in English literature. I was taught American style, but English history was in our résumé. But it was really not at all true, not at all descriptive. Nevertheless, I certainly took it all in, it was spoon-fed to me. Then I started reading these things, not only about the nuclear pollution but also about social issues surrounding the way England has gone. I started reading. I read economics from the late eighteenth century—no, really the early eighteenth century—through to William Beveridge. It took me years. It was such a strange thing to do, you know, sitting in old libraries reading books that nobody had opened for a hundred years. But it was fascinating. Part of what was fascinating about it, I mean, on the one hand the absolute barbarism of the assumptions that generally inspired it, and the fact that it is so repetitive. It is one generation after another with just the slightest change until you get to Beatrice Webb, with her saying what a waste it is that the poor have metal coffin handles on their coffins. I mean, the mean-mindedness of people that we call socialists. Well, they call themselves that. But basically, the whole system was to squeeze and squeeze and squeeze yet more out of the poor, who were considered to be some sort of a burden to the society, like an infestation of some sort.

JL: You didn't go to the UK, when you went in the 1980s, for this, you just kind of found out when you were there?

MR: You'd find these articles on the front pages of the major newspapers. I would say to Americans, "Can you believe this stuff? Can you believe they are dumping this acid and nuclear elements into the sea?" They would not have seen the articles. It's like we just build blind spots into people. There are supposed to be fifty thousand Americans in London on any given day. And I alone escaped to tell you this?

JL: This was just when Margaret Thatcher was coming to power and the American-British relationship was being redefined in terms of Reaganism and Thatcherism. At that point in time, what hit you as an American living in London?

MR: R. W. Apple was the American correspondent for the *New York Times*. And I read his valedictory, and he said, "The great achievement of the British is that they have preserved their environment." And I thought, "What in the world is he talking about?" Sellafield is only one instance. They've got crazy things all over that little island.

SM: But that's the same dynamic you've talked about in other contexts because it doesn't fit in to the preconceived notions that we have. So it's like, "Oh, I don't have a box for that. So I'm not going to see it."

MR: Exactly.

SM: I think that describes the unique form of perception that Sylvie has and that Jack has because they don't have any boxes. . . .

MR: They don't, right.

SM: They see everything. They have this ability to really experience and perceive. And it seems like it's part and parcel of the fact that they are outsiders, that they don't have a place carved out for them in conventional society.

JL: You had written in a couple of places about fear being the passion most to be avoided or contained in democracy, being something that perhaps democracy is particularly susceptible to or particularly in danger of succumbing to. And I wonder if you'd talk some about in what sense fear is a—for lack of a better word—contagion within democratic peoples. How have you tried to handle that, and what do you think can be done to deal more effectively with our propensity to fear?

MR: I don't know how many democratic peoples there are, but . . .

JL: People aspiring in the general direction of that ideal.

MR: I don't know how many of those there are either. But the thing about other cultures, it is very typical of them, other kinds of cultures, that they shape and groom information that comes to the public. And they can feel complacent when they really ought to be afraid. In an open system like ours, we're flooded with information and have very little grounds for making selections among the sources of it. For most people that's true. I don't know where else the kind of attacks that have been made on the government here would be tolerated. Not in France. They have systems for screening these things out. I think that openness creates a possibility of exploitation of the other. A closed system simply means that people whose quality as leaders cannot by any means be guaranteed can manipulate public feeling, and they create fear too. I think that a lot of the hostility toward immigrants that you find everywhere in the world now is politically manipulated. In any case, the combination of democracy on the one hand, that ought to mean that someone who's elected president is president, and on the other hand, the idea that this country generally claims to be Christian or at least religious. And what kind of religion keeps you in a state of existential panic? If these people believe that things are in the hands of the benign God, ultimately, then what excuse do they have for buying semi-automatic weapons?

SM: That's a quotable quote [*laughs*]. I mean I think that's right because those attacks are coming from those who would see themselves as most Christian. On that note about the relationship between a people and their government, what is your sense—you've alluded to this in bits and pieces—but what is your sense of that kind of implicit social contract that should exist between a government and the people? What does the government owe the people, and what do the people owe the government?

MR: Well, again, I think that might be one of those oppositions that is better conceived in terms of a merism. I think that an openness that creates spaces of possibility in freedom for people is basically what should be desired. Sometimes it's a lot harder to persuade the public of that than it is to persuade the government of it. I mean, whose tyranny are we feeling now? But the social compact in a democracy should be negotiated generation to generation. I think that if you're going to have a functioning democracy, you have to have a basic level of well-being and literacy. But beyond that, how another generation will shape the culture, that has to be their choice. That's democracy itself.

JL: The Jeffersonian ideal. "The earth belongs to the living"—every twenty years a new constitution and a new country comes into being.

SM: One of the questions that I wanted to ask is about religion, though not about Calvin. We think it should be noteworthy that we haven't asked any questions about Calvin. We've read all of your interviews and since you're always asked about Calvin, we decided that we would not ask anything about Calvin [*laughter*]. One thing that struck me, though: you do have this incredibly idiosyncratic understanding of religion which is so attractive I think for the way that it penetrates beyond those conventional oppositions, and our conventional ways of thinking about religion. But it seems to me that there's something sympathetic with Eastern religions, in your view of religion because the core of it is this attentive mindfulness, this attentiveness to human experience. It sounds similar to Buddhism. And so I wondered if you have studied Eastern religion and philosophy, or if you see any sympathies between your views on religion and Buddhism, for example? Or is it just that when you penetrate deep enough to any religion that kind of that reverence for human experience is maybe what you get?

MR: I think that's true. I haven't studied Eastern religions. I do think that it's important to remember that Christianity is not a European religion, and it's not surprising if it has these sympathies. I mean, we have a tendency to narrow and harden. Over time cathedrals and all kinds of things undreamed of have become definitive for us. But I think that we do try to get back to the core.

SM: Right. Like Emerson digging deeper into his own religion and finding these unexpected sympathies with Buddhism or Hinduism.

MR: Thomas Wentworth Higginson wrote a wonderful essay called "On the Sympathy of Religions." It's just brilliant, and he is obviously very widely read in Eastern and all kinds of religion. As is so often the case with nineteenth-century people, he is so much more broad-minded than anything you hear now and so much better informed.

JL: You come back to the nineteenth century over and over again. Can you speak to the kind of central importance of the nineteenth century in shaping the literature you read, the way you think about the United States and its prowess? Is it possible to sort of encapsulate what was so special about the American experience in the nineteenth century that makes it in some way such a singularity in your way of understanding our politics? Are there a couple of features that are just so essential to see why that time period is the key to American political development?

MR: The great crisis of the nineteenth century is really very relevant now. Because when Lincoln said that we had to see whether "a country so constituted may long endure," people say he wanted to save the union. And they act as if this meant that he, you know, creating these oppositional things, meant he didn't want to abolish slavery. The question in this country is whether we can remain united at the same time that we disagree with each other. If any side that lost an election could simply withdraw from the union, then obviously the democracy is gone. There was a great deal of thinking around that absolutely crucial question. And there was also immigration. We have this experience that really began fairly early. Eighteen forty-eight was a huge year for immigration, much more than there had been before. So the people that immigrated in that period tended to be people who were very hard-pressed in the places they came from, typically illiterate and so on. So in a way we had a sort of blank slate. "What will people become if . . . ?" And the huge development of educational institutions in this country, which still has no parallel, was meant to find out who people were when they could step out of circumstances that defined them in such restrictive ways. It must have been a wonderful thing to see. In a way that we are no longer aware of ourselves, we were a transformative culture in that sense. And we still are. Here the legislatures are, taking such terrible swipes at the educational system and so on. Yet people come from all over to be educated here. I get students from the Caribbean now. And they have generations of poverty behind them. They've moved to Boston or somewhere. One of them, his brother is a cancer researcher, and he's a very talented writer. People in whom no one ever invested any attention before, never wanted anything from them before except field labor or something. That's amazing, and it's a huge endorsement of equality and generosity, which it repays so lavishly.

SM: That's one of the ways that it seems that despite the rhetoric and despite the pervasive kind of cynicism in American politics today, there is some way that that American dream is still real for some people, that this land of opportunity idea still does mean something for a lot of people?

MR: Exactly, and could be for more of us if we just acknowledge that we have that impulse and history, that we have resources.

SM: It's a matter of whether the desire and will is there, on the part of the people in charge.

MR: The rhetoric. I mean, people talk about immigrants, and that we've let this rhetoric devolve into using this word as a dismissive term. But then when you look at what the country gains, not simply in GDP but in new minds. Everything sounds like economics now because there are those who want to reduce everything to a single vocabulary. But the real economics of it is that they actually enrich the culture literally and figuratively. You just don't hear that talked about.

JL: In that regard, I wonder if you can talk about your commitment to teaching and how it ties into that political understanding of the promise of the lives of people in America in all their complexity and differentiation. How do you see that with teaching? I remember I saw you interviewed at King University a couple of years ago. You said then, you were talking about resigning from a grant and how you felt like something would be missing from your life if you weren't teaching. But can you say something about the politics of being a college teacher in the United States and continuing to teach?

MR: It comes very naturally to me to believe that if you can get people to think in language and consult what is most valuable to them and so on, it's a wonderful thing.

SM: It's also something that's so much more engaged and participatory and so has tangible rewards that are more immediate than writing, which can be solitary and more about delayed gratification.

MR: That's true. Although sometimes students leave and disappear, then they show up ten years later with a lovely book.

SM: Alluding to what you were saying earlier about Joe's question about the nineteenth century being such a rich period for you because of the conflicts that were working out in American history at that time. It seems like 1955, 1956 is another kind of moment in American history you are returning to and again with *Gilead* and I think *Lila* too. What is it about 1955? We know that *Home* takes place after Emmett Till's murder. So we know it's sometime between 1955 and 1956. Is it that same moment of conflict where it's not slavery anymore but segregation with these antimiscegenation laws? What is it that's compelling to you about that moment in history that you stop there again and again?

MR: I've been reading so much middle-western history I wanted to have a narrator who was of an age that he could have known an abolitionist. So it's a little stretch, but that sets the book in about the middle of the

1950s. There is a profound discontinuity in history that I don't really understand. There are many of them, but there is one there, certainly, where one generation was passionate on the subject of abolition and the next generation forgot it, forgot all of the history that surrounded it. You hear these people say things like, "I don't know what to do with them. I've got these civil war uniforms in my attic. I don't know where to get rid of them."

JL: That's amazing, actually.

MR: Yeah, it is amazing. It's hard to bring up old conflicts because they rekindle so readily. Still, it is bizarre that the South's been romanticized, and the North, which lost two soldiers to one, is treated as if it were just some sort of industrial machine that went down there and ground everything up. The southern economy was much more industrial in effect than the northern because they were feeding the industries of Europe. They were completely a by-product of European industrialization, a link in a chain of an industrialized economy.

SM: So much of what you're saying has to do with the American tendency to forget. Americans have the shortest memories. We don't remember things that happen just a few years ago, and that seems to be the part of the forward-looking tendency of this country. Which in some ways is positive, but it also has these really pernicious elements because of the short memories and forgetting of recent history.

JL: You write at one point, I think it's in *When I Was a Child I Read Books,* that the real importance of narrative for Americans is connectivity, that Americans need and thrive on that sense of connectivity. That this happens and this causes this, and this causes this and this causes this. Whereas in *Mother Country* you talk about how the English read the news in snapshots, there's just this series of revelations, "Oh, today, boom. Oh, tomorrow, this." They're not interconnected. When you talk about that forgetfulness, are you trying to reestablish in a way the narrative? Reestablish an appreciation for how one set of events or decisions leads to the next set of events and decisions, and the next set, so that we're awake to our agency? Awake to our ability to participate in things that do have downstream effects? Long-term transformations?

MR: Really. Absolutely. The idea that this country's actually in process and that we have arrived at a place that a couple of generations ago people could not have imagined in all sorts of ways. We can't look at most histories because most countries have constitutions that last seven years at best. Or they have a shadow government with the real mechanisms of power behind it and that sort of thing. But we have historically and actually an interaction between whoever happens to be governing and whatever ideas are potent in the population. This has worked out repeatedly over time. We feel stagnated now, I think. The only model for change that is relevant to us is our own history of change.

SM: I think so often that people think Americans are optimistic because they're always looking toward the future. But it sounds to me like what you're saying is we can draw a lot of hope and inspiration from looking to the past.

MR: Exactly.

SM: That knowing our history is important. Knowing what was possible in the past and how far we've come from then to now.

MR: Right. We've gotten ourselves into a situation where all we're trying to do is get back to where we were, 1970 or somewhere. When we look to the future now, we're looking to some new Apple product that we would never have expected. As far as creating social transformation, we're not really thinking in those terms. We're just worrying about invidious social transformation.

SM: This is a different vein of inquiry entirely, but are there books that had a profound influence on you when you were a child? I think probably my favorite volume of your essays is the most recent one, *When I Was a Child I Read Books*. When you were a child, what were the books that you read that really have stuck with you? Are there books that you read before you became an adult that you feel like you carried with you into adulthood?

MR: I think I read the usual books, *The Secret Garden* kinds of things [*laughs*]. I'm trying to think. I remember my grandfather had a collection of books by Rudyard Kipling. I was bored, and so I read one summer through the complete works of Rudyard Kipling, which just irritated me page by page.

SM: But you kept going?

MR: I did, I did [*laughter*]. But it's funny, I think in my life my reactions against things have been as informative for me as any tropisms that I have felt.

SM: I know people who can only write about the thinkers that they disagree with. Whereas I tend to write about the theorists that I find I feel an affinity with or that I agree with.

MR: I virtually never read anybody I agree with [*laughter*].

SM: Why would you do that? Why would you need to do that?

MR: In the first place, the people that I agree with tend not to be prominent [*laughter*]. I don't have to read them to keep up, shall we say. The other thing is that you find out what you do think by finding out what you don't think.

SM: That's right. Yeah, that's very true. That's something I definitely try to instill in students.

JL: Sometimes with great difficulty. But as part of that robust public discourse of a more ideal democracy that you espouse.

MR: Exactly. We don't treat people we disagree with respectfully now. So we never hear their case. We just say, "Oh, he's a . . . " It's a gross impoverishment of public discourse.

SM: Yeah, it's that same kind of tendency to just categorize. Put something in their box and say, "I know what that's about. I know what that is. I don't have to engage it."

MR: And if somebody says something that could possibly be interpreted as out of the box . . . [*laughs*] . . . then he has to scramble for days to get it back into the box.

SM: Right. It seems to me that this is part of why teaching becomes such an important part of this democratic practice because it really is trying to get students not to think in those terms. Not to think in terms of those conventional categories and boxes. That's important democratic work.

JL: It's good to remember that on a frustrating day, right? [*laughter*]. I guess we can ask one completely random question, which I think actually violates probably about five or six canons of discussing an author's work with her. Don't ask people to explain imagery [*laughter*]. Don't ask people whether there's a subtle hidden meaning to repeated themes [*laughter*]. But one of the things that both Shannon and I always came back to is the imaginary children that populate your novels. Images of the imaginary children that comes up again and again, and again through your novels.

SM: We really wanted someone to write an essay on this theme [in this volume,] and it just hasn't happened. It seems that there are so many imagined children that pop up in *Housekeeping*. There are the feral children that Sylvie seems to imagine. They're out near the house that's on the other side of the lake that Sylvie takes Ruth to and tries to attract the children with marshmallows. That's one of the moments where you're like, "OK, Sylvie, is she eccentric or is she crazy?" But there were also Glory's imaginary children. One of the most moving parts I think, of *Home* are the descriptions of Glory putting up with this fiancé who is basically exploiting her so that she could continue this fantasy, this dream of a home of happy children, her imagined children. So there's Sylvie and Glory who have these possible children, these imaginary children. You kind of sense a possibility. And then there's a category of lost children. There's Ames's daughter who died. There's Robby as a kind of imaginary child because Ames is imagining Robby in the future after Ames has died. And there's also Jack's illegitimate daughter that died. So there are all of these fantasy children and imagined children. So both of us have been sort of trying to think about, OK, how is that significant and does gender play in here at all? Because for the women it seems like children might be this kind of possibility whereas for the male characters they're experienced almost as a loss. Maybe it's not an intentional thing, but it is this theme that seems to pop up again and again.

MR: I think of people as living a great deal of their lives creating narratives for themselves, in a way. None of my characters have dreams of grandeur. I would not have a character who had dreams of grandeur. But they do imagine themselves being realized in circumstances that they can't attain. It's a correct intuition about themselves to want these things, even though as a matter of fact they are . . . I mean, Sylvie wants a child. She doesn't want to be alone in the woods, basically.

SM: So it's like it's an ordinary dream. It's an ordinary ambition. A path that their lives might have taken.

MR: Right. Only much lovelier than that. I mean, "ordinary" I use as a positive word.

SM: And grandeur is in the ordinary for you.

MR: Right.

SM: Since this volume is about politics and literature, and we're both political theorists, and we've spent a lot of time thinking about politics and talking about politics with you today, is there a way that the new book, *Lila*, extends any of those meditations on democracy or meditations on political questions that we've talked about in your mind? Or is it about something else entirely?

MR: I suppose it could be thought of in those terms because Lila is, of course, a waif and she is self-created. And Ames sees her as being beautiful, and he's right. I suppose it's very democratic in the sense that it is taken up with imagining somebody who has virtually no access to anything that, as we sometimes assume, would create depth or create richness. But it is still there.

SM: Switching gears: What is your attitude toward mainstream views of secularism that posit a sharp separation between religion and public life? Do you see a place for faith traditions that are deeply connected to the world and to democratic public life?

MR: This is an issue that always brings the word "merism" to my mind. I feel very deeply—very deeply—that faith is a conversation between God and the individual soul that no one else is in a position to understand or to judge. I cannot say from my own experience that those who espouse religion in the usual sense of the word are better, even more devout, than those who don't. We all know that the churches have done themselves a world of harm in the last few decades. I don't think those who are alienated from them on this account can be blamed for it, or that they are in any meaningful sense less religious than their adherents. I sometimes think the anxiety about secularism diverts the attention of the religious from the consequences of their own failures. Respect for faith traditions is essential to democratic public life, as is respect for those whose experience does not fall within any of the traditions. Who is to say how we as individuals are arrayed on the continuum between faith and disbelief, or where any of us will be on it tomorrow?

SM: You seem to have a deep respect for many traditions and traditional things but are often critical of social conventions. What is the difference between tradition and convention, in your view?

MR: Traditions have been tested. They have a history. They can be judged by their effects, and by the people who have found them to be fruitful and valuable. Social conventions are faddish, very often the behavior of people casting about for other people's approval, and fiercely controlling all the same. The best traditions have shed the conventions of the time in which they emerged. No doubt there are traditions now emerging that will outlast our conventions. We do seem to be making advances in areas of life where the conventions of earlier periods obscured basic justice.

SM: We're so appreciative for the time that you've made for us today, and it's really been a pleasure to talk with you.

JL: We do hope that, as the series goes forward to focus on contemporary authors, other editors will also include interviews like this one. And make that part of the legacy of democratic literature that it preserves. We're very sorry we didn't get the chance to interview Herman Melville, but . . .

MR: You and me both.

[*laughter*]

Selected Bibliography

Fiction by Marilynne Robinson

Gilead. New York: Farrar, Straus and Giroux, 2004.
Home. New York: Farrar, Straus and Giroux, 2008.
Housekeeping. New York: Farrar, Straus and Giroux, 1980.
Lila. New York: Farrar, Straus and Giroux, 2014.

Nonfiction by Marilynne Robinson

Absence of Mind: The Dispelling of Inwardness from the Modern Myth of the Self. New Haven: Yale University Press, 2010.
The Death of Adam: Essays on Modern Thought. 1998. New York: Picador, 2005.
Mother Country: Britain, the Welfare State, and Nuclear Pollution. New York: Farrar, Straus and Giroux, 1989.
When I Was a Child I Read Books: Essays. New York: Farrar, Straus and Giroux, 2012.
The Givenness of Things: Essays. New York: Farrar, Straus and Giroux, 2015.

Selected Essays by Marilynne Robinson

"Connie Bronson." *Paris Review*. www.theparisreview.org/fiction/2766/connie-bronson-marilynne-robinson.
"Fear." *New York Review of Books* 62, no. 14 (2015): 28–32.
"Language Is Smarter Than We Are." *New York Times Book Review*, January 11, 1987.
"The Polemic against Calvin: The Origins and Consequences of Historical Reputation." In *Calvin and the Church: Papers Presented at the 13th Colloquium of the Calvin Studies Society—May 24–26, 2001*, edited by David Foxgrover, 96–122. Grand Rapids, MI: CRC Product Services, 2002.
Preface to *John Calvin: Steward of God's Covenant*, edited by John F. Thornton and Susan B. Varenne, ix–xxviii. New York: Vintage, 2006.
"Sacred Inwardness." *Christian Century*, July 8, 2015, 24–25.
"Writers and the Nostalgic Fallacy." *New York Times*, October 13, 1985. http://graphics8.nytimes.com/images/blogs/readingroom/robinson.pdf.

Selected Interviews with Marilynne Robinson

"The Art of Fiction, No. 198." Interview by Sarah Fay. *Paris Review*, Fall 2008. www.theparisreview.org/interviews/5863/the-art-of-fiction-no-198-marilynne-robinson.
"Interview with Marilynne Robinson." Interview by Bob Abernathy. *Religion*

and Ethics Newsweekly. Podcast audio. www.pbs.org/wnet/religionandethics/episodes/march-18–2005/interview-marilynne-robinson/4226.

"An Interview with Marilynne Robinson." Interview by Jennifer Holberg. *Image: Art, Faith, Mystery*, no. 74 (2013): 69–80.

"An Interview with Marilynne Robinson." Interview by Thomas Schaub. *Contemporary Literature* 35 no. 2 (Summer 1994): 231–51.

"Keeping Faith in Democracy." Interview by Bill Moyers. *Moyers & Company*. Public Broadcasting System. October 17, 2014.

"A Life in Writing: Marilynne Robinson." Interview by Emma Brocke. *Guardian*, May 29, 2009. www.guardian.co.uk/culture/2009/may/30/marilynne-robinson

"Marilynne Robinson on Democracy, Reading, and Religion in America." Interview by Joe Fassler. *Atlantic Monthly*, May 16, 2012. www.theatlantic.com/entertainment/archive/2012/05/marilynne-robinson-on-democracy-reading-and-religion-in-america/257211/.

"On Influence and Appropriation." Interview by Tace Hendrick. *Iowa Review* 22, no. 1 (1992): 3–4.

"President Obama and Marilynne Robinson: A Conversation in Iowa." Interview by Barack Obama. *New York Review of Books* 62, no. 17 (November 5, 2015): 4–8.

"President Obama and Marilynne Robinson: A Conversation in Iowa, Part Two." Interview by Barack Obama. *New York Review of Books* 63, no. 18 (November 5, 2015): 6–8.

Secondary Sources

Acocella, Joan. "A Note of the Miraculous." *New York Review of Books* 52, no. 10 (June 2005). www.nybooks.com/articles/2005/06/09/a-note-of-the-miraculous/.

Bohannan, Heather. "Quest-tioning Tradition: Spiritual Transformation Images in Women's Narratives and *Housekeeping*." In "The Personal Narrative in Literature," special issue, *Western Folklore* 51, no. 1 (January 1992): 65–79.

Burke, William M. "Border Crossings in Marilynne Robinson's *Housekeeping*." *Modern Fiction Studies* 37, no. 4 (Winter 1991): 716–24.

Caver, Christine. "Nothing Left to Lose: *Housekeeping*'s Strange Freedoms." In "Write Now: American Literature in the 1980s and 1990s," special issue, *American Literature* 68, no. 1 (March 1996): 111–37.

Davis, Thomas J. "The Death of Adam, The Resurrection of Calvin: Marilynne Robinson's Alternative to an American Ideograph." In *Sober, Strict, and Scriptural: Collective Memories of John Calvin, 1800–2000*, edited by Johan de Niet, Herman Paul, and Bart Wallet, 357–84. Boston: Brill, 2009.

Delbanco, Andrew. "Her Calling." *New York Times Sunday Book Review*, April 20, 2012. www.nytimes.com/2012/04/22/books/review/marilynne-robinsons-when-i-was-a-child-i-read-books.html?_r=0.

Deresiewicz, William. "Homing Patterns: Marilynne Robinson's Fiction."*Nation*, September 24, 2008. www.thenation.com/print/article/homing-patterns-marilynne-robinsons-fiction.

Ebert, Roger. "*Housekeeping.*" RogerEbert.com. www.rogerebert.com/reviews/housekeeping-1988.

Elshtain, Jean Bethke. "The Incarnational Vision of Marilynne Robinson." *Cresset: A Review of Literature, the Arts, and Public Affairs* 73, no. 3 (2010): 15–21.

Galehouse, Maggie. "Their Own Private Idaho: Transience in Marilynne Robinson's *Housekeeping.*" *Contemporary Literature* 41, no. 1 (Spring 2000): 117–37.

Gardner, Thomas. "Enlarging Loneliness: Marilynne Robinson's *Housekeeping* as a Reading of Emily Dickinson." *Emily Dickinson Journal* 10, no. 1 (Spring 2001): 9–33.

Geyh, Paula E. "Burning down the House? Domestic Space and Feminine Subjectivity in Marilynne Robinson's *Housekeeping.*" *Contemporary Literature* 34, no. 1 (Spring 1993): 103–22.

Handley, George B. "The Metaphysics of Ecology in Marilynne Robinson's *Housekeeping.*" *Modern Fiction Studies* 55, no. 3 (Fall 2009): 496–521.

Hartshorne, Sarah D. "Lake Fingerbone and Walden Pond: A Commentary on Marilynne Robinson's *Housekeeping.*" *Modern Language Studies* 20, no. 3 (Summer 1990): 50–57.

Kaivola, Karen. "The Pleasures and Perils of Merging: Female Subjectivity in Marilynne Robinson's *Housekeeping.*" *Contemporary Literature* 34, no. 4 (Winter 1993): 670–90.

Kirkby, Joan. "Is There Life after Art? The Metaphysics of Marilynne Robinson's *Housekeeping.*" *Tulsa Studies in Women's Literature* 5, no. 1 (Spring 1986): 91–109.

Leise, Christopher. "That Little Incandescence': Reading the Fragmentary and John Calvin in Marilynne Robinson's *Gilead.*" *Studies in the Novel* 41, no. 3 (Fall 2009): 348–67.

Moss, Maria. "The Search for Sanctuary: Marilynne Robinson's *Housekeeping* and E. Annie Proulx's *The Shipping News.*" *American Studies* 49, no. 1 (2004): 79–90.

Peterson, Charles. "West towards Home: Tracking Marilynne Robinson's Intellectual Pilgrimage." *Book Forum,* February/March 2012. www.bookforum.com/inprint/018_05/8874.

Ravits, Martha. "Extending the American Range: Marilynne Robinson's *Housekeeping.*" *American Literature* 61, no. 4 (December 1989): 644–66.

Ryan, Katy. "Horizons of Grace: Marilynne Robinson and Simone Weil." *Philosophy and Literature* 29, no. 2 (October 2005): 349–64.

Ryan, Maureen. "Marilynne Robinson's *Housekeeping:* The Subversive Narrative and the New American Eve." *South Atlantic Review* 56, no. 1 (January 1991): 79–86.

Shy, Todd. "Religion and Marilynne Robinson." *Salmagundi* 155/156 (Summer/Fall 2007): 251–64.

Tanner, Laura E. "'Looking Back from the Grave': Sensory Perception and the Anticipation of Absence in Marilynne Robinson's *Gilead*." *Contemporary Literature* 48, no. 2 (Summer 2007): 227–52.

Wilson, Christine. "Delinquent Housekeeping: Transforming the Regulations of Keeping House." *Legacy* 25, no. 2 (2008): 299–310.

Contributors

Roger Berkowitz is associate professor of political studies, philosophy, and human rights at Bard College, where he is academic director of the Hannah Arendt Center for Politics and Humanities. His research interests include justice and jurisprudence, Arendt, Heidegger, Nietzsche, Kant, dignity, history and transhumanism, as well as politics and aesthetics. He is the author of *The Gift of Science: Leibniz and the Modern Legal Tradition* (2005), and coeditor of *Thinking in Dark Times: Hannah Arendt on Thinking and Politics* (2009) and *The Intellectual Origins of the Global Financial Crisis* (2012). He also edits *HA: The Journal of the Hannah Arendt Center at Bard College* and the *Hannah Arendt Center Blog.* He writes regularly for the *American Interest* and his writing has appeared in the *New York Times; Democracy: A Journal of Ideas;* and *Carnegie Journal of Ethics & International Affairs*, among others. Berkowitz lectures frequently at One Day University.

Anna Hadfield majored in human rights at Bard College and wrote her senior thesis on the crisis of humanism, with a focus on the work of Marilynne Robinson. After graduating, she worked at Al-Quds Bard Honors College in the West Bank. She now resides in New York.

Ralph C. Hancock is professor of political science at Brigham Young University. He is the author of *Calvin and the Foundations of Modern Politics* (1989), as well as *The Responsibility of Reason: Theory and Practice in a Liberal-Democratic Age* (2011). He is also the editor of *America, the West, and Liberal Education* (1999) and has published many journal articles.

Joseph H. Lane Jr. is Hawthorne Professor and Chair of the Department of Politics at Emory & Henry College, where he also directs the College Honors Program. He is coauthor of *The Deconstitutionalization of America* (2004) and coeditor of *Interrogating Nature* (2014). His work has appeared in many journals, including *American Political Science Review; Review of Politics;* and *Political Theory.* He is currently working on a monograph about Rousseau and modern environmentalism.

Christie L. Maloyed teaches in the Office of the First-Year Experience at the University of Louisiana at Lafayette. Her research focuses on religion and civic education in colonial America and the early republic.

Shannon L. Mariotti is associate professor of political science at Southwestern University. Her research focuses on nineteenth-century American transcendental thought and twentieth-century critical social theory. She is the author of *Adorno and Democracy: The American Years* (2016) and *Thoreau's Democratic Withdrawal: Alienation, Participation, and Modernity* (2010). She has published articles on Adorno, Thoreau, Emerson, and Du Bois in journals such as *Political Theory* and *Telos* and in volumes such as *A Political Companion to Henry David Thoreau*.

Lorraine Krall McCrary is a visiting assistant professor of political science at Wabash College. She teaches and writes on topics in political theory, disability studies, and literature.

Emily C. Nacol is assistant professor of political science at Vanderbilt University. Her research interests lie primarily in the history of political thought, especially early modern political theory. Her first book, on the intersection of knowledge, politics, and economy in early modern Britain, is forthcoming in 2016. She has also published articles in *Political Studies* and *Polity* and is beginning a new book on labor, marginality, and risk in the long eighteenth century.

Matthew Scherer is assistant professor of government and politics at George Mason University. His research focuses on the politics of modern secularism, and his work has appeared in *Political Theory; Cultural Anthropology; Modern Language Notes; Politics & Religion; Hedgehog Review;* and the edited volume *Political Theologies: Public Religions in a Post-Secular World* (2006). He is the author of the book *Beyond Church and State: Democracy, Secularism, and Conversion* (2013).

Daniel Skinner is assistant professor of health policy in the Department of Social Medicine at Ohio University's Heritage College of Osteopathic Medicine, in Dublin, Ohio. His work has appeared in journals including *Public Administration Review; Review of Politics; Politics & Gender; Law, Culture and the Humanities;* and *Polity*. His research interests include the politics of health care, gender politics, and political rhetoric.

Alex Zamalin is director of African American Studies and assistant professor of political science at University of Detroit–Mercy. His areas of expertise include African American political thought, American politics, and political theory. He has written on topics such as politics and literature, ethics, social justice, and race and politics. He is the author of *African American Political Thought and American Culture* (2015).

Index

POLITICAL COMPANIONS TO GREAT AMERICAN AUTHORS

SERIES EDITOR

Patrick J. Deneen, University of Notre Dame

BOOKS IN THE SERIES

A Political Companion to Saul Bellow
Edited by Gloria L. Cronin and Lee Trepanier

A Political Companion to Herman Melville
Edited by Jason Frank

A Political Companion to Walker Percy
Edited by Peter Augustine Lawler and Brian A. Smith

A Political Companion to Ralph Waldo Emerson
Edited by Alan M. Levine and Daniel S. Malachuk

A Political Companion to Marilynne Robinson
Edited by Shannon L. Mariotti and Joseph H. Lane Jr.

A Political Companion to Walt Whitman
Edited by John E. Seery

A Political Companion to Henry Adams
Edited by Natalie Fuehrer Taylor

A Political Companion to Henry David Thoreau
Edited by Jack Turner

A Political Companion to John Steinbeck
Edited by Cyrus Ernesto Zirakzadeh and Simon Stow

CPSIA information can be obtained at www.ICGtesting.com
Printed in the USA
BVOW08*2305041016

463029BV00008B/4/P

9 780813 167763